MODERNIST MONTAGE

P. ADAMS SITNEY

MODERNIST MONTAGE
The Obscurity of Vision
In Cinema and Literature

Columbia University Press
New York

Columbia University Press
New York   Oxford
Copyright © 1990 P. Adams Sitney
All rights reserved

Library of Congress Cataloging-in-Publication Data

Sitney, P. Adams.
Modernist Montage:
The obscurity of vision in cinema and literature
P. Adams Sitney.
p.   cm.
Includes bibliographical references.
ISBN 0-231-07182-5
1. Literature, Experimental—History and criticism.
2. Modernism (Literature)
3. Experimental films—History and criticism.
I. Title.
PN771.S58   1990
700'.9'04—dc20   89-25461
                          CIP

Casebound editions of Columbia University Press books are Smyth-sewn and printed on permanent and durable acid-free paper

Printed in the United States of America

c 10 9 8 7 6 5 4 3 2 1

To my father Harry Sitney
in celebration of his eightieth birthday

Contents

CONTENTS

Illustrations appear as a group following page 156.

Preface

CRISSCROSSING AND sometimes converging in this book are two "venerable contradictions," in Wallace Stevens' words. He stressed the modernist poet's need "to make the visible a little hard to see" in his poem against T. S. Eliot, "The Creations of Sound"; and in the essay "The Relations between Painting and Poetry" he identified the "paramount relation between . . . modern man and modern art" as "simply this: that in an age in which disbelief is so profoundly prevalent . . . the arts in general are, in their measure, a compensation for what has been lost. Men feel that the imagination is the next greatest power to faith: the reigning prince."

When I began to see how these venerable contradictions were interrelated this work began to take shape. In writing it I have usually proceeded from attention to minute details to the interpretation of whole works. The details are, for the most part, figurative representations of acts of seeing or of naming what eludes visualization. Throughout this analysis the influence of my undergraduate training in Classical and Indic philology, more than twenty years ago, exerted its ineluctable force. Years of identifying grammatical forms, considering the ambiguities of syntax, noting rhetorical figures before proposing interpretations (and later the discovery of the great German literary historians Curtius, Auerbach, and above all Spitzer) fundamentally affected the way I wrote about film.

This book grew largely out of my teaching the history of cinema as a visual art. Each week for at least fifteen academic years I have lectured at either Cooper Union, The School of the Art Institute of Chicago, or, mainly, Princeton University, on one or a few films, in chronological sequences. Generally, I have attempted to distinguish the generic and syntactical elements a film has assumed by tradition from its unique stylistic organization and variation of those elements. In the study of films in the modernist spirit, I attempted to ask how a particular stylistic feature generates a convincing and original film. That question usually led me to asking what kind of film would eschew that feature, for which another modernist film would provide an answer.

Over the years in which this book was written I have incurred innumerable intellectual debts. Leon Balter encouraged and aided my research into psychoanalysis. During the five years in which Stephen Koch and I shared rooms at Princeton an endless conversation about modernism occurred: much of it is distilled here. Earlier I had written a dissertation at Yale under the direction of Paul de Man, with massive help from Harold Bloom. The chapters on Olson and Blanchot stem from that work. Stan Brakhage first urged me to read Stein and Olson in the early sixties; Noel Burch's scorn for my ignorance of Blanchot, a few years later, brought me to read him. In the twenty-five years I've known Annette Michelson and Richard Foreman the issues discussed here have been the core of our talk. Bartholomew Callopy, without knowing it, revealed to me the centrality of Exodus 33 to my project.

In the many years since the first pages of the book were written David Quint, Noël Carroll, Richard Drake, Rosalind Krauss, David Bromwich, George Wilson, and Joanna Hitchcock have given me ideas and encouragement. Maria Di Battista suggested that I send the manuscript to Columbia University Press, where my editor, Jennifer Crewe, and Susan Pensak have been enormously helpful. A number of anonymous readers, and Bruce Kawin, made suggestions and objections that helped me clarify my argument. My agent, Georges Borchardt, and his staff, especially Cindy Klein, have made many aspects of publication more pleasant for me than if I had to represent myself. Hollis Melton lovingly produced the stills from prints at the Anthology Film Archives, with supplemental help from Cooper Union and Marie Nesthus at the Donnell Library. The genuine surprise that my children, Blake and Sky, have grown interested in the matters I discuss here inspired me. To my wife, Marjorie Keller, I owe the greatest of debts. This book first took shape as a conversation with her. She has advised me and criticized every chapter as it was written and boosted me in all of its setbacks. Even as I write this preface, she is correcting galleys for me.

New York, 1989

MODERNIST MONTAGE

Introduction

Modernity, Modernism

OF THE many contradictory lines of force that intersect to define the horizon of modernism in the arts, two antinomies are central to this book. The first recognizes that innovation is the sole legitimate means of guaranteeing a link to tradition. Typically the modernist artist mines the greatest works of the tradition for irreducible structures which can be made to support new works. That creative activity in an artistic medium, then, heightens and extends insight into what is most durable in the history of that medium. Modernist criticism follows suit, identifying and evaluating these unanticipated routes of historical continuity. At the same time the modernist artist defends a position in history and stakes claims for creative freedom by making works that aggressively assert their autonomy. These works bear signs of rupture from the successful achievements of the immediate past and stylistically distinguish themselves from the works of contemporaries so as to make the authorial signature immediately apparent. The paths from these works to the great models of the tradition are marked by internal allusions, often obscure quotations, and reductive schemata.

The schemata themselves are various and unpredictable; modernists respond to the pressure they have interiorized both to invent new modes of schematization and to disguise, even from themselves, the conse-

1

quencies of their reading of the past. Isolation, negation, amplification, and parody are among the most frequent and fecund of these schemata. Once a stylistic, generic, or syntactical element has been isolated, it becomes the matrix for generating new works.

An elaborate analytical literature explores and debates the consequences, even the existence, of this first antinomy. Until the recent fascination with the spectre of "Postmodernism" the stakes involved in that debate were quite high. Theoretical claims of distinctions between modernism and avant-garde art, between progress and restoration in modern art, between authenticity and theatricality, have offered different resolutions of the evident contradictions within the scope of modernist creativity. However, a second antinomy has not been generally recognized as such. I shall call it *the antinomy of vision.* Modernist literary and cinematic works stress vision as a privileged mode of perception, even of revelation, while at the same time cultivating opacity and questioning the primacy of the visible world. Furthermore, the quest for autonomously generated, medium specific works results inversely in a serial pattern of acknowledgments of (a) the ineluctable traces of the picturing process in language and of (b) both the tendency to respond with linguistic and representational reflexes to visual abstraction. One fascinating dimension of modernism is its apparent need to keep producing allegories of these fundamental antinomies. For the most part this book will consist of readings of several of those allegories.

This, then, is a book of readings of modernist texts and films, not a theory of modernism. There already exists an adequate scholarly literature on the subject.[1] After some preliminary remarks on a poem by Stéphane Mallarmé and a film by Sidney Peterson, I shall concentrate on the later reaches of modernism, from the 1920s to 1980, without the slightest hint of being inclusive. The pioneering achievements of Picasso, Proust, Schoenberg, Pound, Joyce, Stravinsky, et al. were known, even if not universally esteemed, by the artists whose writings and films I examine. In short, modernism or several conflicting modernisms was a historical force for all of them. In writing this book I set out at first to chart the poetics of allusion and to explore the varieties of resistance to vision, in a historical period in which it was commonly asserted that literature stressed the visual and in cinema, where visualization was often taken for granted. In the course of my work, I encountered a series of allegories of artistic creativity. In uncovering the network of allusions in the works that seized my attention, I began to see a pattern of poetic archeology: apparently random echoes and vestiges, even when they were deliberately rendered absurd, turned out to be important indications of the artist's conception of his or her relation to tradition. In

L'Etoile de mer Man Ray and Desnos invoke a powerful poem by Catullus when they play on the common name Cybele; a Scythian warrior is uncovered by the machinery constructing electrodynamic plants in Vertov's *The Eleventh Year;* Judith's cry, *Nescio vos,* in Blanchot's *Au moment voulu,* pretends to be a neutral illustration of Latin grammar, but it actually reveals an intimacy between the *récit* and Jesus' parables.

Dramatic moments of vision occur in these works, in which nothing, or nothing dramatic, is seen. Man Ray's poet staring at his starfish, Dreyer's Gertrud gazing into a fire which consumes her friend's letters, Michel's "figurative" reading of Jeanne in Bresson's *Pickpocket,* Brakhage's "metaphors on vision," Frampton's frenzy over a photograph he neglects to show us, and the comic condensations and displacements of Landow's *Wide Angle Saxon* are all negative epiphanies. The strength and fascination of these works derive from the intensity and variety of ways they restate one of modernism's grand oxymorons: a secular theology.

Cultural modernity reflects the Protestant spirit in the arts. The gradual interiorization of Luther's theology and Descartes' philosophical independence culminated in the "modern" paradox of Kant's formulation of the mark of an aesthetic object: "purposiveness without a purpose." He recognized that aesthetic experience was at once radically subjective and fiercely committed to an ideal of universal assent. In essence, it duplicated the structure of Protestant conviction without reference to a God.

The aesthetics of Protestanism diverges from its economics, if we follow the classical argument of Max Weber. Weber saw the religious notion of a "calling" leading to the secular pursuit of a life of productive work, even while the religious motives were evaporating; but in modernist aesthetics the ancient idea of a *poetic calling* was revived and reformulated with an intensity that actually increased inversely as the theology of election ceased to matter in the accumulation of wealth. Without upholding the religious tenets of modern Christianity, the modern artist came more and more to oppose the commercialism of a society that increasingly displaced a theological notion of human labor onto objects for sale. Therefore, in opposition to the manufacturer, the artist tended to treat his or her works as sources of aesthetic revelation rather than as products for use and profit.

The concept of modernism appeared in the nineteenth century, first in France, at a time when the nature and autonomy of the individual arts was a subject of debate. The Protestant revolution had already reached its artistic apogee with Romanticism. The first articulations of modernism include a highly Romantic anti-Romanticism which put an emphasis on the impersonality of the creative selfhood. This fiction of impersonality encouraged theories of the specificity of particular artistic media as well as illusions about the increased accuracy with which the artist rendered the world. But at the same time a massive challenge to the idea of the autonomy of media came from the triumphal success of Wagner, whom the most influential avatars of aesthetic modernism alternately adored and hated. By the time the cinema was invented, 1895, there were visible modernist movements wherever Western artistic traditions held influence. Painting, sculpture, music, drama, fiction, poetry, dance, and archtecture had their modernist manifestations, despite the lack of any unified modernist style or theory which pervaded the different arts and countries where they were practiced.

Thus modernism in the arts marks a survival of the preoccupations of Romanticism after a prolonged crisis over the authority of subjectivity as a creative principle. At one decisive stage in that crisis art approached the status of a religion for practitioners such as Wagner or Mallarmé. Kandinsky and a number of American poets and painters extended that version of aesthetic Orphism into the contemporary moment.

Lacking a collective theory of artistic vision, the modernists often articulated individual stances on the status and values of seeing. Marcel Duchamp's well-known disparagement of "retinal" painting is a simplified example of the displacement of a polemic against painterliness onto a rudimentary discrimination in optical perception. Historically, it repeats William Blake's insistence that he sees *through* his eyes not *with* them, in his parallel assertion of the priority of figurative design over atmospheric tonality. However, the modernisms of painting and sculpture are as peripheral to the concerns of this book as those of music or architecture. In literary and cinematic modernism, my focus, the matter of the status of vision takes quite complex turns which require careful elucidation, largely because it did not become a subject of open debate; for the most part, the artists I shall discuss formulated their theories of vision in isolation from each other, seldom realizing the centrality of their speculations to their concepts of their own creativity.

In introducing the argument of this book, I want to look in some detail at two paradigmatic works, a well-known sonnet of Stéphane Mallarmé and a short film by Sidney Peterson, a work too little known outside the audience for avant-garde cinema.

Mallarmé's Self-Allegorical Sonnet

FROM A reading of Mallarmé's sonnet, I would derive the following modernist precepts: the evocation of ancient sounds confirms the work of modern poetry; the "purification" of language can retard but not defeat vision; and whatever visual images do break through can be read as an allegory of verbal processes; finally, the allegorical reading itself is as much a reflex of historical conditioning as the habitual joining of stars into imaginary constellations, and it is as fragile a fictive construction. Mallarmé's hermetic transposition of images into signs of language and into an allegory of poetic form points to a dimension in modernism which will be taken up, with radically different effects, by dadaists and surrealists. Marcel Duchamp's only film, *Anémic cinéma,* illustrates this tendency more fully than any other film of the silent period. At the same time the valorization of the interior room of the poet (along with the city street) will extend into both literary and cinematic surrealism. *L'Etoile de mer* by Man Ray and Robert Desnos erotically intensifies the fetishism of what Mallarmé identifies as a "bibelot" in the sonnet as an object of fantasy in the poet's room, while representing the streets of Paris as a theater of sexual encounter.

There are two versions of the sonnet. The earlier one (1868) bore a title:

Sonnet allégorique de lui-même

La Nuit approbatrice allume les onyx
De ses ongles au pur Crime, lampadophore,
Du Soir aboli par le vespéral Phoenix
De qui la cendre n'a de cinéraire amphore

Sur des consoles, en le noir Salon: nul ptyx,
Insolite vaisseau d'inanité sonore,
Car le Maître est allé puiser de l'eau du Styx
Avec tous ses objets dont le Rêve s'honore.

Et selon la croisée au Nord vacante, un or
Néfaste incite pour son beau cadre une rixe
Faite d'un dieu que croit emporter une nixe

En l'obscurcissement de la glace, décor
De l'absence, sinon que sur la glace encor
De scintillations le septour se fixe.

[Approving Night lights up the onyx of her nails in the pure Crime, the lightbearer, of the Evening abolished by the vesperal Phoenix whose ash has no cinerary urn// on the consoles, in the black Salon: no ptyx, unwonted vessel of sonorous inanity, for the Master has gone drawing water from the Styx with all the objects with which the Dream prides itself// and corresponding to the sash toward the empty North, an ill-omened god who believes he is carrying away a nixie//in the obscurity of the mirror, decor of absence, or else on the mirror the septet sets itself out of scintillations.]

The published version of nineteen years later contains many revisions:

Ses pur ongles très haut dédiant leur onyx,
L'Angoisse, ce minuit, soutient, lampadophore,
Maint rêve vespéral brûlé par le Phénix
Que ne recueille pas de cinéraire amphore

Sur les crédences, au salon vide: nul ptyx
Aboli bibelot d'inanité sonore,
(Car le Maître est allé puisser des pleurs au Styx
Avec ce seul objet dont le Néant s'honore.)

Mais proche la croisée au nord vacante, un or
Agonise selon peut-être le décor
Des licornes ruant du feu contre une nixe,

Elle, défunte nue en le miroir, encor
Que, dans l'oubli fermé par le cadre, se fixe
De scintillations sitôt le septour.

[Its pure nails very high offering their onyx, Anguish, lampbearer, this midnight, holds up many vesperal dreams burned by the Phoenix which are not received by a cinerary urn// on the credences, in the empty salon: no ptyx, abolished trinket of sonorous inanity (for the Master has gone to draw tears in the Styx with this one object with which the Nothingness prides itself.)//But near the vacant sash to the north, a gold dies perhaps corresponding to the decor of unicorns rushing from the fire toward a nixie,//She, naked, dead in the mirror while, in the oblivion enclosed by the frame, at once the septet sets itself out of scintillations.]

"Ses purs ongles" (1887) dramatizes the equivocal status of representation that arises from a temporally ambiguous "moment of vision." The poem enacts its own play of visual obscurity as it slowly allows

an interior scene to come into focus. The opening stanza puts up a for-
midable resistance to visualization, but the subsequent three stanzas por-
tray an empty room and, within it, a mirror in which is obscurely reflected what seems to be the image which motivates the poem's beginning.
The circularity of this process is deliberate; for it "allegorizes" the way
in which the poem can be read.

The mirror image in the final lines indicates that vestiges of representation are not easily abolished. An image of the Big Dipper haunts
the poem, obliquely identified in the final word "septuor."[2] When we
follow the circular path of reading that the poem suggests and accept
the first line as a gloss on the fourteenth, the flashing seven stars turn
out to be the fingernails of Anguish as it holds aloft a votive lamp.
Habitually, we see stars in constellations despite the assurance of as-
tronomers that the outlined shapes come from stars far dispersed in the
depths of space. Even as constellations these are mere points; the figures
contain nothing. The poet names this nullity, calling the imaginary shapes
the burned-out dreams of evening, which the Phoenix-like sun destroys
every day. Starting from this negation, the sonnet runs through a series
of variations on the traces that nothingness leaves within an increasingly
concrete setting. Intense reductiveness of this order characterizes the
modernist spirit in poetry.

We have good evidence of the poet's awareness of the visual echoes
in this sonnet. The early version, and its title, come to us from a letter
Mallarmé wrote to Dr. Henri Cazalis on July 18, 1868. He had been
asked for a sonnet to be included in an illustrated collection *Sonnets et
eaux-fortes*. Even though the contribution arrived too late to be included
in the book, the poet spelled out the problems he foresaw in illustrating
the poem. He attested ironically to his acute awareness of the complex
relationship of his language to visual representation by suggesting an
"appropriate" picture in terms that defy visualization:

> I extracted this sonnet which I dreamed up one day this summer,
> from a projected study of *the Word* [*la Parole*]: it is inverse, I have
> to say that the meaning if it has one (but I am consoled on the
> other hand by the dose of poetry it encloses, in my opinion) is
> evoked by the internal mirage of the words themselves. Letting
> oneself murmur it several times, one gets a rather cabalistic sen-
> sation. This is an admission that it is hardly "plastic," as you re-
> quired, but at least it is as "black and white" as possible; and I
> think it would lend itself to being illustrated by an etching full of
> Dream and Void. For example, a nocturnal window open, with
> its two shutters fastened back; a room with no one inside [avec

personne dedans], despite the stable air that the fastened shutters give, and in a night made of absence and interrogation, without furniture, except the plausible sketch of vague consoles, a frame, bellicose and dying, of a mirror hung at the back, with its reflections, stellar and incomprehensible, of the big Bear, which alone connects this room abandoned by the world to the sky. I took this subject of an empty sonnet which reflects itself in every manner [ce sujet d'un sonnet nul et se réfléchissant de toutes les façons], because my work is so well prepared and stratified, representing as it can, the Universe, that I would not have known, without damaging any of my graded impressions, how to take anything out—and no sonnet would have occured.[3]

As if he were anticipating the response that the poem defied illustration, Mallarmé joked about its "black and white" character, meaning, of course, that it was nothing but letters on paper. The paradox "full" of "Void" neatly restates the problematic of the astronomical constellation in the compulsively figurative human eye. The one allusion to a human presence is tortuously ambiguous. Instead of writing "sans personne dedans" the poet wrote "avec," violating conventional French usage to create a middle zone between "without anyone inside" and "with someone inside." Mallarmé's letter reeancts the imaginative erasure of the sonnet, effacing the image as quickly as it appears; significantly the oxymoron "full of nothing" corresponds to the ancient-neologism "ptyx" around which the sonnet pivots.

An Allegory of Genre

THE GENERALLY fine critical literature on "Ses purs ongles" has paid insufficient attention to the degree to which the historical fate of the sonnet form itself is at stake in both versions of the poem.[4] Nothing could be more absurd than the persistence of a fourteen line, carefully patterned literary form, expressive of Renaissance and Baroque wit, into the modern period. Mallarmé recognized the sonnet form as an "aboli bibelot" which can still be made to work, at least in the negative mode, even though its master—himself and the poetic genius collectively— had moved on to more original—and more primitive—structures: "Hérodiade," *Igitur,* and ultimately *Un coup de Dés.* Every modern sonnet likewise forms a "cadre" in whose "oubli" mythological metamorphoses can still take place. The strict rhyme scheme, or "the internal mirage of the words themselves," opens up a space in which poetic history, especially, can be reflected; for, the literary "rêve" is "vespéral" to the extent that the modern lyric is a later, western development of Greek (matinal and eastern) and Latin sources from a time when the flexibilities of syntax did the work later relegated to rhyme. Rhyme emerged in late Latin poetry as the pressure from the vulgur tongues was making word order rather than inflection the basis of syntax. Classical poetry did not know rhyme.

We have a letter the poet wrote to Eugène Lefébure on May 3, 1868, about this puzzling concatenation of Greek looking letters:

> I made a sonnet and I have only three rhymes in ix. Try to send me the real meaning of the word ptyx; I have been assured that it has none in any language, which I would greatly prefer, for that would give me the charm of creating it by the magic of rhyme.[5]

The letter of Lefébure suggests that the poet consulted several sources about the word. He might well have been informed that in Homer, in the only passage which mentions writing [*Iliad* 6.168–69], signs [σήματα] are written in a folded tablet [πτυκτῷ]. And even if the poet only had the most casual acquaintance with the Odes of Pindar he would have seen the First Olympian which begins the standard recensions of the poet's surviving works. There Pindar defines the poet's task as "to ornament with renowned folds [πτυχαῖς] of songs."

If Mallarmé learned anything about the word from his Greek-reading acquaintances, he would have found out that the nominative form, "ptyx" itself, is a philological fiction. All the recorded instances are in inflected forms; so that the final "x" must be merely a deduction from the oblique cases where the Greek uses the letter "chi"; the lexicographers insert the entries under *ptyx on analogy with other Greek nouns that alternate the nominative "x" [ξ] with "chi" [χ] in the oblique cases. In this sense, above all, he could have been assured that the word "does not exist in any language."

I believe that the very process of inventing a hypothetical nominative form for the sake of lexicography has more relevance to the choice of "ptyx" than any single definition. But this "mise en abîme" does not fully account for its role in the poem. There it remains a word without a reference. The suspension of referentiality acts like a vacuum around which the second quatrain organizes itself. The full colon before the word "nul," which performs the syntactical function of drawing the sense of "ptyx" back toward "amphore," graphically marks the moment of suspension. The comma following "ptyx" puts the whole sixth

verse in apposition to it. This tends to confirm our philological observations; for if "ptyx" has no meaning—not shell, book, hill, or urn—
it is an *abolished vestige* recovered only by the grammarians' sensitivity
to *lifeless sonority*. Furthermore, the history of the hypothetical word
allegorizes the history of the sonnet form, itself a pure speculation in
sonority. My conviction that the sonnet form itself is the issue here
draws reinforcement from the coincidence of the phrases "nul ptyx" in
the poem and "sonnet nul" in the letter about it to Cazalis.

Liminal Vision

AS A purely linguistic entity, "ptyx" marks the limit of invisibility
within the sonnet. It is the nucleus of a range of nouns smuggled into
the poem behind a minus sign: *rêve, amphore, crédences, bibelot, Maître,
Styx, objet* are, one and all, not there. The tercets sketch the liminally
visible scene that Mallarmé ironically filled out in his letter. Just as visual representation begins to grow more distinct in the tercets, allusions
to Greek mythology fade away (along with the Greek rhymes), leaving
Romanic and Germanic vestiges instead; unicorns and a nixie supplant
the Phoenix and the Styx—along with the indirect evocations of the
Cocytus (the river of tears), the Lethe (of oblivion), and the Danaiads,
who were condemned to gather water in sieves.

Mythology thus joins visualization, Greek and Latin diction, and the
sonnet form as a not-quite-vanishing component of the modern poem.
The peculiar beauty that it evidences in its waning phase comes from
the fusion (and confusion) the distance of centuries permits the modern
poet. The concatenation of Hadean rivers is a good example of this:
when a god took an oath in Greek mythology, Iris, the rainbow, de-
scended to the Styx to draw a cup of water which the god poured out
as he swore. The modern poet cannot achieve this apotheosis; in the
welter of fluvial associations he becomes a Master who would simultaneously draw from the rivers of tears and oblivion with Danaiad fu-
tility. The suggestion that the Danaiads haunt this sonnet neatly fits the
dipper image, especially when we "see" it as merely seven points which
may take the shape of a ladle but can hold no more liquid than a sieve.
But it is not only, nor even principally, a ladle in the poem. If anything,
it represents a funereal candleholder in the sky and a dipper in the mirror. In his prolonged absence the flickering reflections take the form of
clouded vestiges of medieval myths. Since mythology has dwindled to
the status of poetic decor such phantasmagoria surfaces with the sanc-
tion of our forgetfulness of the original specificity of the myths. This

is yet another version of the negative illumination described naturalistically in the opening two lines.

The "pure" incantation of sound does not abolish the picturing process. The time designation, *minuit,* fosters the acknowledgment that the etymological play of *ongles* and *onyx* may be an evocation of the stars. But the stars are representations reduced to a minimum: points of light against a wall of black, irreducibly distant, not even constellated into a figural outline until the sonnet's final two lines.

So, once again, the "internal mirage of the words themselves" transforms visual imagery into an abstraction of poetic form. Such is the very nature of constellations: mere points of light illusionistically clustered for the earthly observer, they can be coaxed into outlining an infinity of shapes. Such protean versatility rests on the condition that the imagined shape can contain nothing. The revelation of "midnight" is that we cannot keep from constellating the stars, and even associating those outlines with mythological figures. For Mallarmé the stars *are* language, at once music and image, echoing through poetic history.[6]

In Mallarmé's allegorical scheme the departure of the Master corresponds to the impersonality of the poetic act, as though symbolist language excreted its own internal mirage of sounds and inevitable pictorial evanescences once the creative selfhood left the scene. In some of the later allegories of artistic creativity, an emblem of the unconscious plays a crucial role. For example, in Sidney Peterson's 1948 film, *Mr. Frenhofer and the Minotaur,* the Freudian principles of dream work, condensation and displacement, become strategic guides for inventing a cinematic dream about modernist painting.

The Missing Patient

EVEN WHEN they turn their backs on him, late modernists are necessarily more haunted by Freud than Freud's immediate contemporaries were. Peterson has the following observation about the status of Freudian ideas in the art of post-World War II modernism:

> I think if there is one thing that distinguishes the early 20s from the late 40s . . . it is that in the latter period we were no longer being so careful [about not joking about psychology.] I tend to think of the plethora of psycho-shrinking of still later periods as unrestrained joking representing unconscious attempts to reduce to absurdity a once powerful mythology. This is one thing that distinguishes post-WW I Surrealism from that of post-WW II. In

a way, this represents a triumph for Duchamp's doctrine of the ready-made. By regarding the Freudian or neoFreudian model as aesthetically comparable to a 1917 urinal signed by R. Mutt, the identities of both the therapist and his patient were redefined and the latter was, in effect, invited to leave, much as Duchamp, after a brief look at his part of the 1938 Surrealist Exhibition in Paris, a few hours before its opening, had left for England.[7]

To generate the images of his film Peterson deliberately displaced allusions to Balzac's *Le chef d'oeuvre inconnu,* which Dore Ashton aptly called "a fable of modern art," onto a visual network derived from Picasso's etching "Minotauromachie" (1935), while inventing a monologue for the soundtrack that condenses elements of both works in a stream of consciousness narration which draws heavily on the manner of H. C. Earwicker's "allnight newsy surreal" in James Joyce's *Finnegans Wake.*

Balzac's "conte philosophique" imagines an incident in the lives of two historical painters, Porbus and Poussin, and one fictional master, Frenhofer. The latter has been working for ten years on a portrait he believes to be of incomparable perfection, a masterpiece fusing ideal beauty with uncanny realism. The two younger rivals are so eager to see it that they persuade Poussin's mistress to pose for Frenhofer so that he can compare the work of his imagination with a woman of great beauty.

Frenhofer toiled so long on his painting that he totally effaced the image except for a single, perfect foot. At first Porbus and Poussin see nothing in his canvas. Poussin confides to Porbus: "I see only colors there, amassed in confusion and held by a multitude of bizarre lines which make up a wall of paint." Eventually, Porbus locates the foot and reveals it to Poussin. The interview ends when Poussin lets slip that the old master has deceived himself and wrecked his painting. At first Frenhofer despairs, but he regains his confidence:

> "Nothing, nothing! and to have worked for ten years!" He sat down and cried.
>
> "So, I'm an imbecile, a madman! So, I have neither talent, nor ability. I'm only a rich man who can never get where he wants to go! After all that, I've produced nothing."
>
> He looked at his canvas through his tears. All at once he stood up with pride, and fixed a flashing glance on the two painters.
>
> "By the blood, by the body, by the head of Christ, you are so jealous you want me to believe she is ruined so you can steal her

from me! But, I see her! [Moi, je la vois!]" he shouted, "she is marvelously beautiful."[8]

The audiovisual style of Peterson's *Mr. Frenhofer and the Minotaur* owes something to Man Ray's and Robert Desnos' *L'Etoile de mer*, which I shall discuss at length in the next chapter. The entire film was shot with a distorting anamorphic lens, and its soundtrack is a chain of puns and free associations. However, the narrative persona has been changed; instead of an obsessive poet, a female art student and model recites the monologue as if on the edge of sleep or actually dreaming. From within the dream logic we can surmise the following "plot": her lover has read Balzac's *Le chef d'oeuvre inconnu* to her; without losing her sense of irony, she identified with Poussin's mistress in the story and associated Porbus and Frenhofer with the faculty of her art school. Somehow the figures of "Minotauromachie" have come alive in her dream to interact with modern versions of Balzac's characters.

Peterson has said:

It was my decision to do a thing about the Balzac story, taking seriously as the theme of the story the conflict between Poussin's Classicism and its opposite. So, as strained through my mind, it became, really, a way of exploring the conflict stated in [Henri] Rousseau's remark to Picasso: "We are the two greatest painters: you in the Egyptian manner; and I in the modern."[9]

For Peterson, the central conflict within modernism has been the opposition of a visionary quest for revolutionary newness and a continuity with a classical tradition. Frenhofer and Henri Rousseau represent the former; Poussin, Porbus, and Picasso the latter.

Peterson made this film, as indeed most of his films, under the sponsorship of the California School of Fine Arts (now the San Francisco Art Institute) with student and faculty participation during the period sometimes called "The San Francisco Renaissance" when Clyfford Still and Mark Rothko were teaching painting at the school and Ansel Adams and Minor White photography. The film reflects Peterson's polemical refusal to take the notion of abstraction as a decisive issue for modernism. He has claimed that all abstraction is either geometry or biomorphism. Stan Brakhage has carried this dismissal of abstraction to a radical extreme, arguing in *Metaphors on Vision* (1963) that the greatest achievement of the American Abstract Expressionists was the representation of "closed-eye vision" in their paintings. Brakhage's general strategy

13

has been to recuperate the visionary stance from Peterson's dialectical allegory, first, by interpreting all art as representational and, second, by taking the accuracy of the representation of *personal vision* as the measure of artistic quality.

Inviting the Unconscious In

Mr. Frenhofer and the Minotaur is framed by shots of the young woman in bed. At the beginning she wakes in fright at the sight of a cat presenting her with a dead mouse. The film ends with a shot of her asleep. Within the oneiric comedy, the visual equivalent of the continuously punning monologue is the substitution of images derived from the "Minotauromachie" for characters in the Balzac story. The role of the barebreasted Athenian virgin is subsumed by the model herself, but a new figure, a fencer, also enters the film from Picasso's images of the wounded or exhausted female matador. The horse becomes a sawhorse in Frenhofer's studio, and the other figures from the etching populate the studio with an indifference to the central drama that should remind us of Courbet's great painting of himself at work in his studio, which must be yet another source for the film.

When he made *Mr. Frenhofer and the Minotaur,* Peterson provided a characteristically cryptic program note. It ends with an enigmatic clue to its interpretation:

> In the labyrinth in which Frenhofer is supposed finally to have lost himself there is also, of necessity, a minotaur and, also of necessity, a Minotauromachy. As for the detail of *Mr. Frenhofer and the Minotaur,* its interpretation should be on another level entirely. Thus the recurring "kitty" is a reference to Catherine Lescault, the subject of the unknown masterpiece, but although Catherine is Kitty and Kitty Catherine, both are equally something else and so on. This is not complicated, merely diffuse, a sort of indefinite intellectual extension of quantitative atmosphere whereby we are not led to conclude that the film ends where it starts, but in some vast labyrinth of endless reference where it is also possible to encounter Minotaurs, picassoidal or otherwise, which we should have the courage to recognize after first, of course, discovering them.[10]

Balzac's parable of ideal beauty poses the paradoxical question: does the human instance provide the model for the painter or is his idealized vision a standard for measuring reality? Peterson recasts the story as a system of signs when he writes of a "vast labyrinth of endless reference." Of course, that also describes the poetics of allusion which underpins his film. Part bull, part man, the minotaur is an emblem of the principle of collage, the art of displacement and condensation. In the symbol of the minotaur, dichotomies break down; Henri Rousseau's oppositional pair, the Egyptian and the modern, fuse into something that threatens the survival of the artist.

Peterson tells us here that the minotaur is itself the dreaded object of an obsessive quest, like the starfish of *L'Etoile de mer*. Even if Peterson, like Joyce in this too, resists Freudian interpretation, the language of his film encourages it. When the art student and model dreams of her "mini-mini-mini-tower," we may wonder if the reference is to a phallus or the clitoris, but we are nevertheless clearly in the realm of genital fantasy so thoroughly explored by Freud.

Peterson's contemporaries interpreted the minotaur in Picasso's etching as a figure of male sexual aggression, refracted through the perspectives of a curious child holding up a candle and an older, bearded man, looking back in flight from the scene.[11] Two women with doves (birds of Aphrodite) complete the audience of spectators. Blinded by the candlelight, or groping toward it, the minotaur stretches out his hand. Dr. Schneider's analysis of the etching suggests an argument that would later be made by the psychoanalyst Henry Edelheit, which I shall use extensively in chapters 6 and 8. Such scenes represent the libidinal theater of primal scene fantasies.

For Peterson, it would seem, psychoanalysis does not answer questions about the origin of aesthetic creativity; it institutes a "powerful mythology" which the artist must face and challenge. In a sense, the minotaur is the psychoanalytic apparatus, the very system that would unmask the riddle of minotaurs. By collapsing Picasso's imagery on top of Balzac's, the filmmaker has turned a story about the male fascination with observing and depicting female nudity into an allegory of the destructive potential inherent in "inviting the unconscious in" on the creative process.[12]

The consistent use of anamorphosis gives the film a unified look. At the same time, it softens the distinction between the spatial organization of shot–countershot exchanges between art school students and faculty and the parallel scenes from the world of the "Minotauromachie." The ultimate fusion of the two domains occurs when the fencer stabs Frenhofer in the one shot–countershot alternation between the previously independent zones of imagery; but the witty, surrealist image of the minotaur staring at Frenhofer's canvas after the artist's death completes that transfer of meaning from Balzac's world to Picasso's, without ever leaving Peterson's. The painting becomes the object of the monster's groping quest. This shot near the conclusion of the film makes the absence of a countershot significant. Frenhofer's painting must remain visually "inconnu," like the final and climactic photograph in Hollis Frampton's (*nostalgia*). It is yet another version of Mallarmé's "ptyx," a center of gravity under the negative sign.

Like the readers of Balzac's tale that Dore Ashton discusses in *A Fable of Modern Art*—Cézanne, Picasso, Rilke, and Schoenberg—Maurice Blanchot reads *Le chef d'oeuvre inconnu* anachronistically, as if Frenhofer had created a portrait so "modern" that his contemporaries could not see it. In fact, he ironizes the story even further, by suggesting that Frenhofer's failure was that he could not get rid of the realistic foot! Here is how he ends "De l'angoisse au langage," his first long theoretical essay, which he published the same year Peterson finished his film:

> The unknown masterpiece always allows one to see in the corner the tip of a charming foot, and this delicious foot prevents the work from being finished, but also prevents the painter from facing the emptiness of his canvas and saying, with the greatest feeling of repose: "Nothing, nothing! At last, there is nothing."[13]

The vestigial foot is another equivalent of Mallarmé's "ptyx"; it reaches back into earlier modes of representation, forcing a quivering movement within which yet another obliteration of meaning becomes a link to the tradition.

1

The Instant of Love:
Image and Title in Surrealist Cinema

IN FOCUSING on the relationship of some aspects of literary modernism to the stylistics of a number of difficult films made over a span of nearly sixty years I hope to delineate some of the varieties of intertextuality to be found in modernist texts. I shall look at (1) some radical forms of adaptation (Man Ray of a poem, Dreyer of two plays, Bresson of two novels, Straub and Huillet of an opera), (2) some films which foreground the use of language, and (3) conversely, some which abjure the use of words but rhetorically use cinematic tropes. In all these categories the trope of shot–countershot, and above all the figurative methods of *avoiding* or postponing it, plays a distinctive role.

Shot–Countershot

SHOT–COUNTERSHOT OR "reverse angle cutting": the alternation of cinematic images with the direction reversed, along an axis of between 120 and 180 degrees. This has been the filmmaker's standard way of representing a person and what he sees ("eyeline matching") or two people looking at each other. It took some twenty years for this figure of editing to become the cornerstone of a narrative continuity in films. By the end of the First World War, it was a firmly established convention.

Since the filmmaker creates shot–countershot by pointing the camera alternately at one figure, and then at the thing or person supposedly opposite him, the sequence, in the edited film, of the discrete shots has the implicit effect of erasing the presence of the camera. The counter-shot mutely reassures us that the camera is, or, rather, was insubstantial. Together, the two images in sequence declare the integrity of a seam-less, fictional space in which the former intervention of a camera, a director, and a crew has been forgotten. In the past fifteen years, a considerable amount of theoretical writing has focused on the formal, and even psychoanalytical, implications of this illusion of continuous space.[1] The ramifications of that discussion lie outside the scope of this book.

Traditionally, there was a tendency in film theory to take shot–coun-tershot for granted. Alfred Hitchcock, far from questioning its privi-lege, identifies it with "pure cinema." In fact, writing for the 1967 edi-tion of the *Encyclopaedia Britannica,* he covertly alludes to his own film *Rear Window,* a thriller about a photographer reduced by an accident to peeping at people in the courtyard beyond his wheelchair:

> [P]ure cinema has nothing in itself to do with actual movement. Show a man looking at something, say a baby. Then show him smiling. By placing these shots in sequence—man looking, object seen, reaction to object—the director characterizes the man as a kindly person. Retain shot one (the look) and shot three (the smile) and substitute for the baby a girl in a bathing costume, and the director has changed the characterization of the man.[2]

Hitchcock knew he was describing the "Kuleshov effect," named for Lev Kuleshov, who experimented with intercutting closeups of the ac-tor Mosjukhin, all with the same deadpan expression, with a plate of soup, a dead woman in a coffin, and a child playing with a toy. Pu-dovkin made the experiment famous in his book *Film Technique:*

> When we showed the three combinations to an audience which had not been let into the secret, the result was terrific. The public raved about the acting of the artist. They pointed out the heavy pensiveness of his mood over the forgotten soup, were touched and moved by the deep sorrow with which he looked at the dead woman, and admired the light, happy smile with which he sur-veyed the girl at play.[3]

Some sentences before, describing the construction of the experiment, he had written: "It was *obvious* and *certain* that Mosjukhin was looking at the soup" [emphasis mine]. Both Hitchcock and Pudovkin write as if an audience were a well-conditioned machine. This confidence in the simplistic response of film viewers reveals an important aspect of the history of shot–countershot: many of the most distinguished filmmakers, and especially those who did not question the centrality of narrative to cinema, relied on the conventional response to shot–countershot as the foundation of their emotional manipulation of viewers. Furthermore, they constructed fictional characters in terms of what they saw and how they reacted to sights.

This concentration on the act of seeing, thus reduced to a montage formula, is as fundamental to the narrative film as speaking and reading are to the fictional persons in novels. Yet, this distinction is one of nuances and degrees. Novels describe crucial acts of seeing and most films are crammed with information only speech can reveal. It is Hitchcock, again, who underlines a difference of emphasis when he concludes: "The essence of good direction then is to be aware of all these possibilities and to use them to show what people are doing and thinking and, secondarily, what they are saying."[4]

In the chapters which follow shot–countershot will be mentioned frequently in the detailed analysis of a few films of exceptional intensity and originality, which either entirely eschew the technique (or as I prefer "figure") as a worn-out convention or use it in a deliberately eccentric manner to give it a new vitality. I am not suggesting, however, that the abandonment or the original use of shot–countershot is the sole marker of cinematic modernism, nor that modernist films never resort to the conventional figuration.

My isolation of certain seminal films which consciously aspire to forge a cinematic modernism necessarily entails sacrificing an argument of theoretical application to cinema in general. Instead, my approach will be stylistic, examining the uniqueness with which several filmmakers of different periods and nationalities have, on occasion, constructed their films. Insofar as they have made "pure cinema," its definition runs counter to that of Hitchcock. The richness and depth of his deployment of shot–countershot conventions in *Rear Window* and *Vertigo* are functions of the psychological mimesis with which he represents the act of watching within the dramatic narrative. Seeing what his characters see, we come to know them and identify with their curiosity. All the films I shall discuss make the crucial moment of vision problematic, each in a different way.

Shot–countershot, parallel cutting, and the use of intertitles became standard features of international film production after the First World War, a little more than forty years after the publication of Mallarmé's

"Sonnet en yx." From the fragmentary remains of early cinema it is possible to trace these stylistic figures back to the first decade and a half of filmmaking. Historians often employ the unfortunate term "primitive" to describe this period. That labeling by analogy to the traditional arts creates the false impression that cinema had a clearly defined origin. Actually, when Louis and Auguste Lumière first presented their cinematographic machine to the public in 1895, they were operating within a century long tradition of optical engineering, and more significantly, the illusions they projected were subject to a critique of representation that had been particularly intense in France.

The Return to Reason

THE AVANT-GARDE filmmakers working in France in the 1920s inherited a legacy of dynamic debate about cinematic representation that had gone on for almost twenty years. Within this context two well-known films are to be seen in a relationship previously unexamined. They are *Anémic cinéma* and *L'Etoile de mer*. Furthermore, their relationship to each other is relevant to one of the most strenuously debated theoretical issues of their time: the status of the intertitle in silent films. Negatively, these films address the question of the centrality of shot–countershot by utterly avoiding it.

With his development of the rayograph Man Ray drove a wedge between photography and camera work. He placed objects—strings, buttons, tacks, a hand—directly on the surface of photosensitive material before exposing it to light. A positive image gave him a brilliantly outlined white shape on a black background; the negative reversed it. Parts of the surface could even be exposed to a conventional camera negative to create a synthesis of camera and contact imagery.

The rayograph reaffirmed in a modernist register Fox Talbot's early discovery that the camera was not a necessary part of the ontology of photography. Rather, the photosensitive surface was the essential material element. Even though photographic images usually were and continue to be generated by cameras, Man Ray's work stated the claim that the imagery of the lens was a contingent aspect of the art. This theoretical position is comparable to that of the German dadaists and Russian *zaum* poets, who held that sounds and letters of the alphabet rather than words were the fundamental materials of poetry, even though most poems are made up of words.

For cinema, the implications of Man Ray's photography were large and complex. In his first film, *Le retour à la raison* (1923), Man Ray actually applied the rayographic technique: he stuck tacks into successive frames, laid a spring and other objects across several feet of film in his darkroom, and sprinkled granular substances on more undeveloped film. When he exposed this to light and then processed the pieces, the pure white shapes danced in black space because of the slight variations in the positioning of objects from frame to frame. But even by alternating positive and negative strips of these moving rayographs he could only get a minute or so of moving imagery. The process was simply too time-consuming for the needs of cinema. A number of conventionally photographed images—a nude torso striped by bands of light and shadow, a twirling grid superimposed asynchronously over itself, night lights and signs, etc.—also appear in this very short film. The "return to reason" of the title might be taken as a declaration that cinema is fundamentally a play of light on a surface. After almost thirty years of cinema, here was a film that returned to the theoretical starting point of the medium, taking account of its possibility as an art. All the images refer to the interaction of lights, screens, and other surfaces. There is no attempt to construct a fictional space by means of either shot–countershot or intertitles. Much of this material was reused for his longer, more structured film *Emak Bakia* (1926).

My concern here is not exclusively with Man Ray's contribution to the avant-garde cinema and its theory. This rayographic technique could not effectively cope with the repetitiousness of film frames. The investigation into the irreducible elements of cinema, of which *Le retour à la raison* and *Emak Bakia* were parts, proceeded on a much more productive and profound level in two projects in which Man Ray participated: Marcel Duchamp's *Anémic cinéma* and Man Ray's own collaboration with Robert Desnos, *L'Etoile de mer*.

Intertitles

BOTH FILMS respond to the intense debate of the 1920s concerning the status of the intertitle. The German director Lupu Pick made *Scherben* (1921) with only one significant title and *Sylvester* (1923) with none. Charles Ray's *The Old Swimmin' Hole* (1921), Murnau's *Der Letze Mann* (1924), and Kirsanoff's *Menilmontant* (1924) narrate complex stories without titles. And at the end of the decade, Dziga Vertov proudly subtitled his tour-de-force *The Man with a Movie Camera* (1928) "a film without intertitles." Curiously, the suppression of the intertitle became a theoretical issue while the elimination of shot–countershot remained a matter of radical practice that did not reach polemical expression.

However, claims of cinematic purity and of a universal language were often linked to these films without words. In 1924 Jean Epstein wrote:

> The theory underlying the film without titles is obviously logical: cinema exists to narrate with images and not with words. However, one should never push a theory to its limits: their extremity is always the weak spot where it collapses. Looking at a film completely without titles is undeniably depressing, for psychological reasons; the subtitle is first of all a rest for the eye, a punctuation mark for the mind. A title often avoids a long visual explanation, which may be necessary but is boring and banal. . . . Isn't advertising a film as having no subtitles like praising Mallarmé's poems because they do not have punctuation?[5]

Rrose Sélavy

THE SURREALIST poet Robert Desnos published film criticism regularly during the 1920s. In 1923 he devoted an article to "Musique et sous-titres." He saw the title as an integral part of the art of cinema. "Everything that can be projected on the screen belongs in the cinema, letters as well as faces. All means are good when they produce good films, and it is in the mind that the quest for purity must occur rather than in a subsidiary technique."[6]

The first film within the tradition of the avant garde to claim equality of title and image was Duchamp's *Anémic cinéma*. The very language that appears on the screen reflects Duchamp's influence on Desnos. In 1923 Desnos published a long poem entitled *Rrose Sélavy*. It consists of 150 punning sentences. In a footnote to the title Desnos advises us: "The author regrets that he cannot cite the name of the initiator of Rrose Sélavy without annoying him. Curious minds might decipher no. 13." That verse—"Rrose Sélavy connait bien le marchand du sel"—links Marcel Duchamp's name with Rrose Sélavy's by means of a spoonerism. In general, these puns are aggressive, mocking religion and society and, above all, emphasizing sexuality. For instance:

> 1. Dans un temple en stuc de pomme le pasteur distillait le suc des psaumes. (In a temple of apple stucco the pastor distills the juice of psalms.)
> 2. Rrose Sélavy demand si les Fleurs du Mal ont modifié les moeurs du phalle: qu'en pense Omphale? (Rrose Sélavy asks if The Flow-

ers of Evil have changed the customs of the phallus: what does
Navel think about if?)
150. Amiable souvent est sable mouvant. (Lovely is often quick-
sand.)[7]

Rrose Sélavy is the name of a verbal game, an exploration of the
potential of the pun, founded by Duchamp and continued by Desnos.
The sayings of Rrose Sélavy are all examples of language turned back
upon itself, in which new meanings are found in the redistribution of
verbal sounds. The meaning of any of these sayings can be crudely parsed
as I have done, but translation is impossible. And the name too is a
pun. In French the letter r is pronounced er, and thus "Rrose Sélavy"
strikes the ear as "Eros, c'est la vie!"

Part of the wit of Duchamp's elaborately witty film Anémic cinéma
derives from the recognition that by and large the cinematic experience
during the silent period was one of an alternation of reading and looking
at images in an illusionistic depth. Duchamp carries this to an extreme
limit; for every image there is a verbal passage, or between every two
images, a title. In all, ten statements by Rrose Sélavy are shown interspersed with nine nonverbal images. This relationship to contemporary
conventions of cinema is purely theoretical, for Anémic cinéma does not
look like any film that had been made before it. The images are all disks
of eccentric circles within circles and spiral lines. The words are nothing
more than single sentences (in Rrose Sélavy's manner) printed spirally
on disks, winding from outside in.

The viewer's automatic optical response is at odds with the sameness
of the images; for, ontologically, there is no difference between disks
with words and those with spirals. Those with words seem just what
they are—two-dimensional figures printed in spiral form—even when
they are in motion. As they turn clockwise the reflex of the eye is either
to move with them, negating their motion in order to read the words,
or to fix a point from which to read each word as it passes through that
point. The mere presence of the words, as language, in either case engenders a response—reading—which is the willful denial of the disk as
an integral visual entity. This unique conditioning to printed language
causes the first figurative interpretation of the literal surface.

Quite a different reaction occurs each time the disks of spirals and
circular lines appear. The eye seizes them as wholes; their motion induces an optical illusion of three-dimensionality. Some seem to pro-
trude from the flatness of the screen, others look like conical depres-
sions. On the most elementary level, the response to this simple alternating

structure confirms the strength of the conditioning that creates different reflexes within a system that is purely repetitious on the formal plane.

A film composed only of spirals and puns is indeed an example of anemic cinema. *Anémic*, the secret epithet hidden within *cinéma*, is not a French form: *anémique* here has been corrupted by an English spelling. In at least two disks with texts there are similar cases of French infected by English. The title obviously identifies the film we see as a weak, bloodless example of cinema. But it can also be interpreted as a general statement about the art as a whole: cinema is anemic. This is the only film Duchamp ever made, although he experimented with a stereoptical project. It is his one statement in film and about film. It implies that cinema is anemic because it all takes place in the mind of the viewer through automatic responses, as that viewer is duped into believing tha the successive still images move, that their flatness is really depth, th they bear a relationship to their titles. The titles seem, at first, unrelat u to the images:

Bains de gros thé pour grains de beauté sans trop de bengué.

L'enfant qui tête est un souffleur de chair chaude et n'aime pas le choufleur de serre chaude.

Si je te donne un sou, me donneras-tu paire de ciseaux?

On demande des moustiques domestiques (demi-stock) pour la cure d'azote sur la Côte d'Azur.

Inceste ou passion de famille, à coups trop tirés.

Esquivons les ecchymoses des esquimaux aux mots exquis.

Avez vous déjà mis la moëlle de l'épée dans le poêle de l'aimée?

Parmi nos articles de quincaillerie paresseuse, nous recommandons le robinet qui s'arrête de couler quand on ne l'écoute pas.

L'aspirant habite Javel et moi j'avais l'habite en spirale.

The final title presents a fingerprint and reads, "Copyrighted by Rrose Sélavy 1926."[8]

At first sight *Anémic cinéma* would seem to underline the difference between optical and verbal images. The two modes of representation are held together by the figure of the spiral. Yet we automatically apprehend them differently. The eye grasps the eccentric circles as if they were geometrical wholes.

So, from the very start, the viewer sees the illusions of protrusion and depression despite the mental assurance provided by the emphatic identity of every shot setup that each disk has been filmed from a fixed frontal position. While the viewer sees one set of disks as creating depth, he "reads" the other set as flat because of his reflex to the familiar orthography of the Latin alphabet.

Thus, the viewer is the victim of an automatic response at odds with the ontological sameness of the "shots." At the same time, the verbal disks produce an auditory effect in the imagination, thereby introducing another automatism against which the viewer is helpless. Of course, the texts reenforce that auditory effect, spiraling upon themselves in near rhymes.

Something else happens when we begin to allow the puns to have their play. The figurative meaning of "la möelle de l'épée" and "le poêle de l'aimée" overpowers the literal (non)sense. The reference to sexual intercourse could hardly be more evident. Furthermore, once we recognize its figurative character, our reading of the other disks begins to reveal sexual allusions. So "quincaillerie paresseuse" comes to indicate the genitals after intercourse and "le robinet" a dripping penis: even a rudimentary narrative of orgasm and detumescence is suggested in the sequencing of the titles. The welts of the Eskimos in the sixth word disk have a curiously venereal aspect when read in this light; the nitrogen cure (fresh air) suggests a folk remedy for them. Once the mind has attuned itself to such a reading, it reaches out to include all the texts in the film.

This spilling over of figurative meaning not only determines the interpretation of the words. It conditions the way in which the spiral images can be seen. Suddenly the abstract gyrating shapes which rise from and sink into the plane of the screen come to resemble the igloos, breasts, welts, and genitalia evoked by the words. The sexuality is neither in the literal meaning of the words, nor represented in the optical illusions, seen by themselves. The culminating reflex of the viewer's mind reads the figurative meaning of one part into the other. Duchamp suggests that cinema is anemic insofar as it depends upon such guidance.

The final title describes the position of the imaginary author of the words and of the film. "L'aspirant habite Javel et moi j'avais l'habite en spirale." L'aspirant is a candidate. The word is used for a suitor in love and, in a nautical sense, for a midshipman. The sailor as suitor touches upon popular myths of sexual urgency and excess, much as the "esquimaux aux mots exquis" of the sixth title disk hints at the myths of Eskimo hospitality. Javel is a district of Paris. After a beginning which locates the horny sailor in Javel, we should expect a parallel statement of the moi's address with another covert allusion to his sexuality. This is not exactly what we get. *Avoir l'habite* literally means "to have the coat" or "to have the clothes," and the phrase could be construed as "I had my clothes in a spiral." However, another contamination of French usage by English is apparent here; Duchamp is using *avoir l'habite* as if it were *avoir l'habitude,* "to have the habit."

Rrose Sélavy not only wears a spiral suit and has a spiral habit (if we allow the contamination) but he or she has "la bitte inspirale." The phrase contains a vulgarism and a corruption. *La bitte,* which means "bitt," is a vulgar term for the penis. *Inspirale* is a twisting of *inspiratrice.* Rrose Sélavy had an inspiring cock, the spiral cock, and the cock in a spiral, now become a vaginal form. As puns spiral out from this self-identification, the eroticization of the spiral itself finally becomes explicitly thematic, whereas the concluding title had been covert.

Adapting a Poem

MAN RAY'S participation in the making of *Anémic cinéma* was purely technical. Duchamp called upon him, together with Marc Allegret, to help record the movement of the disks on film. But in *L'Etoile de mer* Man Ray made his own statement about cinema's interrelationship of words and images. The occasion for the making of this work is somewhat obscure. In his autobiography, *Self Portrait,* he says that Robert Desnos read a poem before a gathering of friends prior to his departure for a conference in the Caribbean, whereupon Man Ray promised to make a film of the poem in the time Desnos was away. The poem has disappeared. Man Ray records that it was called "L'Etoile de mer," and that it was eighteen or twenty lines long, containing all the images of the film. The claim has been made that "La Place de l'Etoile," Desnos' dramatic "antipoème" was the basis of the film. The only point of juncture is the appearance of a starfish in both the film and the play, making the claim untenable.[9]

A manuscript was discovered in the archives of the Museum of Modern Art in New York, which seems to be a film scenario in Desnos' hand with annotations by Man Ray.[10] The manuscript is remarkably close to the finished film. However, it is fascinating that many of the titles are not included. When were they incorporated into the film? Who wrote them? Hedges plausibly suggests that Man Ray culled them largely from Desnos' poems.[11] I suspect that either they were from the original poem (if it ever existed) or were added with Desnos' collaboration after the images were edited. Here are the titles as they appear in the film:

les dents des femmes
sont des objets
si charmants ...
... qu'on ne devait
les voir qu'en rêve
ou
à l'instant de l'amour.

Adieu

Si belle! Cybèle?

Nous sommes à jamais
perdus dans le désert
de l'éternèbre.

Qu'elle est belle

"Après tout"

si les fleurs
étaient en
verre

"belle, belle, comme
une fleur de verre"

"belle comme une fleur
de chair"

Il faut battre les morts
quand ils sont froids.

Les murs de la Santé

Et si tu trouves
sur cette terre
une femme
à l'amour sincère ...

"belle
comme une
fleur de feu"

Women's teeth
are objects
so charming ...
... that one ought
to see them only in a dream
or
in the instant of love.

Farewell

So beautiful! Cybele?

We are forever
lost in the desert
of eternal darkness.

How beautiful she is

"After all"

if the flowers
were in
glass

"beautiful, beautiful like
a flower of glass"

"beautiful like a flower of
flesh"

One must beat the dead
while they are cold.

The walls of the Sante

And if you find
on this earth
a woman
of sincere love ...

"beautiful
like a
flower of fire"

Le soleil, un pied à l'étrier, niche un rossignol dans un voile de crêpe.	The sun, one foot in the stirrup, nestles a nightingale in a veil of crepe.
Vous ne rêvez pas	You are not dreaming
"qu'elle était belle"	"how beautiful she was"
"qu'elle est belle"	"how beautiful she is"
belle	beautiful

In André Breton's *Nadja* there are two photographs of Desnos taken by Man Ray showing, in successive images on a strip, the poet asleep. Desnos had a reputation for being able to compose poetry in a sleeplike trance produced by self-hypnosis. Many of his finest poems from the 1920s describe dreams, and they often present the poet as a lover in a desperate erotic situation. A commonplace of surrealist literature is the encounter with a strange, perhaps mad, woman. *Nadja* itself chronicles Breton's meetings with such a woman. In Desnos' poetry the fascinating but impossibly distant female is called "la mystèrieuse."

L'Etoile de mer presents another version of the encounter with "la mystèrieuse." This much of the plot is clear: a man meets a woman who sells newspapers on the street. They go to her apartment where she takes off all of her clothes; he leaves immediately. They meet again on the street. This encounter is followed by several scenes of each of them alone. The man has taken from the woman a glass paperweight in which is enclosed a starfish. At the conclusion they meet in a scene almost identical to their initial encounter, but this time another man (played by Desnos) arrives suddenly and takes the woman away with him.

The film's energy is not concentrated in this elementary plot, but in the depiction of the male figure's mind. The most obvious index of subjectivity is Man Ray's use of a stippled lens which distorts many of the images, especially at the opening. Such distortion as a sign of subjectivity had been part of the French cinema since Abel Gance's *La Folie de Dr. Tube* (1919). The most surprising aspect of Man Ray's use of it is its apparently arbitrary intermittence. The sequence of the meeting at the opening of the film is, by and large, distorted optically, but there are details filmed through a "normal" lens. Given Man Ray's skill as a photographer and the manner in which he called into question the status of the camera lens in both photography and cinema, this alternation of optical perspectives cannot be unimportant. The very subtitle of the film, "poème de Robert Desnos tel que l'a vu Man Ray," draws our attention to the difference between text and sight and bids us look for the particulars of Man Ray's vision.

The World Through Glass

BUT "TEL que l'a vu Man Ray" refers not only to the filmmaker's envisioning of the poem, but also to the very nature of camera vision in general. The alternation of lenses points first of all to the very fact that *films are shot through lenses*. *L'Etoile de mer* is a film about seeing the world through layers of glass. The camera always protects its sensitive film surface from the exterior world with a wall of glass. The implication here is that the so-called normal lens is as artificial as the stippled one. This implicit principle of pure theory functions as an essential component of the film's thematics in much the same way as does the claim of the impoverishment, or anemia, of cinema in Duchamp's work. Both stress the abstract peculiarity of illusionistic modes of vision: in both, language is poetically reflexive; in both, sexuality mediates between two extremes.

The self-conscious awareness of the medium of the glass lens in cinematography persistently inhibits the articulation of a fictional space in which "action" can take place. The alternation of conventional perspectives with distortions forces this drama of sexual encounter and its fetishistic obsession into a symbolical space. Furthermore, the utter suppression of shot–countershot (and cutting on glances) is remarkable in a film so fixated upon the theme of scopic fascination.

As the couple begin to walk together early in the film, the woman attracts the man's attention by stopping to fix her garter. The title which interrupts her gesture reads, "Les dents des femmes sont des objets si charmants. . . ." Had we seen an image of her smile this title would have been nothing more than the literalization of a banal convention. Coming where it does, however, it generates a new level of signification, for the image of the woman's thighs, coupled with a mention of her teeth, brings into play the concept of the *vagina dentata*. That concept, a synthesis of picture and text, is only figuratively represented in the film and, yet, it comes to dominate and determine the man's action.

A similar garter image can be found in Breton's *Nadja*, which has remarkable affinities to this film. Late in the novel, Breton discusses his unusual use of pictures to complement the literary text:

29

On this occasion, I realized that most of the places more or less resisted my venture, so that, as I see it, the illustrated part of *Nadja* is quite inadequate: Becque surrounded by sinister palings, the management of the Théâtre Moderne on its guard, Porville dead and disillusioning as any French city, the disappearance of almost everything relating to *The Grip of the Octopus* and, above all—for I regarded otherwise it as essential, although it has not been referred to in this book—the impossibility of obtaining permission to photograph an adorable wax-work figure in the Musée Grevin, on the left, between the hall of modern political celebrities and the hall at the rear of which, behind a curtain, is shown "an evening at the theater": it is a woman fastening her garter in the shadows, and is the only statue I know of with eyes, the eyes of provocation, etc.[12]

A late edition of *Nadja* illustrates this wax figure; it is remarkably like the image of *L'Etoile de mer*. Even the theme of glass [verre] plays an important role in Breton's book. Opening the novel with the surprising question, "Who am I? [Qui suis-je]," the author develops this theme several pages later:

I myself shall continue living in my glass house [maison de verre] where you can always see who comes to call; where everything hanging from the ceiling and on the walls stays where it is as if by magic, where I sleep nights in a glass bed, under glass sheets [sur un lit de verre aux draps de verre] where *who I am* [qui je suis] will sooner or latter appear etched in diamond.[13]

The literary text itself is a glass house on which words are to be scratched, although Breton leaves us uncertain whether the etched letters will be a biography or merely the phrase "qui je suis" blurring our vision of the sleeper within.

Vagina Dentata

The Grip of the Octopus was a film that played a large role in Breton's imagination; its title can be read as an allusion to the *vagina dentata*. The fascination of the *vagina dentata* compels Man Ray's poet to accompany the woman to her room and to watch her strip, but he then bids her adieu and leaves without making love. Instead, he focuses on an object: the paperweight she used to hold down her newspapers. Alone in his room, he contemplates the starfish in the glass paperweight. The pun he utters has an ambiguous referent. Is the woman or the starfish "Si belle"? In uttering the sounds "Si belle!" he pronounces the name Cybèle.

Catullus addressed a long poem, numbered sixty-three in the *Carmina*, to the cult of Cybele. It opens this way:

> Attis, driven over the sea-deeps by swift oars,
> eagerly sought the Phrygian grove, and rushed
> to the dark sites reserved for the Goddess.
> Goaded there by raving madness, his mind adrift,
> he cut off his own weights with a flint knife,
> [devoluit ita acuto sibi pondera silice]
> and then, unmanned, she sensed her loss, and
> as her wound still stained the ground with fresh blood
> she grabbed Cybele's light drum in her snow-white hands . . .

The frenzied follower of Cybele castrates himself and then, to follow Catullus' usage, "she" bemoans her deed for the remainder of the poem.

The starfish which holds the attention of the man possessed by the titillating dread of the *vagina dentata* and Cybelean castration is, significantly, contained within a cylinder of glass. Within the world encased in the camera's glass is a man peering into a glassed-in zone. As he peers, the starfish comes alive. "Après tout," the title declares at this moment. "After all" what? It is for the viewer to decide. After all, as it wraps itself around a sea urchin, the living starfish imitates the dreaded and fascinating *vagina dentata*.

In the more abstract sequence which follows, language and the camera's glass eye are conjoined by a pun: "Si les fleurs étaient en verre." Literally: "If the flowers were in glass." Coming when it does, after the image of a potted flower, the title names, in the conditional mood, that status of the image we have seen, a flower viewed through the glass of the lens. The flower is a sexual organ as well, so that the line refers metonymically to the man's desire to encounter the *vagina dentata* from the same close but protected distance as that from which he studies the starfish. Proximate to this title there is a succession of multiple images of revolving starfish in glass cylinders, roulette wheels, a sword plunged into and pulled out of a scabbard. The composite image in motion is possible only in cinema. And a flower "en verre" or a flower "de verre," as the next title varies it, is possible only in poetry. The pun of *verre* (glass) and *vers* (poetry) fuses the optical and verbal aspects of the film. The space between these two autonomous and reflexive systems is that

31

of figuration in which the dominant but invisible "image" of the *vagina dentata* holds sway.

The invented word *l'éternèbre,* which collapses *éternel* (endless) and *ténèbre* (darkness, shadow), speaks of the constant and hopeless attraction of "la mystèrieuse," as well as the condition of filmic images: perpetual shadows.[14] Man Ray subsequently introduces two new means of optical distortion. The speed of a train affects the camera's view of a landscape viewed through a window. A fog reduces boats seen by the man in a harbor to eerie silhouettes. The filmmaker is letting us see that a stippled lens is not the only source of modified vision: the very speed of the camera's movement and even the atmosphere through which it gathers its light can determine transformation. To these two kinds of distortion he adds still another, presenting a still life in fluid contours, moving from distorted to conventional perspective by merely turning the focus mechanism on his lens. This further establishes that the fluctuation of perspective is built into the glass eye of the camera. And when the still life does come into crisp focus, the two half-sliced bananas on the table beside a wine bottle turn out to be one more displacement of the fear of Cybele's castrating intoxication.

In a reversal of the opening metonymy of thigh and teeth, the first "fleur de chair" we are shown is the woman's face as she removes a mask and smiles: the flower of flesh becomes the bared face and teeth. The second fleshly flower appears on the man's hands as the lines of his palms appear in dark tracings. In *Self Portrait* Man Ray laconically mentions that the French censors required him to remove the title which follows this image of the flower lifelines: "Il faut battre les morts quand ils sont froids" ("One has to beat the dead when they are cold," a variation on the adage, "One must strike while the iron is hot"). The censors had obviously perceived—as two or three generations of art historians and film critics have not—that "les morts" are the genitals of the fetishist, rendered impotent by his fearful fascination. The title is a call for masturbation.

The surrealist hero has chosen to live in the imaginative realm of displacement, fantasy, and mythopoeisis. The scandal of Breton's enthusiasm for Freud, I suspect, was that he was not concerned with psychoanalysis as therapy but with its picture of the imagination, the manner in which it affirmed the lively notion that the dreams of magistrates, presidents of the republic, and archbishops are closer to the visions of Sade than to those of Plato.

The sequence of similes that began "belle, belle comme une fleur de verre" climaxes with the representation of fire. The progression "fleur de verre," "de chair," "de feu" intensifies the frightening imagery of the *vagina dentata*. Fire, a conventional metaphor for erotic passion, becomes horrific when taken literally: the genital of fire would destroy the lover. Man Ray's image, at this point, presents us with the woman's face photographed through a veil of flames. The configuration of the flickering flames, under the pressure of suggestion from the title, looks like a blazing flower. At the same time the filmmaker introduces another natural force for optical distortion. The air around the fire does not let light pass without bending it. The flower of fire generates a stippled beauty.

Optical distortion and Eros are conjoined in the most elaborate and puzzling title in the film: "Le soleil, un pied à l'étrier, niche un rossignol dans une voile de crêpe." The complex metaphor seems to derive from the traditions of Provençal troubadour poetry and the code of courtly love. Two elements of the *aubade,* or poem to the dawn, appear here. The courtly lover hates the dawn because it marks the end of his tryst. The intertitle portrays the sun as a horseback rider. With one foot in the stirrup, the sun mounts the horse; his radiance can be seen glowing around the horse, but the disk of light has not yet appeared on the horizon; it is the glow that precedes the dawn. With the coming of this light, the nightingale which sings at night and sleeps in the morning and is thus a friend to lovers, goes to its nest. The veil of crepe is the crepuscular half-light of this moment. With this metaphor the theme of optical distortion seen in the stippled lens, the train-driven camera, the fog, and the turning focus finally appears in the titles. It announces the end of the nocturnal fantasy and the film's conclusion.

This eccentric intertitle can be teased into sense when we read it as if it were a fragment of a medieval poem. Here, as in the play on Cybele, an allusion from the history of poetry persists within the modernist's seemingly random and spontaneous play of language. *L'Etoile de mer* is haunted by poetic voices as much as Mallarmé's "Sonnet en yx."

Despite the stress on acts of seeing in this film, it is made entirely without shot–countershot. At times Man Ray draws attention to the process of seeing by irising-in on a detail after he has set up a shot of the man looking at something. The early scenes of the protagonist staring at the starfish paperweight take this form. As such, this is the earliest "narrative" film I know that deliberately avoids shot–countershot after the institutionalization of that figure. The denial of shot–countershot, in this particular case, emphasizes the autonomy of those shots which illustrate the protagonist's voyeuristic obsession. By enclosing his stare within the frame, and by underlining it with the iris effect, the filmmaker subtly suggests that his imagination isolates him from the transitive domain evoked by montage.

Desnos seems to have been pleased with Man Ray's film. In his 1929 article "Cinéma d'avant-garde," this work, together with *Entr'acte* and *Un chien andalou,* is spared his condemnation. Of these films he says: "It's not a question of creating a work of art or a new aesthetic but of obeying a new form's deep, original, and consequently necessary movements."[15] That he also takes some credit for *L'Etoile de mer* is apparent in his footnote: "Here the author of these lines assumes a rather modest pose."

The Glass Stare

THERE CAN be little doubt that the question of the status of language in film was a central issue to which both *Anémic cinéma* and *L'Etoile de mer* responded. As well, the status of the lens itself was in question. In 1925 *Les Cahiers du Mois* devoted an entire issue to the aesthetics of cinema. Desnos was one of the seventeen writers consulted on the relationship of cinema to literature and modern thought. The same issue presented two photographs by Man Ray with the following editorial comment:

> We publish at the back of this volume some photographs of M. Man Ray, who has miraculously been able to provoke on sensitive paper the illusions and revelations (close-ups, deformations, soft focus, superimpositions, in short, simultaneity, abstractions, synthesis) that effect in us the sort of feeling one might be tempted to call cinematographic and which would, so it seems, be an a priori paradox to want to achieve with a still image.[16]

Upon opening the issue containing their contributions, Man Ray and Robert Desnos would have found the first article written by the most active theoretician of their day, Jean Epstein, whose rather neglected work is crucial to an understanding of avant-garde cinema in the 1920s. That article, "Le Regard du verre" (The Glass Stare), speaks of a mirror-lined spiral staircase as a metaphor for cinema. The filmmaker's experience is tied, according to Epstein, to an unmasking of the self and its deceptions which is the fundamental gift of cinema:

The mission of cinematography seems not to have been understood precisely. The camera lens is an eye that Apollinaire would have called surreal (with no connection to present-day surrealism), an eye endowed with nonhuman analytical properties. It is an eye without prejudices, without morality, free of influences; and it sees in the face and in human movement traits which we, weighted down by likings and dislikings, by habits and considerations, can no longer perceive.[17]

Both Man Ray and Marcel Duchamp deny the transcendental authority of the cinema's glass stare. For them it constitutes only one moment of cinematic experience. The other is language. The two conjoined reveal the surrealist view that cinema is tied to the power of the erotic imagination.

Mallarméan Cinema

NOT ALL the positions taken in the issue of *Les Cahiers du Mois* devoted to the aesthetics of cinema were as radical as those of Robert Desnos and Jean Epstein. The musicologist and general aesthetician Lionel Landry contributed a conservative evaluation of the claims made for the uniqueness of cinema entitled "The Formation of the Sensibility: The Role of the 'Subject.' " Examining the assertion that "The cinema should be cinema before it is anything else," he acknowledged that the purest advocates for the abolition of intertitles had a point insofar as the plethora of titles contributed to the mediocrity of most films, but he concluded that they were, for the moment at least, a necessary evil: "For if there is anything worse than projecting a text, it is to induce in the minds of the majority of spectators the feeling that a situation is not clear and that it needs a text to explain it."[18]

In thus disposing of the hotly debated issue of the intertitle, he implicitly rejected the validity of both *Anémic cinéma* (mostly a projected text) and *L'Etoile de mer* (in which the situation is opaque and the text hardly "explanatory"). Nevertheless, considering in succession the influence of the novel, poetry, music, dance and mime, theater, and painting on the cinema of his time, and isolating what each of the traditional arts could achieve more effectively than cinema, he concluded that filmmakers should abandon the search for the essence of cinema, as if it were something unique—such as Epstein's "glass stare." Instead, by distilling what they had learned from the other arts, filmmakers would make more powerful films. In the final passage of the article, he wrote:

> So little by little the meaning of the precept cited at the beginning of this study becomes more precise. What properly constitute "cinema" are not modes of expression unknown to the stage, the orchestra, the book; they are those in which the screen specifically succeeds more than the stage, the orchestra, or the book; that is the meaning of cinema finding its own direction. (p. 48)

A very curious allusion had been made by Landry earlier in his article, at a moment when he is trying to discriminate between the sensibility of the reader of poetry and that of the film viewer, he wrote:

> If animated photography creates images more fully than language, it requires a much longer delay for them to be perceived and to produce their emotional effect; and this makes it difficult to compare it to the kaleidoscopic speed of evocation that poetry possesses. To put on the screen the impression which three words from a certain line of Mallarmé (*angoisse, minuit, lampadophore*) give successively, in two seconds, would require three screen images each of which would have to last seven or eight seconds; and even then, since vision adapts itself to such rapid changes much less easily than the ear, the viewer would soon become tired if such a series were prolonged. (pp. 39–40)

The citation of three nouns from the second verse of Mallarmé's "Sonnet en yx" is puzzling here. In the introduction, I treated at length the difficulty of this sonnet and elaborated on the long tradition, dating from the poet's own letters, in which this particular poem has been cited as a challenge to visualization. The mention of this particular poem is more interesting than the aesthetician's failure to realize that filmmakers such as Gance, Epstein, and Léger, in his own time and place, had edited lucid film sequences which contained many shot changes within a single second.

Landry's use of the "Sonnet en yx" demonstrates his resistance to the idea of radical autonomy in any art, not just cinema. By mentioning the poet, if not the very poem, who in the French tradition stands for the hermetic isolation of the verbal artifact, as if one of his most difficult verses universally conjured up three distinct images, Landry aligned himself with aestheticians, like the Italian Croce, who argued the primacy of art over all the particular arts. The presence of a position of this sort in the film issue of *Les Cahiers du Mois* (and in the lecture series at the Ciné-club de France which was the source for the journal) helps us to see more clearly the context for the radicalism of Duchamp, Desnos, and Man Ray. Their contribution to cinema, and to the issue of cinematic modernism, was to test the limits of the autonomy of image and text, and to resist, with as much force and wit as they could muster, a cinema that synthesized the other arts. In so doing, they shared more with Mallarmé's self-allegorizing sonnet than Landry could have recognized.

2

Revolutionary Time:
Image and Title in Soviet Cinema

THE PEDAGOGICAL program of the Soviet cinema in the decade and a half following the Revolution required a version of modernism that counteracted the emphasis on allusion, paradox, and aesthetic skepticism such as we encountered it in the French avant-garde. In practice that meant a vigorous exploration of the parameters of shot–countershot and cautious experimentation with intertitles. Ultimately Soviet cinematic modernism became a critique of visual illusionism by playfully hyperbolizing the power of shot–countershot and the authority of the visible (Vertov's "Theory of the Interval" and Eisenstein's "intellectual montage") or by stressing the allegorical dimensions of cinematic figuration (Dovzhenko).

The major Soviet theoreticians accepted and worked with the principles of reverse-angle cutting. The clearcut distinction between the approach of Kuleshov and that of Vertov derives from their notions of the application of these principles rather than from their theoretical formulations of the principles themselves. For Kuleshov cinematic narrative always seems to take precedence. In his 1929 book, *The Art of the Cinema*, he described the following experiment:

> Khokhlova is walking along Petrov Street in Moscow near the "Mostrog" store. Obolensky is walking along the embankment of the Moscow River—at a distance of about two miles away.

They see each other, smile, and begin to walk toward one another. Their meeting is filmed at the Boulevard Prechistensk. This boulevard is in an entirely different section of the city. They clasp hands, with Gogol's monument as a background, and look—at the White House!—for at this point, we cut in a segment from an American film, *The White House in Washington*. In the next shot they are once again in the Boulevard Prechistensk. Deciding to go farther, they leave and climb up the enormous staircase of The Cathedral of Christ the Savior. We film them, edit the film, and the result is that they are seen walking up the steps of the White House. For this we used no trick, no double exposure: the effect was achieved solely by the organization of the material through its cinematic treatment.[1]

Vertov's 1923 manifesto, "Kinoks: A Revolution," puts the same principle into an address to the reader, but he stresses the disjunction rather than the synthetic illusionism of montage: "You are walking down a Chicago street today in 1923, but I make you greet Comrade Volodarsky, walking down a Petrograd street in 1918, and he returns your greeting." In the same text he expands the montage principle into a poetics of space and a collectivist anthropology:

> I am kino-eye. I am a builder. I have placed you, whom I've created today, in an extraordinary room which did not exist until just now when I also created it. In this room there are twelve walls shot by me in various parts of the world. In bringing together shots of walls and details, I've managed to arrange them in an order that is pleasing and to construct with intervals, correctly, a film-phrase which is the room.
> I am kino-eye, I create a man more perfect than Adam, I create thousands of different people in accordance with preliminary blueprints and diagrams of different kinds.
> I am kino-eye.
> From one person I take the hands, the strongest and most dexterous; from another I take the legs, the swiftest and most shapely; from a third, the most beautiful and expressive head—and through montage I create a new, perfect man.[2]

Kuleshov too tells us how he invented a human figure by combining details from several women; but the point of his experiment was to show that in the finished film she "still retain[ed] the complete reality of the material," so that she seemed to be a single fictional woman put-

ting on makeup before a mirror.[3] Where Kuleshov writes of the effi-
ciency of montage for story telling, Vertov draws a new view of the
world from its principles.

Eisenstein, for the most part, follows Kuleshov's approach to the
synthetic construction of cinematic space. Consider his example about
the editing of films imported into the Revolutionary state which had to
be reedited to change their political message:

> I cannot resist the pleasure of citing here one montage *tour de
> force* of this sort, executed by Boitler. One film brought from Ger-
> many was *Danton,* with Emil Jannings. As released on our screens,
> this scene was shown: Camille Desmoulins is condemned to the
> guillotine. Greatly agitated, Danton rushes to Robespierre, who
> turns aside and slowly wipes away a tear. The sub-title said, ap-
> proximately, "In the name of freedom I had to sacrifice a friend
> . . ." Fine.
>
> But who could have guessed that in the German original, Dan-
> ton, represented as an idler, a petticoat-chaser, a splendid chap and
> the only positive figure in the midst of evil characters, that this
> Danton ran to the evil Robespierre and . . . spat in his face? And
> that it was this spit that Robespierre wiped from his face with a
> handkerchief? And that the title indicated Robespierre's hatred of
> Danton, a hate that in the end of the film motivates the condem-
> nation of Jannings-Danton to the guillotine?!
>
> Two tiny cuts reversed the entire significance of this scene![4]

Although Eisenstein usually employed shot–countershot conventionally, he would, on occasion, use it to bring together spatially disjunctive
fields for dramatic effect. It was Vertov, naturally, who exploited the
potential for inventing artificial spaces most fully in his last silent film,
The Man with a Movie Camera (1929). There he stresses the mediation
of the filmic apparatus, by setting up, then exploding shot–countershot
situations of the cameraman filming (and what he shoots), the editor
looking at shots (and what she sees), and the audience watching the very
film we see in the making (and what they see on the screen).

The Question of Intertitles

THE MAN *with a Movie Camera* was subtitled "a film without intertitles." It was a showpiece of the clarity a complex and dialectical film

composition could achieve without recourse to words, even though—
perhaps especially because—it was made when it was common knowledge that the silent cinema was obsolete. In it, many shots repeat themselves in different montage contexts. The whole fabric is so intricately
constructed that each repetition refers back to and comments upon the
earlier context. As such, the film and the "theory of intervals" which
it embodies are attempts at a tropology of cinema.[5]

The study of the intertitle cannot be severed from the larger issue of
the poetics of montage which dominated Soviet film theory during its
formative period. This is exemplified by Boris Eikhenbaum's important
essay of 1927, "Problems of Film Stylistics," where the validity of intertitles is measured by their effectiveness:

> To treat film as absolutely non-verbal art is impossible. Those
> who defend cinema from the imitation of literature often forget
> that though the audible word is eliminated from film, the thought,
> i.e., internal speech, is nevertheless present. The study of the par-
> ticularities of film-speech is one of the most important problems
> in cinematic theory.
>
> The question of intertitles is connected with that of internal
> speech. The intertitle is one of the essential accents of meaning in
> a film, but it is impossible to speak of intertitles in general. One
> must differentiate their types and functions in a given film. . . .
>
> In any case, since cinema is not an aspect of pantomine, and
> the word is not altogether eliminated from it, intertitles are an
> absolutely legitimate part of a film; and the important thing is sim-
> ply that they do not turn into literature but take their place in a
> film as a natural and cinematographically realized element.[6]

Eikenbaum may have had the theoretical work of Dziga Vertov and
Bela Balazs (a Hungarian Communist, whose book *Der Sichtbare Mensch
oder die Kultur des Films* had appeared in German in 1924) when he rejected the notion of nonverbal cinema. Certainly Eisenstein, the youngest of the major Soviet filmmakers of the period, became a theoretical
polemicist as soon as he made his first film, *Strike* (1925), by dramatically isolating Vertov's and Balazs' theories for attack.

At the climax of *Strike*, Eisenstein had metaphorically intercut shots
of the butchering of a bull with images of the slaughter of striking workers
who had resisted factory owners and their agents, the police. He demonstrated the power of his theory of "the montage of attractions" in
which the conflict of images induces a physical response in the viewer

by skillfully intercutting scenes from the dramatic reconstruction of a mounted police assault (with beatings, the hosing of workers, and even a baby thrown brutally from a parapet) with the shots of the abattoir and the symbolical gesture of a worker under police interrogation who, slamming his fist in resistance on the chief's desk, overturns a bottle of ink on a plan of the city, which, in the montage context, suggests the figurative drenching of the workers' district in blood. But in this early film, Eisenstein only intercuts the single title "Brutalized" to underline the culminating violence (apart from the dialogue captions for the interrogation). At the very end, he adds the injunction "Remember/Proletarians," with two glaring eyes staring out at the audience.

That same year Vertov had released *Kinoglaz (Film Eye)*, an equally explicit demonstration of *his* theoretical position. He too showed the slaughter of a bull, but to opposite effects: by reversing the order of the shots from marketable meat back to the execution of the animal, he emphasized the labor history of food production. Furthermore, he presented the most violent scenes in reverse motion so that the butcher's knife seems to reunite magically the separated halves of the carcass and the killing blow restores the collapsed animal to life. The conventional effect of such reversed motion is comic. Even the cameramen of the Lumière brothers exploited this potential for cinema in the last years of the nineteenth century, although with much less emotionally charged material. Vertov's point was that cinema can transform our habitual reactions to slaughter; by radically altering the temporality of the act— by reversing it—cinema creates a new reaction. His titles cued the viewer to what cinema could do: "Film Eye pushes time backwards/ Beef 20 seconds ago/ Beef gets its intestines back/ Skin is returned to him/ Resurrection of the bull/ Corral./ To Freight cars/ With the herd."

These alternative approaches to the representation of violence were, and remained, characteristic of the difference between Eisenstein's and Vertov's film theories. Yet each insisted that his was the authentically Marxist approach. For Eisenstein, the filmmaker had to direct each film at a particular class audience and seek to effect a particular historical situation. Vertov found that approach a form of commercialization, preferring a cinema that would instruct an audience by exhibiting the limitations of a conventional personal perspective and, at the same time, by showing the inherent aptitude of cinema to overcome that perspective. In his idealization of montage, he sought to uncover its immanent laws, which, he compared to the fixed relations between intervals in music. His early manifesto "We" (1922) announced that theory without elucidating it:

> *Kinochestvo is the art of organizing the necessary movements of objects in space as a rhythmical artistic whole, in harmony with the properties of the material and the internal rhythm of each object.*
>
> *Intervals* (the transitions from one movement to another) are the material, the elements of the art of movement, and by no means the movements themselves. It is they (the intervals) which draw the movement to a kinetic resolution.[7]

The metaphor of the "interval" was fitting, not only to stress the primacy of shot change, but to suggest that the relations between elements were independent of any particular juxtapositions. The intervalic relationship in music is both melodic and harmonic. The scale guarantees that every note in the system has one of a limited number of relations with every other note. Instrumental coloration cannot alter these fixed correspondences. Vertov wrote: "We are searching for the cinematic scale," indicating that his intuition of a finite, immanent set of relationships had not yet fully reached his goal.

Eisenstein, with his usual rhetorical skill, belittled the theory of intervals by calling it a form of pointillism. In his early polemic, "On the Question of a Materialist Approach to Form," he wrote:

> Such frivolousness puts the Kinoks into a rather funny position, since, in a formal analysis of their work, one must conclude that their works certainly and very definitely belong to art, and *what's more, to one of the least ideologically valuable expressions of it—to primitive impressionism.*
>
> *It is from a montage of pieces of real life* (with the impressionists —of real tones) *whose effect is not calculated, that Vertov weaves the carpet of a pointillist painting.*[8]

Of course pointillism, per se, is not under attack. Eisenstein knows that his readers will associate the technique of pointillism (whose schematism superficially resembles the theory of intervals) with pictures of the French bourgeoisie, e.g., *La Grande Jatte,* such as those collected by the Russian aristocracy; and furthermore, in case the association fails, he mixes his metaphors to make his rival a merchant of fancy rugs.

Vertov, in turn, pointed out to his Parisian listeners in the first "Kino Eye Lecture" of 1929 that "More and more, [Soviet] cinema has borrowed the methods of Kino-Eye, superficially, to create what is known as the 'art' film. We cite as examples *Strike, Potemkin* and others."

Marxian Temporality

VERTOV OBJECTED to all cinematic fictions and attempts to represent historical scenes which occurred before the invention of cinema. When he wanted to illustrate the transformation of society under socialism, as in *Enthusiasm* (1931), he photographed "retrogressive" elements around him at the time (religion, drunkenness, Czarist monuments) and edited them in contrast to the "progressive" transformation of churches into clubs. In *The Eleventh Year* (1928), a film on electrification and industrialization in the Ukraine, he ends a series of images describing the Dneiper River with a fossilized skeleton. The titles read: "Halfway between Dnepro-Petrovsk and Zaporozhe roar in the rocks the rapids called 'The Voracious'/ Further down stream/ Catherine's armchair/ The rock 'The Hero'/ 'The Rock of Love'/ 2000 year old Scythian." Here, he implies that the contemporary building of the hydroelectric plants has resulted in the excavation of the fossil. Thus industrial, socialist progress entails the recovery of the ancient past. Perhaps the most extreme demonstration of Vertov's radical theory of the inaccessability of the past to cinema is the figurative structure of the opening of *Stride Forward, Soviet* (1926). The first title announces "Today" followed by images which illustrate the captions "when a Plant/ a factory/ electricity/ running water/ and steam Heating works." Then we are told that the past "looks like a NIGHTMARE" from this perspective. But instead of seeing the direct representation of the past, we get "nightmarish" or unreal figures for it: a loaf of bread slipping away from eager hands in animation, the water faucet turned on to no result, the electric light going out. The titles tell us those were days "without BREAD . . . without water . . . without LIGHT." But Vertov makes no attempt to convince his viewers that they are actually looking into the past.

Modern and Mythological

EISENSTEIN RECORDED his impressions of a preview of Alexandr Dovzhenko's first long film, *Zvenigora*, in 1928:

> As the film goes on it pleases me more and more. I'm delighted by the personal matter of its thought, by its astonishing mixture of reality with a profoundly national poetic imagination. Quite

modern and mythological at the same time. Humorous and heroic. Something Gogol about it.[9]

The phrase "quite modern and mythological at the same time" betrays a hint of surprise at the yoking of the archaic and the modern, a pattern we have found in Mallarmé and Peterson as well as Desnos and Man Ray. However, within two months of seeing Dovzhenko's film (ca. April 1928) Eisenstein was completing his own film of the fusion of pagan tradition and modernity. For *The Old and the New* not only contrasts two ideologies of agriculture; it also suggests that Soviet collectivism is more authentically "traditional" than owner capitalism.

Although Dovzhenko was Eisenstein's senior by three years, he came to cinema at a time when he could take the fullest advantage of the innovations his colleagues had made just a few years before. In addition to seeing Griffith's *Intolerance*, which directly influenced *Zvenigora* as it had the works of the other major Soviet filmmakers before him, he could have seen Eisenstein's *Strike* (1925) and *Potemkin* (1925), Pudovkin's *Mother* (1925) and *The End of St. Petersburg* (1927), and Vertov's *Kinoglaz* (1924), *Leninist Film Truth* (1925), *Stride Forward, Soviet* (1926), and *The Sixth Part of the World* (1927) before he shot *Zvenigora*. Vertov himself had gone to the Ukrainian studio, VUFKU, the most liberal of those in the Soviet Union in the late twenties, where he was making *The Eleventh Year* and would make *The Man with a Movie Camera* and *Enthusiasm*, while Dovzhenko was making his first four features.

Futurist Allegory

ACCORDING TO the filmmaker's account, some of the obscurity of *Zvenigora* came from its original screenplay:

> The screenplay was written by Mike Johansen and Yurtyk. There was a lot of devilry and nationalism in it. So I rewrote about ninety percent of the script. The authors then demonstratively removed their names from the credits. This was the beginning of my parting of ways with the Kharkiv writers.[10]

This is from a brief autobiography that poses its own problems of interpretation. As a Ukrainian artist Dovzhenko was suspect in the Stalinist Soviet Union. His account of his career might have been an attempt to prove his Bolshevik orthodoxy or a sincere apology for his earlier eccentricities and independence. Kharkiv had been the center of the

Ukrainian avant-garde in literature. Even the Russian Futurist Khlebnikov had gone there to live and work from 1919–20. Luda and Jean
Schnitzer first suggested that Khlebnikov's serial poem "The Children
of the Otter" may have been a source for the script of *Zvenigora*.[11] If
that is the case it would represent a mode of organizing historical material quite differently than *Intolerance*, despite some superficial similarities in their structures. In 1916, D. W. Griffith had been the first filmmaker to intercut four stories from different historical periods.
Khlebnikov's poem, written three years earlier, was made up of six parts
in different styles which passes from the myths of the Orochi tribes, to
Alexander the Great in contact with the ancestors of the southern re-
publics of what would soon become the Soviet Union, to the Crimean
tartars of the period of Gogol's *Taras Bulba*, to the sinking of the Titanic
and the meeting of illustrious souls on the imaginary island of Khlebnikov. In 1910 the author had written to another poet, Kamenski, of
his ambition: "I dream of a big novel . . . with freedom from time and
space, with the coexistence of the willed and the unwilling . . . of modern life united with the time of Vladimir the Beautiful Sun . . ."[12]

The complexities of *Zvenigora* are not as vexing as those of Khlebnikov's poem although they are severe in comparison to *Intolerance*. The
"grandfather" who is the film's central character vacillates between a
temporal existence (situated at the beginning of the present century in
which he lives with his two grandsons, Timosh, the revolutionary, and
Pavlo, the reactionary) and an eternal one, manifesting itself once among
the seventeenth-century Cossacks and, later in the film, with the resistance to ninth-century knights. Instead of a Griffithian interlacing of
separate but parallel stories or a Khlebnikov-like sequence of discrete
episodes, *Zvenigora* has a series of bracketing devices which ambiguously enclose eccentric episodes within an overall allegorical structure.

The first historical episode has no bracketing introduction other than
its intertitle: "Soaked in blood, sealed in secrecy, shrouded in legend,
the treasures of the country have been buried for ages in Ukrainian soil."
Here we meet the grandfather as he encounters a troupe of Cossacks
on horse who are trying to ferret out Poles, who are themselves searching for the treasure of Zvenigora, the magic mountain. The opening
epithets might as well apply to the occulted center of the film as to the
symbolical treasure. Another title describes the grandfather, the human
vehicle of that symbol: "The centuries old guardian, preserver of an-
tiquities, a moss covered grandfather, watches now as he watched when
Cossack robbers roamed the country 300 years ago—1,000 years ago."

Like the old-timer of Homer's *Iliad*, Nestor, the grandfather describes heroics in *Zvenigora* which verge upon parody. With a single gunshot he fells three Poles from a tree. A series of religious and ritualistic images culminate in a revelation of his superstitiousness. First a monk, like an icon of Death, issues from the mountain to curtail his treasure hunting; then he spies upon a group of maidens "for centuries—year after year—" the title informs us, performing a midsummer rite, floating wreaths and candles down a river; and finally, in the modern period, he wakes from the dream of the monk, or Death, and demands that his grandsons cross themselves. Characteristically, the reactionary obliges grotesquely while the revolutionary calmly refuses. The rite the grandfather has witnessed is the pre-Christian rite of Kupalo which the Church assimilated to the feast of John the Baptist. A festival of eros and fertility, it has been associated with the activity of evil spirits in the folkloristic imagination. The clandestine approach of the grandfather suggests the story from Old Testament Apocrypha of Susanna and the old men who peep at her, just as the later narration of the heroics of the medieval Oksanna recalls the Apocryphal story of Judith and Holofernes. We must bear in mind that in the Ukrainian churches, both Catholic and Orthodox, these texts remain in the biblical canon.[13] Here Dovzhenko is developing a subtle point: the biblical texts which were introduced by the Christian conquerors in the Middle Ages repeat native legends and usurp their authority. His modernity entails a recovery of the archaic Slavic traditions, implicity isolating Christianity as an alien phase of foreign imperialism. Something of this return to the pre-Christian world can be found in Khlebnikov and other Futurists, as well as in Stravinsky's "Sacre du Printemps."

The Irony of the Intertitle

THE TITLES in *Zvenigora* are at times illuminating and at times obfuscating. In the sequence immediately following the dream of the monk, we see a bucolic gathering, with a nude boy urinating in a stream, but the titles do not clarify its position in the already obscure temporal sequence of the film. Instead it reads: "You see, they would have lived and grown as corn in the fields—if only—" and a cut brings us elliptically to 1914 and the war. Here the grandfather turns prophet: "Nation after nation, country after country, revolted. An enemy of humanity rules over us." Then a proverb about the slavery of capitalism appears on the screen: "Dogs are not fed when taken hunting. They build roads when they are at war."

In the course of his mythologizing, the grandfather describes how the treasure of the Ukraine became invisible. Here, through the language of the titles, the central symbol begins to shift its meaning. Before the medieval episode, there had been a contemporary scene that was analogous to the story the grandfather tells although he is not aware of the parallel. We see Timosh condemned to death for rejecting the czarist authority on the war front. But when the officer commands his firing squad to shoot, they refuse, an act which in the grandfather's words was a prelude to revolution: "In rebellion nation rose against nation, country against country, brother against brother." The medieval episode that follows is not meant to be a simple tale of hyperbolical heroics, as the grandfather interprets it, but a parallel to Timosh's supposed treason. Oksanna, like Judith, seduces the enemy general in order to kill him. The sequence of episodes illustrates, despite the grandfather's unconsciousness of it, that "treason" and "heroism" are names that can be given to the same political action from different parties. Such large-scale contrast of episodes is typical of the film.

The Higher Mathematics of Cinema

IN HIS brief autobiography Dovzhenko later wrote:

> The artistic audience was quite enthusiastic about *Zvenigora* when it came out, but the general public did not accept it because it was difficult to understand. Yet I was proud of the film and even remember boasting that I was more like a professor of higher mathematics than an entertainer. I seemed to have forgotten why I came to the cinema.[14]

The opposition of mathematician and entertainer was actually illustrated in two crucial scenes in *Zvenigora*. After the war, Timosh went to a technical university. We see him working out a problem in calculus on a blackboard under the instruction of a gray-bearded professor. The montage moves from the classroom to the fields and factories in a long, rhythmical intercutting of industrial and agricultural production which suggests that the higher mathematics of the scene of instruction bears direct fruits in the organization of labor. At the same time, the sequence itself illustrates the higher mathematics of pure montage, reminiscent of Vertov's editing of *Stride Forward*, *Soviet* or *The Eleventh Year*.

The sequence which follows it represents the opposite pole: the reduction of cinema to bourgeois entertainment. Pavlo puts on his suicide act before an enraptured aristocratic audience. The shot–countershot between his patently boring speech and the paroxysmal contortions of the men and women in the audience, whose voyeuristic and sadistic anticipation of his suicide increases with each addition to his speech as he slyly applies the brake to the promised denouement, parodies the suspense film and mocks the climax of *Intolerance*. Just as in Griffith's epic there is the last minute "rescue": the police break in on the act to arrest Pavlo and frustrate the paying crowd to the point of rioting. The police turn out to be Pavlo's accomplices. Together they reap the benefits of this exploitation of upper-class sadism, just as Dovzhenko might have accused the American cinema of exploiting suspense and violence for profit. The contrast of the montage styles of Timosh's and Pavlo's social effects indicates Dovzhenko's positive valorization of abstract montage and his insight into the psychodynamics of the cinema of entertainment, which he locates in shot–countershot exchanges.

Both the reactionary and the revolutionary tendencies of the two brothers have their roots in the character of the grandfather. He had promised Pavlo to blow up the train of the Communists. Before he could carry through his promise, he realized his error: the treasure he has sought for a millennium is not buried in the ground, but manifests itself in the workers and their revolution. Upon realizing this the grandfather stops the symbolic train just before it hits the mine. In "The Class Struggles in France" Marx had written: "Revolutions are the Locomotives of history."[15] The revolutionaries on the train welcome the grandfather as a link to the legends and traditions of the Ukraine. The allegorical emblem of the train of revolution plays an elaborate role in Dovzhenko's subsequent film, *Arsenal* (1929).[16] Pavlo, seeing the stopped train, repeats the closing line of his phony speech, "Ladies and Gentlemen, thank you. I have finished," and, at last, he does kill himself.

As an allegory of cinematic creativity *Zvenigora* indicates the place of the mythological voice in revolutionary, modernist cinema. Dovzhenko rejects the economic exploitation of legendary and violent material, which under the euphemism of "entertainment" caters to audience sadism, while hawking spectacles as if they were "real life." Instead, in this film which marks his artistic incarnation as a filmmaker of ambitious dimensions, he identifies himself with Timosh, and associates his allegory with higher mathematics; his film claims to be a didactic calculus of legend, history, and revolutionary metaphors.

Parallel Montage

IF WE turn from *Zvenigora* to consider briefly the film Eisenstein was working on at the same time, *The Old and the New*, some of the differences in their parallel approaches to the intertitle, religion, and the archaic past, can be highlighted. Eisenstein was much more explicit in declaring the theme, its relevance, and the mode of fictional representation at the outset of his film. His long opening titles apologize the theme: "It is necessary to modernize and mechanize our ancient agrarian system./ The heritage of the old social order: many ignorant, backward peasants!/ Still today there are many backward places in our land!" Then, as he shows the absurdly literal division of a small farm, he spells out the message of the symbolical illustration: "When brothers separate/ They divide their farms/ In half./ The economy is shattered–/Divided–/And they become poorer still!" Finally, before we learn his fictional heroine's name, we read "One of many–" and then "Marfa Lapkina." Throughout the film the intertitles guide the viewers in translating the specificity of images into political and economical generalities.

In *The Old and the New*, the episode of the cream separator illustrates Eisenstein's theory of conflicts, and, implicitly, the difference of his approach to Dovzhenko's. A religious procession, through parched fields in order to pray for rain, precedes the exhibition of the cream separator. The two scenes are intimately correlated. In the first the rhythmic flow of editing is repeatedly frustrated by what the author called "metric montage"—static shots held on the screen for a fixed time—to convey a physical sensation of failure which the glaring sunlight and the images of dusty people and thirsty animals reinforce. The momentary passing of a cloud, and with it only a few drops of rain, intensifies the frustration. At the end of the sequence, shot–countershot establishes the suspicion and growing hostility of the peasants in the procession to the officiating priest.

Griffith's parallel cutting clearly delineates two or more independent realms of action. He meticulously avoids any possible confusion between these realms, usually by beginning the transition with an establishing shot. Often an intertitle and even a change of color tint underlines the transition. While emphasizing the parallel situations, or even just changing realms to increase the suspense in the one from which he cuts away, Griffith takes pains to minimalize ambiguities or confusions. In *Zvenigora*, Dovzhenko accentuates ambiguities with his intertitles. At the beginning of the cream separator sequence of *The Old and the New*,

Eisenstein uses a shot–countershot situation to make parallel cutting look like a spatial and temporal continuity.

He cuts, directly from closeups of the suspicious peasants in the fields to closeups of peasants in the hut where the cream separator is to be tested, so skillfully across the shot–countershot axis that we do not realize the shift of scene until another countershot locates the cream separator. Then the montage of the whole scene *reverses the structure of the previous scene, detail for detail*. The metric montage of skeptical farmers and static machine parts gradually gives way to the rhythmic editing of the machine and smiling faces. Just as there had been a momentary fulfillment of the prayers which only heightened the failure, there occurs a brief hitch in the cream making, marked by a return to metric montage, which makes the ultimate success more dramatic. The dark interior, with its fixed shadows, suddenly scintillates with beams of light flashing off the metallic cream separator on to the smiling faces of the convinced (converted) peasants. In the end white jets of cream spout from the machine in an overtly sexual allusion which marks a contrast to the sterility of the religious procession.

The specular construction of the two–part sequence in *The Old and the New* attempts to correlate meaning with physical responses; as such it closes the interpretative gap which characterizes allegory. In "Perspectives" Eisenstein described his intention thus: "Art must blow up the Chinese Wall that stands between the primary antithesis of the 'language of logic' and the 'language of images.' "[17] Where the antithetical episodes in *The Old and the New* are distinctly marked as parts of a dialectical whole, the juxtaposition in *Zvenigora* of the Vertovian montage issuing from the education of Timosh with the parody of a bourgeois suspense and rescue film seems at first a radical change of pace; only an effort of interpretation can elucidate the allegorical significance of their antithesis.

The elaborate antithesis Eisenstein wove into the rain-making and cream separator scenes of *The Old and the New* indicate a confidence in the articulatory power of symmetry in cinema. Dovzhenko stresses his own eclecticism in his matched scenes. They are generically incompatible. Dovzhenko seems to be interested in exploiting the internal contradictions within the art.

Somewhat later in *The Old and the New*, Eisenstein effects another ambiguous transition from Marfa's dream (in superimposition as she sleeps) of a stud bull for the farm to a futuristic collective farm with the intertitles "Now you may think this is only a dream . . ./ Nothing of the kind!" From this model collective farm, she gets a young bull whose growth is represented by a montage of five very quick transitions to the grandeur of his mature mass. Like *Zvenigora*, *The Old and the New* evokes a pre-Christian era of native paganism, most obviously when the bull is married to a cow, in a mock wedding procession. Of course, Eisenstein introduces an ironic dimension foreign to Dovzhenko when he hints that the bull is an erotic fantasy of his heroine.

If we read *The Old and the New* as an allegory of cinematic creativity, it becomes a witty model of erotic sublimation. Marfa succeeds where the priest fails. The archaic myth of a fecund rain god impregnating the earth, incorporated into the rites of the Orthodox Church, has no apotheosis in the open-air theater of the faithful, but the dionysiac transformation of milk into cream occurs to Marfa's ecstatic satisfaction as she directs two virile men, the second younger and more handsome than the first, in the operation of the machine. Human labor and engineering mark the advantage of vision over traditional faith. Even in the displacement of the creative principle onto the young bull, the mediating role of the collective farm and its scientific breeding suggests the advantage of collective labor.

The viewers represented in these Soviet films are neither poets nor visionaries like the "homme" of *L'Etoile de mer*; they are synecdoches for the Soviet audience of a didactic cinema. The eyes which end *Strike*, the witnesses to the unveiling of the cream separator, the workers and farmers who see and hear the results of Timosh's learning, the audience that begins and ends *The Man with a Movie Camera* are required to complete the work of the film. Thus the Soviet modernist critique of the status of the filmic image and intertitle did not serve the quickening of poetic power for the filmmaker but the "higher mathematics" of modernity, mythology, and collectivity in a secular rhythm interlocking iconoclasm with what Richard Stites has called revolutionary "God-building."[18]

3

Moments of Revelation: Dreyer's Anachronistic Modernity

Death, as we may call that unreality, is the most terrible thing, and to keep and hold fast what is dead demands the greatest force of all. Beauty, powerless and helpless, hates understanding, because the latter exacts from it what it cannot perform. But the life of the mind is not one that shuns death, and keeps clear of destruction; it endures death and in death maintains its being. It only wins its truth when it finds itself utterly torn asunder. It is this mighty power, not by being a positive which turns away from a negative, as when we say of anything, it is nothing or it is false, and, being done with it, pass off to something else: on the contrary, mind is this power only by looking the negative in the face, and dwelling with it.

—Hegel, The Phenomenology of the Mind, *"Preface"*

THE TRANSITION to sound cinema fundamentally altered the poetics of the intertitle. After the mid–1930s written titles *only* had a poetic function. With the domination of speech, dialogue exchanges became a privileged function of shot–countershot. At the same time, the play and the novel—both always popular sources for films—became even more central to the artistic development of the cinema. Poetic modes and sources—which were always marginal—became the preserve, by and large, of the avant garde which emerged after the Second World War with the economic flexibility offered by 16mm production.

Although Carl Theodore Dreyer is known to have said that he would have preferred to have made his last silent film, *La Passion de Jeanne d'Arc* (1928), as a talking film, the work as he executed it utilizes the power of the intertitle innovatively. Dreyer emphasized the exchange of questions and answers between Joan and her interrogators from documents then recently discovered. In closeup after closeup the viewer can read the speaker's lips as they utter the entire speech presented in the title, which comes on the screen in the middle of the visible utterance. *La Passion de Jeanne d'Arc* monumentalized the silent intertitle.

The films of Carl Theodore Dreyer and Robert Bresson made after the Second World War are among the most sophisticated and cinematically intelligent adaptations of literary works. Dreyer took stage plays as his sources; Bresson worked with novels and novellas. They each used shot–countershot for stylistic emphasis, interpreting their sources through their eccentric employment of it, as I shall discuss in this and the following chapter.

I shall argue that Johannes in Dreyer's *Ordet* and Gertrud in his *Gertrud* have visionary experiences we cannot share, even though they are dramatized before our eyes. The most direct correlate of the inaccessibility of their visions would be the filmmaker's refusal of shot–countershot until very late in each film. Only when the protagonist is ready to act, to make a gesture for which he or she is prepared, reluctantly or resignedly, as a consequence of the visonary experience, does shot–countershot montage take over. Although both films derive directly from plays that would not be called modernist, they succeed in reformulating their sources in terms of the limitations of cinematic representation so that they exemplify and even derive their extraordinary power from the aesthetic incongruity of stage and cinema.

Furthermore, we should bear in mind that in the Nordic tradition modernism was often associated with developments in the theater and with realism. Georg Brandes (1842–1927), the Danish avatar of modernism, was primarily an exponent of realism. Kaj Munk, the author of the play *Ordet*, and Söderberg, the author of *Gertrud*, were important figures in the development of Scandanavian realist theater. Shortly after releasing *Ordet* Dreyer gave a lecture on cinematic style in which he asserted that "If it imposes and strikes the eye, it is no longer 'style' but 'manner,' " and in an interview about the film, he warned, "one has to be cautious in talking about old-fashioned and modern rhythm, for the old-fashioned one can under certain circumstances be the most modern."[1] Dreyer's deliberate avoidance of an obvious modernist manner disguises his formal radicalism as if it were old-fashioned theatricalism. This poses an interesting problem in the light of the centrality of theatrical innovation in Scandanavian modernism. In *Ordet* (and later in *Gertrud*) Dreyer derived an innovative cinematic style from the incorporation of theatrical principles in his long, moving camera shots: repressing master shots, he made multiple entrances and exits into and out of the frame, with fluid and static moments, the basis of his mature style. Thus the theatricalism of Dreyer's adaptations of these plays was, to his mind, at once a traditional and modern style. In this chapter I shall examine the circumstances under which the old-fashioned rhythm can be the most modern.

Bresson's adaptations of Bernanos, Dostoevsky, and most recently Tolstoy, assume the inadequacy of finding a visual correlative to the subjectivity the authors of his sources represented: he either isolates the affective language in dialogue or, more characteristically, in voice-over, or supresses it, marking its absence by an ellipsis, a synecdoche, or a metonomy. His elliptical framing and rhetorical montage constitute a method for "hiding the ideas" which his protagonists and his audience, alternately, must labor to discover. Thus he is more in line with the mainstream of modernist narrative than Dreyer.

The four films of Dreyer and Bresson I shall discuss will illuminate the context of the one by Bergman, *Persona*, which I shall analyze subsequently. At that point, I shall try to show how the fictional agon between two women is designed as the tentative, perhaps therapeutic, projection of an authorial consciousness fragmentarily and allusively outlined within the film. These three chapters on modernist narrative correspond crudely to the classical trichotomy of dramatic, epic, and lyrical forms, if we assume the novel to be the modern epic genre.

Ordet, made in 1955, is one of the great anomalies of film history. Apparently conservative in form, truly religious in motive and theme, it is a film without obvious precursors and with little influence, unless one looks to other films by Dreyer himself.

Rhythm–Bound Restlessness

DREYER SAW Munk's play *Ordet* (The Word) when it premiered in 1932. The next year he published "The Real Talking Film," in which he distinguished "the distance between theater and film" as "given with the distance between *pretending* and *being*." I shall quote the relevant passage in total:

> Characteristic of all good film is a certain rhythm-bound restlessness, which is created partly through the actors' movements in the pictures and partly through a more or less rapid interchange of the pictures themselves. A live, mobile camera, which even in close-ups adjusts flexibly and follows the persons so that the background is constantly shifted (just as for the eye, when we follow a person with our eyes), is important for the first type of restlessness. As for the interchange of images, it is important when the manuscript is adapted from the play that the play provide as much "offstage" as "onstage" action. This creates opportunities for new rhythm-making elements. Example: the third act of Kaj Munk's *The Word* takes place in the drawing room of the Borgen family's farm. Through the conversation of those present, we learn that the young woman who is to give birth has become ill suddenly and put in bed and that the doctor who has arrived in haste

fears for her life and for the baby's life. Later, we learn first of the baby's death and after that of her death. If *The Word* were to be filmed, all these scenes in the sickroom, which the theatre audience gets to know only through conversation, would have to be included in the film. The actors going to and from the sickbed would contribute to creating the two types of restlessness or excitement that condition the rhythm of the film to an essential degree.[2]

Twenty-one years later Dreyer filmed that sickbed scene, making it the turning point of his film. The episode is a model of "rhythm-bound restlessness." The camera slowly moves, adjusting its orientation from a closeup of the stricken Inger to include Mikkel, her husband, as he tries to comfort her; then it catches the midwife as she sweeps busily into its mobile frame; finally it settles on the doctor, who stands 180 degrees from the original position. It could be said that the entire episode consists of just one shot; for after a brief interruption so that we can see the elder Borgen driving his wagon quickly to get to her side, the scene continues from the point where it had broken off, as if the two long fluid shots were actually one continuous camera take. The second part of the episode gives it its resonance. It is in fact the most brutal scene I know in the history of the art. The scene, which in Dreyer's words "would have to be included in the film," is the abortion of Inger's baby.

To my sensibility the sickroom scene of *Ordet* is the most excruciating of Dreyer's scenes of pain, perhaps because so much is hinted at and relegated to the soundtrack. When the doctor learns of the failing condition of Inger's heart, he acts quickly, silencing her husband's, Mikkel's, questions. As viewers sharing Mikkel's perspective we can only deduce what he is doing. First he takes the shorter of two pairs of scissors and without difficulty performs an episiotomy. We do not see the operation itself, but as we watch the doctor's face and arms, a piercing cry from Inger underlines the act of cutting. Then, more obscurely he takes the long scissors. If the viewer does not realize that he is about to abort the child, that fact will be brought home in the scene which follows: Mikkel, sent for a pail, confronts his father, who asks if the child is the grandson he has eagerly awaited. The bitterest line in Munk's play remains in the film (although it is suppressed in the American subtitles); the alienated Mikkel tells his father that it is indeed a boy, "in four pieces" in the pail. This exchange of dialogue must be the very speech to which Dreyer refers when he writes of the indirect evidence of the sickroom in the play. In the scene he conceived twenty-one years before filming, however, we must watch as the doctor exerts his full strength to cut with his scissors, four times, each one accompanied by a scream from Inger, as if she could feel fully the severing of her baby.

It is crucial to understand that there is no question of sacrificing Inger. Dreyer did not make a "right-to-life" movie; the theological issue of the priority of mother or child never enters the film. Everything that has passed on the screen up until that moment prepared us to agree with the doctor's immediate decision and to wish for the best. Now we must consider why Dreyer *had to include* this scene in his film of the play.

Shift of Moods

DREYER CAREFULLY placed this scene at a point in his "drama" when the tone shifts suddenly from comic to tragic. Until then *Ordet* had been a charming, meticulously realistic, comedy of antiquated rural manners. It was in fact a pastoral love story of Anders, the youngest of the Borgens, and Anne, whose father belonged to a rival wing of the Danish Church. Inger's diplomacy had moved old Borgen from his bigoted refusal to accept a young woman from the fundamentalist, Inner Church sect into his Grundvigian family. Just as Inger's complications began, he was arguing with his rival, Peter the Tailor, in favor of the marriage. Despite the stubborn pride of the two old men, all of the traditional signposts of the genre indicated that the young lovers would succeed in the end. Thus, the good humored conflicts of the first part of the film turn out to be a deceptive foil for the sudden turn of events.

Dreyer makes us pay a heavy price for the very optimism and playfulness he induces us to enjoy in the first part of the film. Yet, for all of its sudden unleashing of terror in the middle of what had been a pleasant but trivial exercise in historical realism, the abortion scene seems for a time to have purchased the survival of Inger, the film's most vital character. The witnessing of the surgery—Dreyer's innovation—is an extended cinematic meditation on the powerful description of the "four pieces" of the boy's body which Munk had allowed to stand for the whole scene. Munk was more interested than Dreyer in the tension between Mikkel and his father, between the embittered elder son, an atheist who wants to be finally free of the family farm and have a place wholly his own, and his lovable father who makes of his religion a metaphysics of pride and conveniences. By filming the sickroom scene as he did, Dreyer forcefully posed the issue of death as a sudden and immense reality in the middle of his film.

In fact, when Peter the Tailor does bring Anne to Inger's funeral and offers her to be Anders' wife and the woman of the Borgen household, the irony is the more poignant because the issues of the whole film have so shifted. The comedy of the opening scenes was the story of Anders and Anne. But the tragedy of the later part of the film centers around Inger and Mikkel's mad brother, Johannes; the former had been a delightful agent and the latter a minor, and pathetic, obstacle in the pastoral comedy. In the cold light of Inger's death and Johannes' lunatic disappearance—and probably death too—the domestic happiness of Anders and Anne seems insignificant; surely most viewers must feel the paltriness of their union as a recompense for the tragedies which have fallen on Borgengaard.

Cinematic Hypnotism

IN MY exposition so far I have been liberal with the attribution of intentions to the filmmaker. At this point let us examine a statement he wrote about the film:

> The aim of the film must be to induce in the audience a tacit acceptance of the author's idea, as expressed in the closing stages of the film, namely that a sufficiently strong faith confers on its possessor the power of performing miracles.
>
> With this aim in mind the audience must be gradually prepared, beguiled, inveigled into a mood of religious mysticism. To make them receptive to the miracle they must be led to that special sense of grief and melancholy which people experience at a funeral.
>
> Once they have been brought to this state of solemnity and introspection, they can more easily allow themselves by degrees to be persuaded to believe in the miracle—simply because in being made to think about death they are led on to think about their own death—and so, unconsciously, they hope for the miracle and therefore jettison their normal attitude of skepticism.
>
> The audience must be made to forget that they are seeing a film, and must be persuaded (or, if you prefer, hypnotized) into thinking that they are witnessing a divine intervention, so that they go away gripped and silent.[3]

This text is most remarkable for the way in which Dreyer insists upon a vocabulary of illusionistic persuasion that uninhibitedly borders upon duplicity. The verbs "induce," "prepare," "beguile," "inveigle" climax with "hypnotize" and "witness." It is a document that establishes first of all that Dreyer was conscious of the need for special strategies of manipulation to achieve the kind of conviction he wanted *Ordet* to have.

The language of deception which he uses to describe his relationship to the audience is more than a mere self-congratulation for his powers as an artist. The lapse into error, the "hypnotism" to which he alludes, is an integral part of the experience of the film. Moreover, the profundity of *Ordet* arises from the intimacy and complexity with which its religious content and its artistic self-consciousness are coupled. This intermeshing reveals itself, under scrutiny, at the very moment when Inger dies.

I find a curious support for the intensity of self-consciousness I attribute to this short text in the unrealized script he wrote for the film he wanted to make more than any other, *Jesus*. *Jesus* is an extraordinary script in many ways, not the least being its almost obsessive insistence on the strictly Jewish nature of Christ's theology. Dreyer had been a passionate enemy of anti-Semitism (a revulsion which he shared with Kaj Munk) since at least 1921 when he made *Die Gezeichneten*. The *Jesus* script goes to great lengths to show the fundamental sympathy of the Pharisees and high priests for the teachings of Jesus. In this context he creates a fascinating portrait of Judas Iscariot. According to Dreyer he was an over-zealous young follower, who desperately wanted to be convinced Jesus is the Messiah but was "irresolute." On the night of the betrayal the Pharisees argue with him that if he is indeed the Messiah "God will not let him die." Notice the terms by which Dreyer describes his fatal lapse into error:

> Apparently Judas is swayed by these new ideas and he is like one hypnotized when the Pharisee turns to him and says
> *It is in your power to make possible that sign from Heaven. What a deed you will have done. . . .*[4]

Later in the office of Caiaphas, whom Dreyer treats with sympathy as well, he "almost triumphantly" proclaims "Jesus is the Messiah." He has succeeded in deluding himself that he is about to become the instrument for revealing this to the Jewish nation at large. In the script we read: "Caiaphas shakes his head discouragingly. As a realist, he feels that all this is absurd."

The *hypnotized*, irresolute enthusiast and the *realist* are blinded interpreters of the Christ event in *Jesus*. They also represent two stages the ideal spectator of *Ordet* must pass through, according to Dreyer's note. In both the original play and the film, Johannes is an extreme type of the apparently deluded enthusiast, while the doctor and the humanistic priest give the audience two versions of the "realistic" position. However, before I elaborate on their symbolical roles in the film, I want to consider what artistic realism meant for Dreyer and how he exemplified it in *Ordet*. My guide in this excursion will again be his essay "The Real Talking Film."

Abstraction

POINT FOR point *Ordet* exemplifies the principles first enunciated in that essay, written a year after the release of *Vampyr,* Dreyer's first sound film. He began the essay by asserting the value of real locations, "the streets," over stage sets for sound films.

> The real talking film must give the impression that a film photographer, equipped with camera and microphone, has sneaked unseen into one of the homes in the town just as some kind of drama is taking place within the family. Hidden under his cloak of invisibility, he snaps up the most important scenes of the drama and disappears as silently as he came.[5]

Today that sounds like a prophecy of *cinéma verité,* or less radically, of Italian Neo-Realism. Yet everything else in the essay indicates that Dreyer did not envisage a filmed reality, but the artful imitation of that reality with meticulous attention to details. The central points are clear enough: (1) information conveyed in a play through conversation should be visualized; (2) dialogue should be "compressed" into "lines that . . . have present value" because the film audience, unlike that of the theater, does not have time to "recollect" and "compare remarks"; (3) makeup should be minimalized, or better, abolished; (4) films should be shot inside real houses, not studio sets; (5) apparently irrelevant, incidental sound should be incorporated on the soundtrack. He writes: "While I am writing these lines, I can hear church bells ring in the distance; now I perceive the buzzing of the elevator; the distant, very-far-away clang of a streetcar, the clock of city hall, a door slamming. All these sounds would exist, too, if the walls in my room, instead of seeing a man working, were witnessing a moving, dramatic scene as background to which these sounds might even take on symbolic value—is it then right to leave them out?;" and finally (6) the voice and diction of the movie actor should be adapted to the intimacy of the screen rather than reflect the need to fill a theater.

This early response to sound cinema, written by an artist who had won great distinction in the silent film, and above all for his expressionistic *La Passion de Jeanne d'Arc,* is clearly a realist manifesto. Its greatest curiosity is the assertion that the adaptation of a novel or a play is more valuable than an original script. Dreyer had too much experience of the limitations of cinematography to believe that films could be effectively made inside people's houses. What he might have meant, although he did not spell it out, and indeed what he actually did in *Ordet,* was that real houses should be reconstructed under studio conditions to facilitate filming. For *Ordet* he bought a Jutland farm house, transported it in pieces along with precious antique furniture he borrowed from farmers, to the Palladium studios and rebuilt it, including the original floor, on a sound stage. Only in this way could his fluid camera weave about among the actors as they moved within the actual farm house.

Once he had reconstructed the farm with all of its furnishings, with a complete kitchen as well, he began to remove items. In the 1955 essay "Imagination and Color" he called this process "simplification." "The cinematic representation of reality should be true, but purged of trivial details."[6] The two surgical scissors and the proto-stethoscope of the sickroom episode are typical of the filmmaker's heightened use of realistic details. Old Borgen's pipe, the grandfather clock, and the framed portrait of Gruntvig become memorable images in *Ordet;* they exemplify the principle that through "simplification the motif is transformed into a symbol."

In the 1955 essay he also calls for a process by which the "artist shall abstract from reality in order to reinforce its spiritual content, whether this is of psychological or purely aesthetic nature."[7] The acquisition of a Jutland farm and the use of authentic furniture were but part of the filmmaker's almost obsessive concern for the spiritual realism of his film. In his casting of the roles and in his subsequent direction he put into practice all of the prescriptions of "The Real Talking Film." He strengthened the intimacy of the cast with the script by turning to actors who had been associated with the original production. Munk had written the role of Borgen with the actor Henrik Malberg in mind. In 1932 he could not accept the part because he was attached to the National Theatre. At eighty-one years old he came out of retirement to play the part originally written for him. Dreyer got Ejnar Federspiel, the original stage Borgen, to play Peter the Tailor, Borgen's nemesis. Emil Hass Christensen played Mikkel, the eldest brother, in the film, but he had played Anders, the youngest, on stage. For Anders and Anne he chose amateurs. Yet the summit of Dreyer's obsessive casting was Birgitte Federspiel, the daughter of Dreyer's Peter, whom he chose to play Inger largely because she was to give birth while the film was in production.

Dreyer accompanied her into her labor room and recorded her cries. The screams he so carefully and horrifyingly synchronized to the episiotomy and the abortion were sounds she made while giving birth (without complications) to her child.

For Johannes, Dreyer wanted to recapture the voice quality of a schizophrenic he had known. For this role he went to his cast of *Vredens Dag*. He so transformed Preben Lerdorff Rye that many viewers, familiar with Dreyer's films, fail to recognize the handsome young Martin of the earlier film in the deranged Johannes.

Another striking realization of the principles of "The Real Talking Film" is the incorporation of incidental noise. Even in the most momentous and tragic scenes within the farmhouse, the mooing of cows, and other rural acoustic intrusions, remind us of the fictional continuity of the world outside the scene of action, and in so reminding us, symbolically emphasize the fact that pathos and tragedy are uniquely human possibilities. The filmmaker even added a scene to Munk's plot which capitalizes on the unseen presence of the animals: Old Borgen, pouting over Anders' decision to ask Peter for his daughter's hand without first consulting him, stalks off to the barn to sit beside the sow that is about to give birth. The untroubled fecundity of the sow forecasts a distinction from Inger and thereby reinforces the symbolical isolation of the human world.

Sequence Shots

I KNOW of no narrative film made before *Ordet* that so radically dispensed with shot–countershot in the presentation of dialogue. Yet, between the very opening and the very end of the last scene there is hardly a single instance of it. Furthermore no film before it had used camera movement in every shot; yet in all but a half dozen brief and insignificant shots the camera glides about the rooms, pans the rare exteriors, and takes over the role traditionally assigned to montage (again excepting the very end of the film).

Dreyer's interiors are not naturalistic; we do not think the camera is hidden in a Jutland farm—that aspect of the 1933 manifesto has been abandoned. Still, the set we see is unusually accurate. The filmmaker starts his work with an immediate acknowledgment of his authority, yet he appears to be operating within rigid conventions. This appearance of conventionality turns out to be a foil for the more startling religious aspirations of the film.

The conventions of the horror film genre can provide us with a useful counter-example here. The early episodes of many horror films are punctuated by unspecific hints that an occult disaster is imminent. Although the fictional characters may be blind to the pattern of these hints the viewer must dwell upon them and experience dread of their consequences. The situation is almost reversed in *Ordet*. In the early parts of the film, the characters discuss the power of faith and the nature of miracles, but the viewer is encouraged to ignore these remarks. The reassuring markers of pastoral comedy guide the viewer to interpret the theological issues as part of the texture of historical realism. The real issue seems to be the power of love over bigotry, so that questions of faith turn into props through which the bigots define themselves. Rather than making us eager to see a miracle, the filmmaker quickly sets to work to assure us that miracles are the chatter of hypocritical old men who insist that their faith is the only true one because they actually have no faith.

One effect of the gliding camera which isolates a figure or a small group within a room, allowing them to hold a conversation without recourse to editing, and then moves away to pick up another character who changes the tenor of the action, is to deny the viewer an overall image of the set. In the theater the artificial room on stage is always totally before us. We can concentrate our attention on a part of it, but no one can enter or leave the set unseen by us without the most elaborate ruses. Most films insist on reassuring audiences of the reality of the scene of action by firmly fixing part/whole relationships. Conventionally, we see the whole room first, in a master shot, and return to that shot every now and then, while the medium shots and closeups are coordinated with these establishing shots. To cut from a face in a paroxysm of emotion to a larger field which includes the face, or vice versa, is to operate fully within the conventions of filmic narrative. In *Ordet* we never see that trope (again, the very end is the exception). The gliding camera, with its "rhythm-bound restlessness," does not give us the impression that we can see all that is going on; rather, it convinces us that it is presenting us with everything that is important.

The camera movement and the diminution of shot–countershot of Renoir's *Le Règle du jeu* is certainly as innovative as *Ordet*'s but it is not as systematic. By holding off the more conventional structures until the very end of the film, rather than dispersing them architectonically throughout the whole, as Renoir does, Dreyer transforms the mode of representation. This transformation is also effected by, and actually seems to require, a correlative suppression of action in depth. Dreyer's camera does not plunge into, pull back from, or reel about within the field of action. In gliding and reframing continuously it seems to discover events in relief and, by turning to them, animate them as if they had been waiting frozen offscreen to come to life with the goad of attention. On the other hand, life, in Renoir's world, overruns the perspective from all sides and the camera is breathless to capture all that it can.

The camera movements of *Le Règle du jeu* enlarge and expand the depth of field which is already crammed with parallel actions criss-crossing in the foreground and background. Such complex articulations of depth function similarly to the part/whole economy of establishing shots and closeups in confirming the spatial coordinates of representation. Dreyer's shift from a spatial, or rather pictorial, mode of representation to an expressionistic one, in which the camera's movement rhythmically pinpoints the phases of action *over time,* does so through a reduction of the dramatic possibilities of the dimension of depth. In "Imagination and Color," a lecture presented at the Edinburgh Film Festival seven months after the premiere of *Ordet,* the filmmaker speculated on possible use of color to achieve "abstraction":

> Perhaps there is an idea for an interesting abstraction in the conscious elimination of atmospheric perspective—or, in other words, by giving up the much-coveted illusion of depth and distance. Instead, one could work toward an entirely new image construct of color surfaces, all on the same plane, forming one great, aggregated surface of many colors from which the notion of foreground, middleground, and background would be completely dropped. In other words, one could move away from the perspectivistic picture and pass on to pure surface effect.[8]

Here, as elsewhere, Dreyer's radicalism was a matter of nuance, not aesthetic revolution. I would argue that he had begun to work with his version of the "pure surface effect" in *Ordet.*

We cannot afford to forget that Dreyer was one of cinema's greatest masters of moving camera cinematography, and perhaps even the artist with the greatest innovative range in that domain. *La Passion de Jeanne d'Arc* systematically alternates broad sweeping pans of the judges with closeups of the heroine. Long stretches of the film use this alternation to create the impression of Joan as the unmoved center of a circle whose circumference is her agitated accusers. At points of dramatic intensity the camera will plunge along the imaginary radius to Joan's face or out to her inquisitor. Historical accuracy and precision of detail also contribute to the forcefulness of this silent film. But it is by no means within the realistic style. Dreyer drew upon the expressionistic tradition and even hired Hermann Warm, one of the designers of *Das Kabinet des Dr.*

Caligari, to build the castle in which Joan would be imprisoned and tried. Yet he underplayed the expressionistic elements to create a film in which Joan would be characterized as a creature of a decidedly different spiritual order than all those around her. The relationship of camera movement to montage dramatized both Joan's isolation and her privileged substantiality.

A similar situation occurs in *Vredens Dag* when the witch, Herlofs Marte, must undergo an interrogation by torture from the Cathedral Chapter. Her moral status is considerably more ambiguous than that of Joan. Therefore, Dreyer formulated a significant variation on the camera strategy of the earlier film. We are introduced to the interrogation by a long and complex camera movement that may actually be a 360 degree sweep of the room. Instead of establishing a space in which what the script calls the "feverish agitation" of the priests is clearly focused upon their victim—as the trope of the circumference and the center of a circle does in *La Passion de Jeanne d'Arc*—the spatial ambiguity of the camera movement and the lighting moves Herlofs Marte closer to the priests. The camera discovers her along with them. This ambiguity, of course, fits the moral ambivalence of the dramatic situation, in which Absalon is implicated in the evil he has sworn to uproot so brutally.

In its intricacy of chiaroscuro, offscreen voices, camera movement and shifting directionality, this long shot recalls the very opening of the film in which we see Herlofs Marte concocting a magic potion in her den. In the language of the script: "The sequence opens with a closeup of Herlofs Marte, a wrinkled old peasant woman. . . . By means of a track-back—or a new shot—we realize that Herlofs Marte is not alone." This "realization" of space and of its occupants is inherently anti-theatrical. Twelve years later, making his next film, Dreyer will employ it without relief until the final scene of *Ordet.* Dreyer's camera halts as much as it tracks and thereby substitutes a series of the filmic frames for a single theatrical set. One of the characters can enter into the frame or pass through it, making us "realize" he or she had already entered the room. If, in its limited employment in *Vredens Dag,* the function of this spatial ambiguity is to suggest the moral continuum between the so-called good and evil characters, it operates similarly in *Ordet,* where it is used constantly, to disguise the spiritual authority of one of the characters.

In *Ordet* the intricate sequence shot which follows that of the abortion posits old Borgen alone with each of his three sons in separate phases; Mikkel occupies two, in fact, beginning and terminating the lengthy shot. All the comedic good humor of the opening of the film has evaporated as we glimpse the world of the male Borgens without Inger. The carefully orchestrated entrances and exits into the mobile frame abut upon one another in shifting registers of despair; they fuse into one another without calling attention to themselves as entrances and exits must on the stage. Mikkel's nervous anxiety turns to bitter irony after he sees, offscreen, the severed body of his aborted son in the pail; Anders cannot divorce his despair over Anne from his worries about Inger; Johannes solipsistically wanders across the frame as usual, but retrospectively we come to realize the accuracy of his vision of Inger's death. Each entrance frustrates Borgen's need for a moment of solitude, until the very end of the series.

In order to achieve the spectacular transformation toward which the whole of *Ordet* moves, the filmmaker has to allow, even encourage, the audience to misinterpret Johannes. He is the figure who lurks outside the frame, who can suddenly enter it and change its tone. His stiff movements and strange voice always rupture the rhythmic harmony that the other characters share with the gliding camera. The filmmaker even manages to hide the fact that he is the film's central character until the very end. First the story of Anders and Anne, later the tragedy of Inger, occupy the foreground while the preparations for the revelation of Johannes' importance are smuggled into the film.

Adaptation

THE MOST important deviations from the Munk play concern the identity of Johannes. Munk lets his audience know, through a conversation between Mikkel and the priest early in the play, that Johannes' madness is the result of a tragic love. In the play this fact unites the three Borgen sons in contrast to their father as men whose lives are shaped by love. So we learn that Johannes was engaged, against his father's will, to the daughter of a judge while he was still a student of theology. One evening they attended a play whose subject was miracles. Johannes was so struck by the play that he stepped distractedly into the street upon leaving the theater. He would have been killed by a car had not his fiancée pushed him out of the way. In saving him, she was killed. At her funeral he attempted to resurrect her, inspired by the play they had seen. He failed and remained incurably mad since then. Dreyer cut all of this from the film. Instead he laconically cites the intensity of his theological studies, especially Kierkegaard, as the cause of Johannes' delusions. The need for suppressing the theme of the play within the play will concern us shortly. Two other modifications of the original should be mentioned before that. In the play the doctor, an atheist and exponent of modern rationalism, expresses the idea that Johannes can be cured if he suffers a shock parallel to the one that caused his illness. Therefore, he encourages him in his delusions, calling him "Rabbi," and even at the funeral of Inger urges the priest to let him try to raise the corpse from the dead in order to shock him back to sanity. This is one of the two ways in which Munk hedged on the final miracle. The other dodge concerns a running argument between the priest and the doctor about the efficacy of death certificates signed by clerics. Therefore, in the play, when Inger does rise at Johannes' invocation of the Word, the doctor feels vindicated in his claim that only a scientist can pronounce someone dead. This leaves the audience uncertain about the status of the miracle, as does, for example, the conclusion to Bergman's *The Virgin Spring*. Dreyer wanted no ambiguity about the miracle. Therefore, he excised all remarks about psychotherapy and death certificates. In its place he substituted a series of subtle theological points.

Dreyer smuggles a sublime visual model for the end of the film into a comic scene of his own invention by having the tailor's wife separate Anders and Anne by showing them alternately an illustration of the Bible. One of the few insert shots in the whole film thus presents us with an image of the raising of Lazarus, where it would be least likely to intimate prophetic relevance.

In Dreyer's version Johannes' collapse results from a modern theology of doubt. He opens the film with a sequence in which the three other Borgen men find him preaching to the wind on the dunes adjacent to the farm. His theme is faith. Yet, ironically, it is the scene that guarantees the incredulity of the film audience. When Johannes howls "Woe unto you, because ye believe not in me, the risen Christ," we are naturally encouraged to share the perspective of the Borgen family and consider him mad. This position is confirmed late in the film when he enters the sickroom and collapses in his failed attempt to resurrect Inger. (This scene is in the play.) Shortly after that he disappears in the night leaving a note which is another of Dreyer's innovations to the plot. We read on the screen:

> I go my way, and ye shall seek me.
> Whither I go, ye cannot come.
> (John 8.21.)

The twenty-first and twenty-second verses of the eighth chapter of the Gospel of John read:

> Then said Jesus again unto them, I go my way, and ye shall seek me, and shall die for your sins: whither I go, ye cannot come.
>
> Then said the Jews, Will he kill himself? because he saith, Whither I go, ye cannot come.

In giving the location of the text Dreyer introduces a subtle note: here, for the first time, Johannes makes a reference to the evangelical authority rather than quoting the words of Christ in his own voice. By quoting the fourth Gospel, he recovers his own name, Johannes. The shift from the delusion of being Christ to the identification with His evangelist is crucial to the theology of the film, but the drama requires that we not notice this change. It strikes us first as just another confirmation of his delusion. Even more significantly we are led to believe, with the Borgen family, that he has (mercifully) died after days of disappearance. This error, which we share with the characters of the film, repeats the misinterpretation of line 23, "Will he kill himself?" which follows immediately upon the quotation Dreyer puts on the screen.

Throughout *Ordet* we are encouraged to view things "realistically." Like Caiaphas in the *Jesus* script we so easily recognize the hysterical delusions of another (in his case Judas, according to Dreyer's invention) that we blind ourselves to the truth which is not encompassed by either position. Dreyer's skill in incorporating scenes which demonstrate the peculiar strength of Johannes' vision which the viewer deliberately overlooks is remarkable. Two such scenes precede the failed resurrection. They are masterfully buried in the film. The first is a dialogue between Johannes and his young niece, Maren, about her dying mother; the other defines the actual moment in which Inger dies.

The beautiful pathos of the conversation between the deluded prophet and the innocent child distracts our attention from the strangeness of what is going on before our very eyes. Maren approaches Johannes' chair from behind. Throughout the dialogue she speaks over his shoulder so they never face each other. At one point she slightly reorients herself, shifting to the other shoulder. They are in the familiar living room. As the camera fixes them in the center of its field it slowly pans around them. But that is impossible! They continue to occupy the center of the frame, staring out beyond the camera, while the room revolves around them. David Bordwell, in *The Films of Carl-Theodore Dreyer*, usefully identified this mysterious shot as an arching turn of the camera while the crab dolly moves in the opposite direction.[9] However the movement is so strange that it seems as if Johannes and Maren were on the dolly with the camera. There is no other shot like this in the film. For the first and only time we see Johannes occupying the center of the screen while the camera movement to which we have become accustomed by this point in the film only affects the background space. Everything up to that moment has prepared us to see the film realistically and to pity the madness of Johannes. The filmmaker seems to require that, for the time being at least, we remain blind to what we are witnessing.

This, I take it, is what he means when he writes that "the audience must be made to forget that they are seeing a film." At first reading, Dreyer seems to be saying that this forgetfulness is to be achieved through the extreme of naturalism. But that does not reflect his practice. The gradual preparation he describes as a prelude to "hypnotizing" the audience, has to be the careful conditioning of expectations, the reinforcement of realism, so that a shot which emphasizes the creative, rather than mimetic, function of the camera movement, has to be ignored. The moment that he invites us to question the realism of the film and the veracity of its psychological perspective, he expects us to prefer to stick to the erroneous pattern of interpretation. This moment significantly coincides with the first occasion in the film when someone—Maren—believes what Johannes is saying.

The intervention of a purely cinematic, anti-realistic construction of space may account for an important deviation from Munk's play. I am referring, of course, to the omission of the play alluded to within the play. At the end of Munk's *Ordet,* the play, the audience finds itself in a situation similar to Johannes when he has seen a play. Dreyer could have retained this story and sacrificed the irony of the parallel situations. I believe he found the more profound solution in inscribing the irony within the film. The first stage of that inscription would be the almost circular pan around Johannes and Maren. The second he would have found already in the play of Munk. When Inger dies, Johannes tells his family that "the man with the scythe" is cutting off her life, but since they, and we, have been assured by the rationalistic doctor that she is sleeping and recovering, we take this to be further proof of his madness. This occurs just as the doctor is driving away. Johannes sees the lights of his car as "the man with the hourglass" going through the wall and hears the sound of his car as the hacking of his scythe. Anders tells him what we as viewers *know:* "It's only the doctor, now he's backing out."

This is the moment that we must "forget we are seeing a film;" for a film is nothing but light projected on a wall and sound. It can be said that any seeing of people and things in photographs or films are acts of interpretation of configurations of light, however automatic. Moreover, in sound films we tend to interpret the simultaneous perception of image and sound as the emanations of a single event whenever possible. We are given two interpretations of the light and the sound, Johannes' and Anders'. The tone of the film puts all the authority on Anders' side; this reenforces the circular error of the realistic interpretation, confirming the decay of faith Johannes has been preaching since the very opening of the film. It is as if Dreyer were asserting that faith, which is a mode of interpretation, and cinema were incompatible.

The natural argument against the weight I have given this scene as a parable of cinematic perception would be that it comes directly from Munk's play. I have no argument against that fact. Yet, I believe that Dreyer may have recognized the self-reflexive cinematic potentials of that scene from the very moment he saw the play. It was doing precisely what the "real talking film" had to do by creating an image instead of offstage light and offstage sound. In the script Dreyer calls for a "blinding white light from the headlights" to sweep "from the wall round the room." The actual image is less dazzling. Still, the script direction betrays the filmic emphasis on this scene.

Johannes' prophecy occurs in a complex sequence shot. He recedes offscreen but the shot does not end. No sooner does he move away than Mikkel emerges from the sickroom to announce that Inger is dead. Dreyer so skillfully handles this transition that the tragic seriousness of Mikkel's revelation overrides any connection to Johannes' prophecy, *as if the two events of the single long shot had no logical connection.* This pivot of attention, which is both rhythmic and dramatic, diverts the viewer's attention from the ironical meaning of juxtaposed scenes. In *Ordet* the subsequent failure of Johannes' first attempt to resurrect Inger seems to confirm the delusionary status of his prophetic vision of her death. Only later do we come to understand the theological import of his failure: so long as he believes he is the Savior, rather than an agent of the Word, and so far as he acts alone, rather than bolstered by the faith of a child, he is powerless. Dreyer confirms this theology in several ways, and even adds a speech to the original when he has Peter the Tailor, overwhelmed by the final miracle, say to Borgen: "Morten—He is still the God of old—the God of Elijah—eternal and the same." He refers to the two books of Kings in which Elijah and Elisha have ressurectionary powers (1 Kings 17, 2 Kings 4).

This failure precipitates Johannes' midnight flight from the farm and the note which we, like the witnesses of John's Gospel, misinterpret as an announcement of his death. Therefore, when he shows up in the middle of the funeral, visibly recovered from his delusions, walking and speaking normally, capable of recognizing his father, we jump to the conclusion that he has been "cured" of his religious delusions. There is

70

no evidence, other than the elliptical suggestion of the departure note, that his transformation has been around a subtle theological axis, that he has recognized his role as a vehicle for the Word, rather than as the Word Incarnate.

As Johannes calls upon the power of the Word to raise Inger, montage and shot–countershot suddenly enter the film. The doctor and the priest are astonished at what is going on; as the priest moves to stop it, the doctor restrains him. A suddenly static camera isolates them. It cuts back to Johannes, again without moving. Then it cuts to the corpse of Inger. Another static shot. This is the first conventionally edited sequence in the film. Dreyer's "realistic" use of camera movement had successfully disguised his radicalism up until and perhaps through this moment. As viewers, we have been conditioned to expect the camera to move in every scene; we have seen no montage, no shot–countershot since the opening shots of the film. Within the synthetic space created by static camera shots and the coordinates of shot–countershot montage something special is about to happen. Johannes prays for the Word. In a long still shot Inger's corpse reacts. At first the twitch of her hands is so slight we can suppress acknowledgment of what we are seeing. But then she visibly moves. This event is emphasized by yet another cinematic convention which had been withheld until this moment: the cutting in of a closeup. From a shot of Johannes and Maren standing side by side, witnessing the signs of Inger's revival, the film cuts to the child's face as she breaks into a smile. This is the only instance in the film of a change of shot which isolates a detail of the previous shot. While representing with consummate mastery the miracle of the Munk play, Dreyer has engineered a cinematic miracle of his own: he has succeeded, in 1955, in making the most elementary of cinematic tropes, the closeup, have the overwhelming emotional force it is said to have had in the work of D. W. Griffith, one of Dreyer's first masters. In a way, he somehow managed to "resurrect" it, and shot–countershot montage as well, long after it had lost its vitality.

Picturing Death

ACCORDING TO Dreyer's note, of which I have made so much, *Ordet* should induce a meditation on death "unconsciously." The final miracle sustains belief as a wish fulfillment for the overcoming of death on the part of the audience "simply because in being made to think about death they are led to think about their own death." The four episodes I have stressed in my analysis of the film confront us with death: the abortion and the resurrection utilize cinematic realism to achieve their effect, while the discussion of death between Johannes and Maren and Johannes' prophetic announcement of Inger's death give death an allegorical or emblematic dimension.

There is no intrinsic priority in cinematic representation of the literal (realism) over figurative (allegory). Dreyer's strategy in *Ordet* is to beguile the viewer into anticipating a realistic film so that he will be blinded until the climax to the figurative truth of Johannes' speeches. Behind this strategy there lies a meditation on death which is the unceasing concern of Dreyer's major films. In his first sound film, *Vampyr,* the figural mode controlled the film. But there the filmmaker made every effort to transform the rupture between life and death into a continuum. An interlocking system of tropes emphasize that continuity. On the soundtrack voices become musical, music imitates the sounds of nature; wind and thunder chant in nearly human tones; and the whole aural environment reflects the spiritualization of a world in which living and dead cross over. The foggy atmosphere, aided by crepuscular photography and gelatinous filters, obliterates the distinctions of harsh black and white, situating the image in an intermediate zone. The precariousness of this continuum is marked by the astounding independence of bodies and their shadows. Yet, above all, it is the predominance of doors, archways, and windows in shot after shot which suggest the fluid transition between inside and outside in both psychological and architectural terms. In this system the camera operates like the shadows, sometimes physically linked to the movements of the strangely "absent" protagonist and his acts of bewildered attention, and sometimes veering off as if it were a disembodied consciousness.

Furthermore, it was a stroke of genius on Dreyer's part to organize so many crucial scenes around the emblem of the window. Through the window in Grey's coffin the camera participates in his abruptly terminated funeral; the unsubstantial image of the dead Bernard's face flashes like lightning in the blind woman's window before the sinister doctor; finally, in the scene which appears twice in the film—once explicitly as a dream—Grey, himself translucent in this episode, sights his love, Gisele, tied up in a room through a glass window. According to the script, "The glass is murky and dusty, but sufficiently transparent for him to see that there is somebody in the room."[10]

In the realistic atmosphere of *Ordet,* however, the death is represented by the corpse, either the quartered body of Inger's baby which we never see, or her own corpse which holds the center of the screen in the final scene. The figurative emblems of death, in Johannes' speech to Maren and in his revelation to Anders and old Borgen, take on the appearance of madness. In the end, of course, that realism breaks down. When Inger actually stirs and then rises in her coffin, she attests to the solidity of "life" with rapacity. The shock of *Ordet* comes from the recognition that "life" is not a given in cinematic realism, but that only the most intense confrontation with death can make it palpable.

The Light of the Past

IN ITS overall formal schema, *Gertrud* more or less repeats the structure of *Ordet:* a continually gliding camera, framing and reframing scenes within its long takes, transforms a well made, but rather conventional play, into the spatial dynamic of "rhythm-bound restlessness"; the suppression of shot–countershot montage gives added weight to its employment in the final shots of the film. That suppression, however, is not absolute in the main body of the work: there is one encounter of Gertrud and her husband, Kanning, in which their dialogue is rendered in alternating matched slots. *Gertrud* is unique in its lack of violence or the direct representation of dying. In fact, had the filmmaker not pulled a few fragments together from Söderberg's play and built them into an epilogue, otherwise wholly of his own making, the theme and thrust of the film would have been utterly different.

The play has five scenes, a pattern which Dreyer largely follows before concluding with the sixth, his epilogue. In the first Gertrud counters Kanning's announcement that he will be made a cabinet minister with her own admission that she is about to leave him. Then, she meets her young lover, the musician Janssen, in a park. The center of the play transpires at a public gathering to honor the poet Lidman, Gertrud's former lover. In an anteroom of the banquet hall, he bemoans their separation and tells her of the pain he has felt hearing Janssen brag about his conquest of her. From this point, the play retraces its scenes: again, in the park, Gertrud confronts and breaks off her relationship with Janssen; then, back in the living room of her home, where the play began, she refuses Lidman's invitation to go off with him. In the last few minutes of the play she leaves Kanning, despite his desperate efforts to keep her. The theme of the play is the heroic impossibility of idealized love. Striving for this ideal, Gertrud becomes a ferocious creature.

Although the formal pattern of *Gertrud* resembles that of *Ordet*, and the same historical realism dominates the style of both, the relationships to the audience that the two films project are opposite. Nowhere is this more apparent than in the moments when realism is violated. I have labored to stress the significance of the scene of Johannes' conversation with Maren while the camera circles the room of which they are the center. Just as Dreyer strives to hide the expressionistic deviation from realism in this shot, he goes out of his way to call attention to the artificiality of the two flashback scenes he inserted in Gertrud to visualize episodes that had been conveyed by dialogue in the play. The first of them makes the artificiality inescapable. Gertrud recalls for Janssen their first meeting when she went to his apartment to sing his "Serenade." The flashback is illuminated with a light markedly more intense than any of the "present" scenes in the film; but more than that, the camera passes without cutting from outside his door into the room where it sweeps around the piano as they perform in a complete circle; in passing from the corridor to the room, it moves right through a wall, demonstrating that the scene takes place in a specially constructed set. A similar intensity of light floods the flashback which later occurs when Gertrud, in the anteroom of the banquet hall, tells Lidman that she left him when she found a note in his room on which he had drawn her profile and written, "A man's work and a woman's love are enemies from the start." Even the way these scenes interrupt the slow and deliberate action of the obviously "theatrical" film call attention to their difference from the otherwise realistic representation.

The Temporality of Language

THE MOST striking addition to the original is the epilogue which moves two elements from the play—Gertrud's poem and her epitaph —into a considerably more emphatic position, and then amplifies them with a new context and more dialogue. But almost as important to the film as the epilogue is the invention of the ceremony celebrating Lidman's return to his homeland. All this occurred offstage in the play. Finally, the two flashbacks, and Kanning's visit to the opera in search of Gertrud, which are the occasions for voice-over monologues, constitute the kind of visualizations of dialogue from the play which Dreyer called for in his early meditation on the labor of Inger when he was projecting the filming of Ordet. The first of those flashbacks presents us with still another innovation, Janssen's "Serenade," which is one piece in a fabric of musical allusions Dreyer added to the original.

The play starts and ends with Gertrud's name: Kanning calls her onto the set to talk with him in the first scene, and he hollers after her definitive departure—where we do not know—through the door in a desperate effort to get her back. Its turning point occurs in the third scene when Lidman tells her that Janssen has not only denied her request to avoid a soirée, but has actually bragged about making love to her before the guests. Lidman hates the young musician especially because "he uttered the name" of his latest conquest. The name comes to symbolize the use and reduction of Gertrud by the men she has loved. Later she tells Lidman that when she dies her gravestone will be nameless; instead the phrase "Amor Omnia" will signify what she was and meant.

The men of the play have all made or are making "big names" for themselves: Kanning has just been named to the Ministry, Lidman returns home as a poet with an immense reputation, and Janssen is talked about, his music heard, even in Rome. Söderberg plays the anonymity of Gertrud's erotic idealism against the publicity of the artists and the politician. Dreyer took over all of this examination of the value and vacuity of words and deflected the theme; so that his film centers upon *the temporal density of words and people.* When he displaces the description of the gravestone from its original context to his own epilogue, he changes its meaning, so that we think not only of Gertrud's impossible idealism, and not mainly of that, but of her death. The tension between public recognition and private satisfaction which Söderberg had foregrounded becomes the backdrop against which Dreyer considers the problem of death in secular and artistic society.

Gertrud is a "real talking film" that poses the problem of the inadequacy of both visual representation and language (collaterally, music as well), the fundamental media of cinema. From the play, the filmmaker accepts the curious gifts of Lidman and Kanning to Gertrud: they each have given her mirrors, as if acknowledging that the incompleteness which haunts her, and which makes her attractive, could be rectified by the sight of herself, as if they were giving her their views of her.[11] Under Söderberg's stimulus Dreyer uses the mirror to construct a series of shots, wholly cinematic, utterly impossible on the stage: after Lidman has lit a candle, as if to a votive icon, on either side of the mirror, Gertrud appears framed in it. The camera captures the mournful poet beside the gilded image. Both he and Gertrud collapse into the bitterest moment of despair the film presents. Ritually lighting and framing the image will not undo the erosion of love since their last meeting. His attempt to repeat the past renders him bathetic. After he leaves, Gertrud extinguishes the candles and the camera frames the wall with the mirror which reflects only her back. Thematically, the use of the mirror is identical in the play and the film, but Dreyer's careful filming of that icon of loss and temporal instability suggests, as the play could not, that Gertrud's "love," oddly lacking narcissism, cannot be realized because it cannot be imaged. Dreyer has reinvented the very trope of liminal representation with which this book opens, Mallarmé's visual echo of the "bibelot aboli d'inanité sonore" in the "Sonnet en yx."

"Nothing"

THE ENCOUNTER of Gertrud and Lidman in Kanning's home, the climax of Söderberg's play, enacts the fullest collapse into despair in both the play and the film. All through both works, the characters talk past each other, but nowhere so dramatically as in this scene. Dreyer's most startling cinematic analogue to this verbal fact is his eccentric orientation of actors who seem to cast their gazes everywhere but at each other. In *Ordet* he had significantly modified the symmetry between dialogue and eyeline matching; in *Gertrud* he made the discrepancy radically obvious, but again nowhere more so than in this final meeting of Lidman and Gertrud. Very much like the figures in the Munch print "Two People" behind them on the wall, they seek out a far horizon with their eyes. They never look at the camera, but they fix their gazes in and through the unfilmed space in which the director and his crew work. The text gives us a nearly obsessive repetition of the word "nothing," much as *Ordet* talks repeatedly of "miracles" until the term seems a banality, further distracting us from the revelatory miracle of the ending. In *Gertrud,* at the perigee of despair, the characters seem to insist that they are looking into, staring at, or facing up to: Nothing. It is the void which eludes coming into sight; it cannot be painted, dreamed, reflected, filmed.

Neither Dreyer nor Söderberg privilege verbal over visual representation. "Nothing" does not define or control the elusive horizon of the film or the play. Throughout both, language is systematically circumscribed and silence periodically bears the weight of dramatic confrontation. At one extreme, the idle chatter of Kanning's mother, who shows up in both scenes at Kanning's house, reduces speech to gossip. At the other, poetry and song, especially in the filmmaker's original extensions of the play, cannot escape irony. The entire ritual which celebrates Lidman's return did not appear in the play. Undoubtedly it is a demonstration of pomposity, triviality, and parochialism. Yet it is strangely moving. A few years before making *Gertrud,* Dreyer himself had been honored similarly by students of the University of Copenhagen. Dreyer is too keen an observer to sentimentalize an event of this sort. Yet he was sufficiently touched by the ceremony to carry its power into his film.

Dreyer recast the entire play from the point of view of a future which he fantasized for Gertrud. His epilogue not only gives us a picture of the heroine thirty-five years later, on the threshold of her death; more importantly it focuses the theme and the style of the previous scenes upon the filmmaker's obsessive problem: death.

The epilogue has a lighting similar, although not precisely the same, to that of the two flashbacks in the film. It is brighter than the rest of the scenes in the present tense, but the light does not bleed out sharp outlines. Its immediate effect is to isolate it from all but the flashbacks. The entire epilogue is structured as a commentary on the intensity of its light. Axel Nygren has come to give Gertrud a book he has written as a memoir of their companionship in Paris. Dreyer makes it perfectly clear that their relationship had never been erotic. By symbolizing their days in Paris, it presents the opportunity for Gertrud to comment upon the significance of her studies after she rejected both Lidman's invitation to return to him and Kanning's marriage. By accepting the book as a beautiful object, and by speaking of their experience in Paris only nostalgically, Gertrud indicates that her studies did not change in any fundamental way her view of "love."

The only deviation from realism in Söderberg's *Gertrud* occured at the point, in the third act, where Dreyer inserted the ceremony honoring Lidman. Gertrud, sitting alone in an antechamber, is visited by a "ghost" of herself at sixteen years old, who recites to her a poem she wrote at that time. It is at this point that Dreyer performs an astounding transformation of the scene of Gertrud's meeting with her "ghost" in the play, a piece of cinematic alchemy which suggests, more than any other moment, what potential he might have seen in Söderberg's play. He has Gertrud read the juvenile poem that the "ghost" recited to her in the play. But here it does not serve to motivate Gertrud to pursue her mad quest for absolute love; it becomes purely retrospective.

The filmmaker sets up the reading of the poem by an act of breaking with the past. Gertrud gives Nygren back the letters he wrote her. This is the first clear sign that she recognizes her imminent death. This scene is emphasized by a remarkable circular camera movement making a complete tour of Gertrud's cell-like study. She explains her gift: "It would be a pity to let fall into strange hands what were for me the greatest and warmest words of your life." Nygren asks permission to burn them, which she grants. We watch them stare at the fire which consumes them. Here is where Dreyer originally intended Nygren to request and receive the gift of a song. With that scene removed, the epilogue moves directly to Gertrud's poem. Nygren asks if she ever wrote poetry. She admits

that she wrote one poem when she was sixteen. At his request she reads
the three strophes.

> Look at me.
> Am I beautiful?
> No.
> But I have loved.
>
> Look at me.
> Am I young?
> No.
> But I have loved.
>
> Look at me.
> Am I alive?
> No.
> But I have loved.

This piece of doggerel has been placed so exquisitely in the penultimate
moment in the film as to generate a powerful and tragic catharsis. We
realize that when written the poem was not only trite but a series of
lies. It is difficult to believe that the woman who attracted the heroes
of political and artistic society in her maturity and who remains beautiful at seventy was not beautiful at sixteen! By all standards she was
young when she wrote the poem. To say she is not alive is a paradox.
Furthermore, everything in the play indicates that her affair with Lidman and her imaginative fantasy of one with Janssen were the powerful
loves of her life. The poem, then, could be little more than the idle
jotting of a beautiful, young, lively girl looking forward to erotic passion.

As Gertrud reads the poem, we recognize the charm of its fibs in the
mouth of a sixteen-year-old girl. But at the same time we understand
how time has turned the frivolous lies to truth. It is the declaration of
a once beautiful woman in her old age as she faces death. All through
the film she had turned away from her interlocuters, staring and in-
ducing them to stare into a blank space which the camera requires to
make its images. Now she solicits the gaze of her friend, and ours as
an audience.

Having reoriented the poem from a manifesto of love to a vision of
death, the filmmaker is ready to introduce in his epilogue another than-
otopic allusion from Söderberg's play. Gertrud tells Nygren that she
has ordered her tombstone upon which only "Amor Omnia" will be
inscribed.

Dreyer wrote a final speech for Gertrud and followed it with a final cinematic figure. She tells Nygren: "One day even your visit will become a memory . . . like the other memories I save. Every so often I take up my memories and I immerse myself in them as if I were staring into a fire that is dying out. Goodbye, Axel. Thank you for the visit and for the book." Here, in the final words of the film, Gertrud finally identifies the object of her gaze: the dying fire. The superabundant projector light which illuminates this scene and which flooded the flashbacks corresponds to that last glow of the fire, which can be called either "love" or "life." It will consume Gertrud soon as it consumed Nygren's letters.

The unnamed, unpictured, unreflected object of sight which has haunted the film and its protagonist looms in the end as human temporality. It is not against the invisibility of "nothing" that it comes into sight, but against the horizon of death it figures itself.

The film ends in a remarkable series of images in shot–countershot. Only in the painful and hopeless conversation between Gertrud and Kanning when she announced her separation and in the ironical facing off of Lidman and the student eulogist had this basic structure appeared earlier in the film. As Nygren leaves Gertrud's isolated house he must pass from her study through a hallway to the outer door. This hallway is the starkest interior in this stark film. The repeated alternation of Nygren and Gertrud waving to each other across the long hallway confirms the plea of her poem. He looks directly at her, acknowledging her mortality, which finally comes to be represented by her closed door. In this film, utterly lacking in the violence of the deaths in Dreyer's earlier sound films, he has given us his fullest image of dying. Gertrud's epitaph "Amor Omnia" comes to reverberate as Dreyer's unuttered motto "Mors Omnia." The reservation of shot–countershot for the conclusion of both *Ordet* and *Gertrud* had dramatic importance for Dreyer.

In *Ordet* we share the critical, visionary moment with Johannes, but in *Gertrud* all the characters gaze blankly offscreen, as if hypnotized by an obscurity of meaning for which the final countershots are merely signs of its opacity. By fashioning his last films in this way, he found a stylistic figure to drive home the monumentality of facing up to death which had been his cinematic obsession.

If we think schematically of the important differences between seeing a play and a film based on a play, the possibility of shot–countershot becomes one of the cardinal points of distinction: the director of a play organizes the visual field for a spectator fixed in one place; the film-maker can invent a synthetic space through reverse-angle cutting. In *Ordet* and *Gertrud* he guides and delimits our field of vision by restlessly maneuvering the camera to reframe the image without violating the illusion of the frontality of the spectacle. Once in each film the camera describes a large arc or circle of the set. But it is only at the very end of each film that he allows the cinema to claim its unique privilege of orchestrating the exchange of glances dramatized on the screen.

4

Cinematography vs. the Cinema: Bresson's Figures

"THE IDEAS, hide them, but so that one can find them. The most important will be the most hidden."[1] Sometime between 1950 and 1958 Robert Bresson wrote that note to himself. In 1975 he published the slim but thrilling volume of *Notes sur le cinématographe* which he had accumulated between 1950 and 1974. In a style recalling Joubert's journals, he revealed his painterly approach to filmic issues and he provided several hints about his theoretical orientation toward his medium, most importantly, his distinction between "le cinéma," a debased version of theater, and "le cinématographe," a high art in which "intelligence" is defeated by "automatisme," sound invents silence, emotion takes precedence over representation, and one sees "models" rather than "acteurs."

Suture

IN 1969 Jean-Pierre Oudart introduced the term "suture," from Lacanian psychoanalytic theory, to film criticism, extolling the unique use of shot–countershot in Bresson's *Le Procès de Jeanne d'Arc*.[2] He argued that the emphasis on reversed fields in the exchanges between Jeanne and her judges, with the camera often placed at an oblique angle to the heroine, demonstrated Bresson's peculiar understanding of cinema's illusionary space. "Suture" is the act of joining the matched fields of shot–countershot which the viewer automatically performs.

Oudart's thesis was developed in a number of articles he wrote in the early seventies for *Cahiers du Cinéma*. Soon it became the basis for a theory of identification in cinema in general, which Stephen Heath, among others, elaborated. Oudart claimed, in his initial article, that Bresson lost sight of the discovery he had made in editing *Pickpocket* and turned into a structural principle in *Le Procès de Jeanne d'Arc,* when he made his next film, *Au Hasard, Balthazar,* in which shot–countershot plays a diminished role.

Oudart ignores the fact that the style of *Le Procès de Jeanne d'Arc* reflects the unusual prominence of verbal exchanges in that film. Generally, shot–countershot in Bresson's films underscores the significance of acts of seeing. In this chapter, I shall concentrate on two of Bresson's films in which the process of seeing demands special attention. In the first, *Mouchette,* I shall compare what Mouchette sees in shot–countershot to what we sometimes see of her and about her through camera movement and framing. Then, I shall consider the centrality of seeing in *Pickpocket.*

In 1969 I wrote an article on Bresson's films for the magazine *Changes* which I revised and published in *The Essential Cinema* in 1975 before reading *Notes sur le cinématographe.* Rereading my essay, I am surprised and disappointed in my unwillingness or inability to pursue the implication of the stylistic features I had pointed out as typical of the filmmaker. The most hidden ideas remained securely out of sight in that article. For example, I described a sequence from the middle of *Mouchette* which I had chosen because of its neutrality, its apparent segregation and autonomy from the movement of the film's plot. That sequence and my obtuseness to it will be the starting point for a reconsideration of Bresson's narrative style and its relationship to the questions of form, cinematic language, and modernity I have been exploring in this book. Of modernity, the filmmaker has published only one remark, in the negative mode: "Novelty is not originality nor modernity," to which he footnoted a line from the opening of Rousseau's *Confessions,* "I did not try to conform to others nor the opposite." Here Bresson proudly joins company with a great original and radical modernist; the negative mode is often his most forceful means of expression, as when he writes, "Cinematography, the art, with images, of *representing* nothing."[3]

Synecdoche and Imitation

I HAD described eleven shots from the moment Mouchette deliberately splashed mud on herself before entering church until an anonymous woman gave her a token for a bumper car ride. Here is my description of the fourth shot in the sequence:

> A quick fade out as loud circus-like music comes in. The music continues with different intensities mixed with the calls of barkers throughout the sequence of shots described below.
> 4. Medium shot of hands washing glasses in a bar; the camera dollies back to reveal that it is Mouchette. She dries her hands on her apron, takes the apron off, arrogantly tosses the sponge into the sink and comes forward so that her middle again fills the screen. In the foreground, before Mouchette, someone opens a cash register, gives her a few coins in payment, and closes it. She comes foward and leaves the screen by the left.[4]

I had terminated my description of the sequence with the eleventh shot because it is followed by a dramatic scene and an important innovation by Bresson to the plot of Bernanos' *Nouvelle Histoire de Mouchette,* which he adapted rather closely: Mouchette engages in an innocent flirtation with a teenage boy in another bumper car. He waits for her after the ride, but before she can speak to him her father suddenly descends upon her and slaps her face. We never see the boy again in the film. Shortly after that, the barmaid Louisa and the poacher, Arsène, are seen enjoying the rides of the fair together.

The plot itself can be quickly summarized. Mouchette's mother lies dying at home with an infant to care for. Her father and brother, both alcoholics, deal in illegal wine, which we see them delivering to the bar where Louisa works. She has an ambiguously defined relationship to Arsène, the poacher, while M. Mathieu, the gamekeeper, who is married, pursues her. After school, where Mouchette is ostracized by the other pupils, she witnesses a fight between Arsène and Mathieu, gets lost in the woods during a downpour, and is eventually found and raped by Arsène. In a fit that may be alcoholic or epileptic he believes he has murdered the gamekeeper. Mouchette comforts him and agrees to cover up the murder with him before returning home. There her mother dies before she can tell her what has happened to her. The next morning she is given something to eat by a prying shopkeeper and a shroud for her mother by an old woman obsessed with death. After visiting Mathieu's home and telling him and his wife that she is Arsène's lover, she wraps herself in the shroud and commits suicide by rolling down a hill into a pond. It takes her three tries, and seems, to the viewer, like a game until her body disappears under the water.

Within this sordid and squalid drama of provincial life, the brief sequence I had described in detailed shots seemed an insignificant interlude. Yet when examined in the light of the whole film the details of the cinematic construction, even in this passage, can tell us a great deal about Bresson's interpretation of Bernanos' novel. The fourth is particularly revealing. When the fourth begins, the viewer naturally assumes that he is watching Louisa, because she is the only person we have seen behind the bar before this. Yet before the camera has tracked back very far we realize that Mouchette is working there instead. Is there a significance to this momentary deception by the filmmaker? Now it seems to me that that complex and exciting shot embodies a subtle insight into Mouchette's psychology[5] and a clue to the mystery of her suicide; and that the ambiguity prods the viewer to recognize it. Her suicide is a mystery not because it lacked motivation; the poverty, cruelty, ostracism, loss of her mother, and, above all, rape provide an overabundance of causes. Yet it is mysterious because Bresson, unlike Bernanos, gives us no warning of its occurrence and no exposition of the girl's mental acts leading up to it. The same is true for his next film, *Une Femme douce* (1969), in which the narrator compulsively recounts the history of his wife's suicide in the vain hope of finding sufficient cause. In *Le Diable probablement* (1977) the situation is somewhat transformed: a young man, fixed upon the idea of killing himself, cannot find a sufficient reason for living while testing the sexual, political, and moral passions of his peers.

Mouchette kills herself essentially because of the utter collapse of the crude hopes her world offered her. Bresson invented Louisa from an unexplained remark in the novel by Mathieu to Arsène during their fight—"Stay away from Louisa";—he cast her as a plain and physically unremarkable woman, whose age, perhaps thirty, is difficult to read; yet, for Mouchette, she must have been the only model for an erotically attractive and somewhat independent woman. The rivalry of Arsène and Mathieu invested her with that value. The only indication Bresson gives us of the tenuous identification of Mouchette with Louisa is the momentary ambiguity of the fourth shot from the sequence I have isolated. The image of Arsène and Louisa on the fair ride takes on an added significance after this hint of identification between the two women. *She* is able to enjoy the fair publicly with her lover, but Mouchette is brutally humiliated and stopped before even speaking to a boy who was attracted to her in the bumper cars.

Furthermore, if Louisa is invested with sexual value, so is Arsène, if only because of his success with her. He too has none of the physical attributes we associate with erotic heroes in films. Surely, an identification and a rivalry with Louisa is behind Mouchette's acceptance of his sexual violence toward her. When he collapses in a fit, she tries to soothe him by singing the very song her disgusted schoolteacher chastised her for singing offkey. The next morning she tests the social value of her experience by boasting to Mme. Mathieu that she has become Arsène's lover. But that defiant declaration fails to secure for her the status of maturity and sexual desirability she had unconsciously anticipated as Louisa's successor. Instead, she receives the less than generous attention of two women who pity her for the loss of her mother. Her suicide occurs when she feels the poverty of her aspirations and the vacuity of their fulfillment.

Bresson illustrates the collapse of her illusionary values with a metaphor derived from *Le Règle du jeu,* a film of erotic triangles and social values quite remote from the world of *Mouchette.* Just before her death Mouchette sees a hare, shot by a hunter, writhing and finally dying. The montage of the hunt recalls the opening of the film in which Mathieu spies on Arsène as he sets his snares for small game birds. Together the two sequences, with their meticulously detailed compositions and rhythmical editing, pay homage to the magnificent central hunt scene of Renoir's film in which the shooting of hares is coupled with the killing of birds by huntsmen in blinds.

The death Mouchette accepts for herself shares a quality of sport or game with the hunt she watched. After the dismantlement of her models for imitation, the dying hare presented the first impression Mouchette could grasp with vigor. The montage and isolation of the episode, together with the shot–countershot of Mouchette's immediate reaction to it, underline the importance the filmmaker gave to it. Unlike the subtlety of the identification with Louisa which belongs to the occulted infrastructure of the film, the graphically depicted shooting of the hare concedes the sudden consciousness of a new option. In killing herself Mouchette acted again upon her need to imitate. This last touch was another of Bresson's additions to Bernanos' story. It fulfills cinematically the demands of Bernanos' pessimistic naturalism, demonstrating the awful power with which the patterns and perspectives the individual inherits and discerns in his or her world curtail freedom.

Bernanos' Frighteningly Sudden Event

ONLY READERS of Bernanos' novella would know that the old woman who gave Mouchette the dress had encouraged her suicide. Bresson has eliminated the story she told Mouchette about the original owner of the dress, a young girl who died. Out of the simile which ends Bernanos' description of the old woman, the filmmaker seems to have made his hunting episode: "She had curled up in her chair, and her fingers were moving so restlessly and quickly along her black dress that her hands were like two small grey animals hunting invisible prey." Again, in the last chapter, which describes Mouchette alone in the quarry where she will kill herself, there is a version of that simile: "At that moment, the deep, secret impulse toward death seized her again. It was so violent that she was almost dancing with anguish, like an animal caught in a trap."[6]

By transforming these metaphors into a concrete situation and giving them the status, not of cinematic analogies as Eisenstein might have done, but of elements in a shot–countershot encounter, Bresson has found a filmic substitution for the access to interiority that Bernanos' language has. Passages such as the following would find no place in Bresson's cinema:

> And now she was thinking of her own death, with her heart gripped not by fear but by the excitement of a great discovery, the feeling that she was about to learn what she had been unable to learn from her brief experience of love. What she thought about death was childish, but *what could never have touched her in the past now filled her* with poignant tenderness, as sometimes a familiar face *we see suddenly* with the eyes of love makes us aware that it has been dearer to us than life itself for longer than we have ever realized. . . .

> People generally think that suicide is an act like any other, the last link in a chain of reflexions, or at least of mental images, the conclusion of a supreme debate between the instinct to live and another, more mysterious instinct of renouncement or refusal. But it is not like that. Apart from certain abnormal exceptions, *suicide is an inexplicable and frighteningly sudden event,* rather like the kind of rapid chemical decompositions which currently-fashionable science can only explain with absurd or contradictory hypotheses.[7]

Bresson so thoroughly empties out the projection of intention, conflict, and other signs of interiority that would require interpretation from the actors he calls "models" that the sort of elaboration and even editorializing that characterizes the passages from Bernanos' final chapter seems very remote from his art. Nevertheless, the phrases I have emphasized indicate how closely he has followed the text, or rather, how he has found correlatives to his own epistemological model in it. The sudden sight of the dying hare, which would not have touched Mouchette in the past, now motivates her suicide, which seems "an inexplicable and frightening event" on the screen. His narrative style is so radical because he invests the act of seeing—and therefore the shot–countershot structure—with the full burden of fictional psychology. This radicalism has the effect of making events, which are inexplicable and frightening, seem like the natural consequences of previous events in the chain of images. Furthermore, the very ascesis of psychological projection by the actors gives to each image an equal, neutral value which accentuates this appearance of logic. He gnomically says this when he writes:

> Flatten my images (as with an iron) *without attenuating them*. . . .

> To edit a film is to join persons to one another and to objects by glances.[8]

Again, the *Notes* suggest an important nuance:

> Because you do not have to imitate, like painters, sculptors, novelists, the appearance of persons and objects (machines do that for you), your creation or invention confines itself to the ties [liens] that you knot between the various bits of reality caught. There is also the choice of the bits. Your flair decides. (p. 35)

For Bresson the art of cinematography is not simply that of pictures and sounds; it is the art of making connections (*liens*) or montage. He grants to the mechanical reproduction of the camera a crude access to reality that is denied to human perception. However, he acknowledges that the truth (*le vrai*) immanent in cinematographic reality emerges when the machines correspond to human perception. The filmmaker must first give himself over to the machinery and then, through montage and fragmentation, construct his film according to the emotional dimensions of the images and sounds he has recorded. This process implies an employment of intuition and improvisation on the level of shooting and a willingness to let the camera "correct" the errors of the script. The problem, he writes, "is to make seen what you see through the mediation of a machine which does not see as you see. And to make heard what you hear through the mediation of another machine which does not hear as you hear."[9] Without the middle term, submission to and redomination by the intervention of the machinery, there is no cinematography.

Bresson's addiction to shot–countershot editing puts him at the opposite pole to Dreyer. In *Mouchette,* for example, he built an episode in a shop of a woman, who offers Mouchette breakfast just after her mother's death, around a long take of the girl intercut with seven countershots. Here, as often in his films, he seems to have reduced direction to a matter of telling the "models" to look up, look left, look down, etc., so that the sequence could be constructed in the editing. The principle is the same as Hitchcock's, as cited in chapter 1, but the effect is more like Kuleshov's in that Bresson's montage elicits an emotional reaction to figures who do not mime emotions.

Framing the Hand

THE FLATTENING and accentual neutrality of Bresson's images increases their potential for exchange within the rigors of his visual economy. But economy, in the literal sense, is also a central issue for him. Both *Pickpocket* and *Une Femme douce* (in which the husband is a pawnbroker) offer elaborate versions of the ambiguous sexuality of the exchange of goods and money. In the eleven-shot series I mentioned at the beginning of this chapter there are four apparently casual exchanges. In the fourth shot—which is crucial to the identification of Mouchette with Louisa—Mouchette receives money for her work at the bar. She passes the money to her father in the sixth. In the tenth a woman buys a token for a ride which she slips to Mouchette in the eleventh. She uses it immediately afterward to ride the bumper car.

Earlier, Mouchette's father had responded to her automatic surrender of the money by passing his wine glass to his daughter. The interchange of wine and money describes the parameters of his economy; for it reverses his illegal labor. In strict adherence to the confines of naturalism, which emphasizes the determinism of heredity, Mouchette's brother repeats the patterns of his father.

Correspondingly, the woman with the infant who buys the token for Mouchette is a countertype of her mother, who also has an infant.

It is important to keep in mind that the viewer cannot know the woman's intention until her act is completed. Such attention to manual, undramatic action is a variation on the significant framing of Mouchette when we first see her at the bar. The close framing of her purchase in shot ten of the series does not isolate her from the figures who constitute the bustling environment of a fair. Only in shot eleven do we realize what she has done. This ambiguity is of a different order from that of shot four; we cannot assume, even for a moment, that the person buying the token is her mother. The association with the mother, which the presence of the infant reinforces, is purely formal; it calls our attention—if we notice it at all—to what the mother *cannot* do for her daughter. The ellipsis of the framing and the consequent anonymity of the benefactor separates this woman from those malicious and sinister women who will later offer gifts on the morning after her mother's death.

Even this innovation of Bresson's can be traced to a very different source in the novella. Returning to the final chapter, we find that the involuntary memory of a single act of kindness returns to the girl just before she kills herself. The paragraph is worth quoting in full because it demonstrates the extent of the filmmaker's transposition:

> It had happened one holiday-time at Trémières. She was taking back to Dumont's café the fish which the old man had caught during the day—a basketful of eels. On the way a big fair-haired girl had bumped into her, and turned around and asked her her name. Mouchette had not answered and the girl had gently and absent-mindedly stroked her cheek. At first Mouchette had thought nothing of it, and indeed, the memory had been painful until evening and she pushed it out of mind. It had returned suddenly, changed almost unrecognizably, just before dawn when she was asleep on the ragged mattress Madame Dumont, on evenings when the café was full, put down for her in the narrow corridor littered with empty bottles and cans and smelling sharply of sour wine and heavily and greasily of paraffin. In some strange way, while she was half-asleep, she felt herself cushion her face in the crook of her arm and smell the imperceptible perfume of that warm hand, and indeed she seemed to feel the hand itself, so near and so real and living that without thinking she raised her head and put up her lips to be kissed.[10]

This memory is prefaced in the book by the assertion that "Her mother had never been affectionate and Mouchette had never received many caresses from her hands," and followed shortly by an essential link: "Until her chance meeting with Arsène she had never, despite such fleeting moments, been able to overcome the strange rebellion against tenderness which made her so solitary."

The anonymous woman with the baby receives none of the emphasis that Bernanos gives to the girl who stroked Mouchette's cheek. Through the filmmaker's art, that woman is absorbed within seconds back into the crowd from which she scarcely emerged. Furthermore, her kind act ironically instigates her father's sudden attack, more violent than his earlier shove in the church; for after seeing her flirting with the boy in the bumper car, he rushes at her, pushes her, and slaps her. Another factor in Bresson's systematic orchestration of gestures would be the bumper car scene itself, in which the superficially violent bumps become signs of play and eros.

More crucial than the quick disappearance of the woman with the infant is the withdrawal of Mouchette's own mother. Her intense pain and imminent death prevent her from listening to her daughter's urgent wish to disclose her rape. The mother's death abandons Mouchette to her unformulated mimesis of Louisa. Instead of responding to her daughter as a child, traumatized by the brutality of her sexual initiation, the mother asks the girl to play another role beyond her age by warming the baby's bottle, which she does against her breast.

The Self-Correction of the World's Fragility

PICKPOCKET IS Bresson's prime example of the moral value of perception freed from the confines of intelligence.

Georg Lukács in *The Theory of the Novel,* invoking an intricately developed yet useful Hegelian argument, identified the ironization of subjectivity characteristic of the novel in the following way:

> The self-recognition and, with it, self-abolition of subjectivity was called irony by the first theoreticians of the novel, the aesthetic philosophers of early Romanticism. As a formal constituent of the novel form this signifies an interior diversion of the normative creative subject into subjectivity as interiority, which opposes power complexes that are alien to it and which strives to imprint the contents of its longing upon the alien world, and a subjectivity which sees through the abstract and, therefore, limited nature of the mutually alien worlds of subject and object, understand[s] these worlds by seeing their limitations as necessary conditions of their exis-

tence and, by thus seeing through them, allows the duality of the world to subsist. At the same time the creative subjectivity glimpses a unified world in the mutual relativity of elements essentially alien to one another, and gives form to this world. . . .

The irony of the novel is the self-correction of the world's fragility: inadequate relations can transform themselves into a fanciful yet well-ordered round of misunderstandings and cross-purposes, within which everything is seen as many-sided, within which things appear as isolated and yet connected, as full of value and yet totally devoid of it, as abstract fragments and as concrete autonomous life, as flowering and as decaying, as the infliction of suffering and as suffering itself.[11]

Perhaps more than any other filmmaker with a serious reputation, and certainly more than any discussed in this book, Bresson has adapted important novels and novellas to the screen. The most ambitious literary source he approached was the model for *Pickpocket:* Dostoevsky's *Crime and Punishment.* Perhaps the very scale of that ambition accounts for his refusal to acknowledge the intimate relationship between the novel and his film. Dostoevsky's novellas have been the bases for two of his other films, as have two novels of Bernanos. Visconti is the only other major modern filmmaker that comes to mind who has been confident in translating serious fiction into cinema. In discussing *Mouchette* I have attempted to show how Bresson implemented and interpreted his literary source and, more crucially, how he inflected it cinematographically by structuring both into the film, and into the film's fictional bearer of subjectivity, an openness to a privileged moment of audiovisual stimulation. That moment is the point at which the filmmaker as "the normative creative subject" "glimpses a unified world" within the duality he has reflected. Yet, apt as Lukács' brilliant description of novelistic creativity is for Bresson's self-conscious art, there are critical differences between the verbal modality of the novel and Bresson's cinematic fiction. It is in *Pickpocket* that these differences are most richly and complexly manifested.

The Function of Repetition

THE NEARLY identical repetition of the film's beginning in its final minutes highlights the nullity of its central development. In the opening episode the pickpocket presents us with his first theft. Like Dostoevsky's Raskolnikov, he commits a crime in order to prove to himself his superiority over other humans and their law. He never intended to become a pickpocket, simply to commit a single crime to substantiate his theory. We find out all this only after the first theft has been accomplished and the thief apprehended but released because of insufficient evidence.

The presence of a racetrack is evoked elliptically by a composition of figures staring slightly beyond the camera, while on the soundtrack the sound of approaching horses grows louder and then begins to wane. Just as the sound intensity passes the crowd, the pickpocket, Michel, among them, glances to the left as if following the horses. Both at the beginning and at nearly the end of the film this configuration of image and sound is all we see of the actual race. In neither do we get the countershot.[12] Each time this elliptical trope occurs, Bresson intercuts details of the theft Michel commits while everyone's attention is diverted by the drama of the race. The first time, he gently snaps open a woman's purse as the race commences, and, just as the horses pass, he lifts out a wad of bills, pockets them, and turns away from the camera, exiting from the composition. During all of this, a voice-over commentary describes his emotional state: anxiety leading to elation.

When the trope recurs, Michel is the victim of a police plant. By now he has learned the fine points of picking pockets, so that he can unbutton a man's jacket at the start of the race, and remove his wallet with two fingers just as the horses pass. But this time, the man handcuffs him as he completes the operation. The virtual repetition of the earlier shot is a clue to the more elaborate repetition of the crime and its consequences. Both times he was caught by the police; both times the act failed to confirm the theory; both times the failure created a possibility for a visual stimulus to take on a meaning for him. The difference between his reaction to the first stimulus and the second breaks the chain of repetition and constitutes the meaning of the film. Its exposition will require some elaboration.

At the very beginning of the film, which purports to be the pickpocket's journal, he writes and tells us that there are two kinds of men: those who act and those who write about actions; he, however, claims to be both in one. The statement may be interpreted either as a simple boast of his uniqueness or, more profitably, as a paradox. The initial aphorism does not admit what follows it. Of course, taken literally his boast is a fiction, for Michel himself is a fiction who neither acts nor writes outside of the film in which the filmmaker disposes him.

The Journal

THE PRETEXT of the journal, here as in *Le Journal d'un curé de campagne,* justifies the voice-over which puts the action of the film into the past tense, emphasizing its finality at the start, and pretends to be an intimate or at least interior account. Maurice Blanchot astutely observed in the passage on "The Recourse to the Journal" in his essay, "Le Solitude essentielle," that journal writing involved a literary paradox:

> What does the writer have to remember? Himself, who he is when he is not writing, when he is living a daily life, when he is alive and real, and not dying and without truth. But the strange thing is that the means he uses to recall himself to himself is the very element of forgetfulness: the act of writing. . . .
>
> The Journal shows that already the person writing is no longer capable of belonging to time through ordinary firmness of action, through the community created by work, by profession, through the simplicity of intimate speech, the force of thoughtlessness.[13]

Blanchot was writing of the journals kept by novelists and poets, but what he observed applies as well to the fictional journal, which as a novelistic form is, in Lukács' phrase, "a self-correction of the world's fragility." One of the ironical displacements of subjectivity characteristic of the novel is the notion that a person is the sum of what has happened to him. The fictional journal invites us to share the "well-ordered round of misunderstandings and cross-purposes," again Lukács' phrase, with the invented protagonist.

Bresson makes the case more complex by using a ploy common to the authors of fictional journals, the preface. Before the film actually introduces us to Michel, we read on the screen:

> This film is not in the police genre. The author has to express himself though images and sounds.
>
> The nightmare of a young man driven by his weakness into an adventure of picking pockets for which he was not made.
>
> Only this adventure will reunite through some strange paths two souls who, without it, perhaps would never have known each other.

The difference between a film and a written text obliges Bresson to give up the convention, as old as the novel form itself, of pretending that the journal is a found object, unless he were to make the radical move of treating the images and sounds as found material. The words "This film" immediately underline the fictional status of the journal, which the preface never mentions. Furthermore, it diverts attention from the perspective of the first person narration by referring to the inter-subjectivity of the two souls. The key term "cauchemar" [nightmare] predicts the passive acting style of the "model" as well as the thematic recurrence of the initial theft and prepares us for the recognition—under the metaphor of waking—that distinguishes it from the cycles of repetition. Significantly this preface can only be understood retrospectively; for it predicts so much more than it can elaborate in a single paragraph.

The double inscription of preface and journal reflects the importance of reading in the film. The most obvious instance of the power of reading within the plot itself is the recurring allusion to the autobiography of a pickpocket called "Barrington" which Michel has read and which he recommends to the police inspector, with whom he plays a cat and mouse game. Barrington's book must be another example of the possibility of acting as well as writing. Michel's blindness to this is another way the filmmaker has of putting into question the opening aphorism. A more subtle, and metaphorical, variation on the theme of reading, however, is the event which turns Michel from being the executor of a single paradigmatic crime to a professional thief. Because he has picked one pocket, he sees differently. On the metro he sees a man reading a newspaper and his life is changed. He has "read" the newspaper reader figuratively. Rather than accepting the sight before him, as we see it in the shot, he interprets the newspaper not as something to read but as a tool. The reader, he realizes, is a pickpocket who covers his face behind the paper and uses the paper as an excuse for bumping into another rider. Folding up the paper, he has enclosed the snatched wallet within it. The film viewer, who has not directly experienced Michel's anxiety and elation at the first theft, cannot interpret the filmic image of the subway scene as he does. Only afterward, when the scene shifts to Michel's tiny room, do we realize how he read that scene; for he is practicing the use of a newspaper to disguise the act of picking pockets. Fate, he tells us, directed his steps to that subway. What he figuratively read in the common sight began his education as a thief. Like the sub-jectivized images I discussed in *Mouchette* this sight of the man with the newspaper takes on a special meaning for the consciousness open to it.

Bildungsroman

MOST OF *Pickpocket* details Michel's education as a criminal; its form suggests the *Bildungsroman*. Eventually this subjective reader is himself read by other trained eyes. Another, more experienced thief has seen him and invites him to join him and an accomplice as they practice the art of picking pockets at its most elaborate and refined level. We must deduce this sequence from the fragmentary episodes Bresson gives us. One evening Michel notices a man pacing back and forth before his door. His manner suggests that of a cruising homosexual. Michel follows him onto a street car and, again in a scene suggesting an erotic liaison, tacitly becomes his partner as they enter a café. This suggestion of a pickup extends the erotic tone of the thefts themselves, which resemble caresses and usually involve reaching into men's clothes.

A parallel development turns on another act of reading. Jeanne, who lives in the same building as Michel's mother, and who is the girlfriend of his friend, Jacques, has left a note for him telling of his mother's condition as she approaches death. Exhausted from a vigorous day of robbery, he steps over the note without seeing it. He reads it too late, the next morning. His mother has died. The police have known Michel since a robbery occurred at his mother's house. The unconfirmed suggestion is that Michel had committed this larceny before the period of the film began. We are led to infer that the theory of superiority and its practical consequences entail a self-justification of that initial crime against his own mother.

In the middle of the film Bresson presents us with a depiction of the team of thieves working the Gare de Lyon, an orgy of precisely calculated robbery which is matched by the choreographic precision of camera movements and a breathtaking rhythmic montage in a tour-de-force of cinematography. It functions analogously to the hunt scene in the center of *Le Règle du jeu* which I assume to be an abiding inspiration to Bresson.

An account of the sequence of twenty shots will illustrate the intricacy of the montage and camera movement, which in its precision and virtuoso timing corresponds to the combined skills of the thieves.

A closeup of a notebook entry (1): "I have become extremely daring . . ." dissolves into a moving sequence shot (2), which begins with Michel entering the train station and weaves among characters we take to be his possible victims after he passes out of the image, until it settles on a woman buying a ticket. The next three short shots (3–5) detail Michel deftly substituting a rolled newspaper for the purse under her

95

arm, then passing it to an accomplice; the third dumps the empty pocketbook in a waste basket. Then another sequence shot (6) made up of a long shot and a moving series of closeups shows an accomplice removing bills protruding from a victim's billfold and passing them to Michel. That shot ends with Michel's glance, matched by a countershot (7) of a plainclothes detective, while the voice-over asks "Where did I meet him?" before the tracking camera spots a new mark.

Eight more shots describe the elegant teamwork involved in taking this mark's wallet: A hand taps his shoulder (9), but when he turns to look, a thief from the other side lifts the wallet from inside his jacket, and drops it into Michel's waiting hand (10), as the man turns in the other direction (11). Next, in the most elaborate sequence shot of the film (12) Michel slips the wallet into a tourist's pocket (in close-up). The camera tracks back to identify the innocent carrier for us, and follows him through the ticket gate to the quays where it focuses on two detectives coming in the opposite direction. Panning to follow them, it swivels until it is 180 degrees from where it began, catching Michel passing through the ticket gate in pursuit of the tourist. There follow seven shots taken from inside a train coach. First, the carrier climbs on followed by Michel (13). In a compartment Michel removes the hidden wallet as the man lifts his baggage to the overhead rack, and passes it to an accomplice, who carries it down the aisle (15) to pass it to the third member of the team in a nearby compartment. No sooner has this wallet reached its final destination than attention shifts to a heavy man who had been in the background. In a breathtaking exchange of three short shots, the third man lifts a wallet from the breast pocket of the heavy man as he passes down the aisle. He holds it with three fingers against the inner window for half a second (twelve frames) (16), then removes the money which he passes to an accomplice and slips the wallet back into the same breast pocket as the man returns down the aisle (17–18). In the final three shots of the sequence, Michel helps a man onto the train (19), removes his watch and receives a purse passed to him (20), and climbs down from the coach to deposit the empty purse under the wagon (21).

The second, seventh, and the spectacular twelfth shots are long. They set up the actions which follow. The ninth, tenth, and eleventh shots follow each other rapidly: they describe the single, quick gesture of distracting the traveler by touching his shoulder. By the time he has looked in two directions, he has been robbed and the wallet has changed hands. The elegant tenth shot of Michel's hand catching the wallet sets up our expectations for the breathtaking sixteenth shot in which the stolen wallet hovers—as if in midair—visible only to the thieves and to us.

Fated Vision

FATE AGAIN provides Michel with an important sight, this time a
stark and blatant one that we have no trouble interpreting with him:
his two accomplices, who had preceded him to a railway station, are
arrested before his eyes. He escapes from Paris for a couple of years.
Bresson cuts from his departing train to an image of him returning.
The interval allows for a complication in the plot. Jeanne has had a baby
and refused to marry Jacques, who has disappeared. Michel takes a job
and gives Jeanne most of his salary to support the child. The filmmaker
loses little time in illustrating Michel's normal life. Soon we find him
in a café, looking at a man reading the racing paper. This time he is
unable to read the reader. When he tries to pick his pocket the next day
at the track, we realize that he is a police agent who has entrapped Michel.

The story of a criminal who performs his act to confirm his superiority, discusses his theory with the police, and gets involved in helping
an unfortunate, kind woman comes directly from *Crime and Punishment*.
The variations are fascinating, because through them Bresson demonstrates the difference between "cinema" and "cinematography." Axe
murders, like Raskolnikov's, abound in commercial films. Bresson has
substituted a nearly invisible act (which the camera can unveil with great
compression and even erotic power) for the lurid horror of a scene of
blood and violence. Less brilliant, but nonetheless interesting, is his
translation of Dostoevsky's saintly prostitute, Sonia, into Jeanne. Her
situation is more believable; her decision, in Catholic France in the 1950s,
to have her child out of wedlock is certainly not revolutionary, but it
evidences behavior according to principle more humanely than Michel's
fusion of theory and practice. But more significantly, the substitution
of Jeanne for Sonia reduces her dimensions in this film in order to enclose us in the solipsistic mind of the pickpocket while it withholds the
crucial intersubjective moment to the very final shot.

Every shot of the epilogue is decisive. Even though it is the closest
transcription of Dostoevsky in the film, it is uniquely and wholly Bresson's. Immediately after his arrest, the camera presents Michel sitting
on his cell bed. But the cell is so like his tiny room that, for an instant,
we might think he has been released and sits brooding at home. The
sound of a metal door opening and the echoing corridor confirms that
he is in jail. The epilogue to *Crime and Punishment* has two chapters. In
the first, we learn of Raskolnikov's trial and sentence quickly, and then
of the death of his mother and the correspondence between Sonia, who
accompanied the murderer to Siberia, and his sister. Bresson moved the

97

mother's death to the central narrative of the film. He did not want that to complicate Michel's solitude. But he did reproduce the behavior of Raskolnikov in his model. Dostoevesky wrote:

> Sonia wrote simply that he had at first shown no interest in her visits, had almost been vexed with her indeed for coming, unwilling to talk and rude with her. But that in the end these visits had become a habit and almost a necessity for him, so that he was positively distressed when she was ill for some days and could not visit him.[14]

The first of Jeanne's visits to Michel produces the same hostility. When she suggests that the court will be lenient because of his confession, he tells her he will recant it, almost to upset her. Of the jail he says, "I do not see it." Here Bresson adapts his original closely. In the second chapter of the epilogue we read: "In prison, of course, there was a great deal he did not see and did not want to see; he lived as it were with downcast eyes" (p. 467).

But although the transposition is faithful, the sense is different. So much of *Pickpocket* turns on fortuitous moments of seeing, that Michel's declaration reveals the intensification of his solipsism in the formula, "I do not see it." For him the walls of the prison dissolve and only his "idea" of superiority, and consequently the sense of his inferiority at having blundered, remains visible. This too comes right out of the second chapter of Dostoevesky's epilogue:

> At least he might have found relief in raging at his stupidity, as he had raged at the grotesque blunders that had brought him to prison. But now in prison, *in freedom,* he thought over and criticized all his actions again and by no means found them so blundering and so grotesque as they had seemed at the fatal time. (p. 466)
>
> ". . . many of the benefactors of mankind who snatched power for themselves instead of inheriting it ought to have been punished at their first steps. But those men succeeded and so *they were right,* and I didn't, and so I had no right to have taken that step."
>
> It was only in that that he recognized his criminality, only in the fact that he had been unsuccessful and had confessed it.
>
> He suffered too from the question: why had he not killed himself? (p. 467)

Michel repeats the question to himself after his first interview with Jeanne: "Why live?"

After a fade-out, the initial jail scene repeats itself. Michel is in the same position and we hear the same sounds but this time Jeanne does not come. Instead, he gets a letter telling him that the baby was ill and that Jeanne will come in a short time. This too parallels Sonia's illness and the letter in which she explains her absence. "His heart throbbed painfully as he read it," according to Dostoevsky. Michel informs us of the same reaction to reading Jeanne's note. Again, the isolation of the sequences, the paring down of the plot, and most crucially, the weight given to acts of reading in the film, make this admission of emotion much more dramatic in *Pickpocket* than in *Crime and Punishment*.

The scene fades again and in the next shot we see that Jeanne had kept her promise. As Michel sees her through the grating of the prison meeting room, he tells us "Quelque chose illuminait sa figure." This phrase was not in the original script. The American subtitler, for an unknown reason, remains closer to Dostoevsky than Bresson here; for the former had written: "But at the same moment she understood, and a light of infinite happiness came into her eyes" (p. 471).

Figura

THE CHANGE is critical. It is with this phrase that Michel announces his conversion. The question, "Why live?" prepared him to read the letter with more meaning than its simple apology could contain; and the sight of the letter created the condition in which he could see Jeanne as the answer to his question. Literally, his description of the moment would be translated: "Something lit up her face." *Figure,* from Latin *figura* means, first, a shape or an outline. A French listener would hear it as "face" without difficulty. I take the change of Dostoevsky's line, and the choice of "figure" instead of "visage" as meaningful. The image of Jeanne is not significantly different from those we have seen of her before. Bresson did not literalize the line with a flood of light, as some conventional filmmakers might have.

Michel sees Jeanne's face and reads it *figuratively*. She is a trope for his redemption from the cyclic repetition, demonstrated by the two racetrack scenes, and demonstrated again by the sameness of the scenes in the jail cell. "Quelque chose illuminait sa figure," also refers to the cinematic image: it is an illuminated trope, a projection of light and shadow. Bresson has written in his *Notes:* "How hide from oneself the fact that it all winds up on a rectangle of white fabric hung on a wall? (See your film as a surface to cover.)"[15]

The viewer of "le cinématographe" is invited to read images figuratively, to escape from the nightmarish blindness to the commercial "cinema's" literalness, to see the two models, according to another of the metaphors of the preface, as "souls." *Figura* has a religious as well as a rhetorical dimension. In typology the Old Testament prefigures the New. Read from the pivot of the Christ event, the histories and the prophecies of Israel encode promises of salvation.

As film viewers, we had been forced to read the crucial repeated scenes figuratively. The very separation of picture and sound makes a trope of the composite. In the *Notes* this is the definition of economy:

> *Economy*
>   Make known that we are in the same place by repetition of the same noises and the same sonority. (p. 41)

Once Michel has read the image of Jeanne figuratively, the grammatical person of the narrative changes. The recourse to the journal, which had dominated up to this moment, no longer functions. As Michel and Jeanne kiss each other's fingers through the bars, the voice-over addresses her for the first time: "O Jeanne, what a droll path we took to find each other."

This shift of person, to the almost prayerful mode of address, can even be found in the final entry in Bresson's short book to which I have referred so often.

> DIVINATION, this word [*nom*], how can I not associate it with the two sublime machines which I use to work? Camera and recorder, take me far away from the intelligence which complicates everything. (p. 72; translation modified)

The obsessive Michel, throughout all of *Pickpocket* until the final shot–countershot exchange of the film remained a figure for the crippling intelligence which complicates everything. His redeeming vision of Jeanne is an act of divination. The space of Bresson's fictions is a trap for capturing meaning which, for him, is always figural.

5

The Récit and the Figure:
Blanchot's *Au moment voulu*

NOEL BURCH, in his influential and polemical argument for the
priority of modernism in film aesthetics, *The Theory of Film Practice*,
cites Maurice Blanchot's tales as the quintessential models for the modernist fictional film subject:

> This . . . type of subject involves what we might call "the psy-
> chology of intimation." It is not the characters' external behavior
> or the nature of the external events determining their acts that is
> kept hidden, but rather their innermost motives, the principles un-
> derlying the rather strange world they inhabit, the factors that
> Maurice Blanchot calls "the secret center of everything. . . ." To
> adapt one of Blanchot's narratives to the screen would be a pat-
> ently absurd enterprise; Blanchot's subjects can function only within
> a specifically *literary* set of coordinates. But other subjects fulfill-
> ing analogous functions can doubtless play comparable roles within
> a specifically *cinematic* set of coordinates.[1]

Blanchot's *récits* present us with a paradigm of modernist fiction. As
he reworks earlier texts, continually mixing and shifting allusions, Blanchot stresses the moments of depletion when the waning of meaning is
most palpable. Since Blanchot frequently deprives his reader of a linear
plot, doubles and even elides the identities of his characters, and often

101

dissolves fictional faces into disembodied "pure" images under the pressure of an obsessively dialectical narrating voice, we should not be surprised to find him invoked in a chapter that Burch devotes, at least in part, to Bergman's *Persona,* a film in which two characters fuse into a single composite face for an instant. I shall discuss the intricacy of *Persona* in the next chapter. Here I want to explore the "hidden" dimension of Blanchot's fiction, as Burch puts it, and its relationship to both "figura" and the form of the parable.

The Nothingness of the Image

AU MOMENT voulu will be my narrative counterpart to Mallarmé's "Sonnet en yx" in this discussion of representative modernist strategies. Like that sonnet, this *récit* so draws upon the power of linguistic negation that it declares, via its negative route, the profoundly historical nature of modernist narrative; it suggests that the spatial and temporal coordinates of stories retain vestiges of theological parables which the serious writer cannot entirely escape. In his first theoretical book, *Faux pas,* Blanchot proposed the fantasy of a Mallarméan novel as a model for modernist fiction. In his *récits,* he seems to have given us instances of what such narratives would be. I choose to give an extensive reading of one of his *récits* as my sole example of the modernist novel because I know no other fictions which challenge more rigorously the conventions of novelistic picturing.

Blanchot's explicit formulation of his concept of the literary image might sound like an echo of Mallarmé: "But what is the image? When there is nothing, the image finds in this nothing its necessary condition, but there it disappears." Thus "The Two Versions of the Imaginary" begins. Blanchot stresses the negative dimensions of images, that they are *not* the things they resemble; their strangeness is that of corpses, forcing us to recognize that the dead person is not there; he has "departed." Blanchot calls this "the unbearable image and figure of the unique becoming nothing in particular, no matter what." Here "figure" displays its full semantic range in French as shape, face, and trope.[2]

As a trope the image is an oxymoron: "present in its absence, graspable because ungraspable, appearing as disappeared." But it is also pure metaphor: "and if the cadaver is so similar, it is because it is, at a certain moment, similarity par excellence: altogether similarity, and also nothing more. It is the likeness, like to an absolute degree, overwhelming and marvelous. But what is it like? Nothing."

Blanchot's theory of the image is a reflection on language. In his earlier essay, "Literature and the Right to Death," he had invoked Hegel in his presentation of the annihilating power of words:

> Hegel . . . writes "Adam's first act, which made him master of the animals, was to give them names, that is, he annihilated them in their existence (as existing creatures)." Hegel means that from that moment on the cat ceased to be a uniquely real cat and became an idea as well . . . God created living things but man had to annihilate them. Not until then did they take on meaning for him, and he in turn created them out of the death into which they had disappeared . . .[3]

In "The Two Versions of the Imaginary" Blanchot skews this theological parable of language into a paradox of creation:

> Man is made in his image: this is what the strangeness of the cadaver's resemblance teaches us. But this formula must first be understood as follows: *man is unmade according to his image.*[4]

The negation is less astounding than the displacement of the possessive adjective. The echo of Genesis (et creavit Deus hominem ad imaginem suum) teases us into reading Blanchot's man as a passive god made, or rather annihilated, in *his own* image. In fact, the author dwells on the reflexive pronoun—lui-même—in this essay; first doubting, then extolling the appropriateness of the expression "resemble himself" for the enigmatic presence of the corpse. When he writes "Man is made in his image," Blanchot hints we should substitute the myth of Narcissus for the story of Genesis. Ultimately both are delusions because "the image has nothing to resemble." So like a ghost or a word it wanders (errer) because of "the premonition of the *error* which now [it] represents."

The theoretical essay's substitutions—image for language, void for image—and their fusional oxymorons—corpse as resurrected body, absence as presence—find their freest embodiments in his remarkable *récits*. That may be why they present notorious difficulties for their readers. Occupying a region between the form of an extended prose poem and a fantastically elliptical novella, the Blanchotian *récit* bears superficial resemblance to its Surrealist progenitors, Breton's *Nadja* and Aragon's *Paysan de Paris*. But unlike those wonderfully seductive documents of the late 1920s, Blanchot's short fictions are not thinly disguised autobiographies; they do not give us a vision of a viable city and a community of artists. Instead, they offer the barest kernel of a story, a mere situation which might lead to a story, but with a passion and an insistence that can fascinate the reader into believing that the story—whatever it might be—must be of the utmost importance. In a sense, his are stories about the nature of story telling and listening, brought to an extreme of reduction. Through the work of interpretation they will sometimes appear to be nearly obfuscated variations on the Bible or other monuments of literary history.

Even Blanchot's brilliant theoretical writings on the nature of the *récit* (in his view *Moby Dick, Une Saison en enfer,* and *Nadja* are the central texts of the genre) do not fully prepare us for the interpretation of the genre as he practices it himself. Sometimes it seems as if the fictional work begins at the point where the theoretical essay leaves off, as if literary practice were a higher coefficient of theory. In the reading of *Au moment voulu* which follows I shall call upon Blanchot's theoretical texts, particularly from the volumes *L'Espace littéraire* and *Le livre à venir* which were written for the most part in the decade following the composition of the *récit,* whenever they offer potential glosses to difficulties encountered in trying to read the story.

Nothing about the plot of *Au moment voulu* is clearer than its beginning, even though it begins with a declaration of absence and a paradox of "surprise": "In the absence of the friend who lived with her, the door was opened by Judith. My surprise was extreme, inextricable, surely much greater than if I had met her by chance."[5] The three characters instituted by these two sentences are the entire population of the *récit*: Judith, her friend, Claudia, and the unnamed narrator, a man, act out the events of this tale in a small apartment on the right bank in Paris; hardly anyone else is even mentioned.

The narrator, it seems, has come for an extended visit after a long absence. The purpose of his stay eludes us. The erotic relationships between the characters are not defined, but nevertheless they are not totally effaced: Judith may have been the narrator's lover once; she may now have a sapphic attachment to Claudia; the narrator's invitation to Claudia to go south with him may be an amorous suggestion. In place of any direct allusion to sexuality, Blanchot presents us with a chain of jealous reactions in an apartment with very limited sleeping conditions: a living room or studio, one bedroom, a kitchen, and a bath are mentioned. The narrator is ill, so ill at times that he thinks he is dying. He is often bedridden, in the studio; he has trouble walking through the house.

The *récit* has dialogue, the exchange of glances and stares, and a long meditation on the idea of "an ending." Judith quickly fades out of the picture as the narrator and Claudia engage in a series of elliptical, antagonistic encounters from which they acquire a mutual respect. Late in the tale Judith reasserts her presence, and in the climactic scene, may even die.

The Temporality of an Ending

THE RÉCIT continues long after the disappearance of both women in the narrator's sustained meditation on the meaning of his encounter with them. If we jump to the last paragraph of the text, we find the schematic story reduced to a reflection on the temporality of writing:

> I believe that there is the absolutely dark moment of this in-
> trigue, the point where it constantly returns to the present, where
> I can no longer forget nor remember, where human events, around
> a center as unstable and as static as myself, indefinitely construct
> their return. I can recall what that path made me do and how I
> broke with almost everyone—and in this sense as well I forgot
> everything—, why, as distant as I was, I had to recoil and to recoil
> again to the heart of an instant where I wandered like an image
> tied to a day which passed statically through the day and to a time
> which at a certain point always breaks off from time. I can recall
> that, however long that path was and whatever might be its de-
> tours across the empty repetition of days and moments, nothing
> could keep it from being again and yet again the corridor which
> separated the two little rooms and where it happened to hold me:
> the quivering darkness where I had had to endure the greatest pain
> and nevertheless encountered the truest and the most joyous mo-
> ment, as if I had been hit there not by the cold truth, but by the
> truth which had become the violence and the passion of the end.
> I can recall all that, and to recall it is doubtless only one more step
> in the same space, where going further is already linking myself
> to the return. And nevertheless, although the circle already binds
> me, and even if I have to write it eternally, I will write to erase
> the eternal: Now, the end.[6]

The final two words, "Maintenant, la fin," receive an emphatic stress. Earlier in the concluding monologue he has considered the strangeness of the word for "now," as we shall see later in this chapter. In order to account for the narrator's peculiar thoughts about "maintenant," I want to pause to dwell on this uniquely French adverb. It is, of course, the present participle of the verb "maintenir," coming from the late Latin *manutenere,* which, like it, means "to support, to sustain." Etym-

ologically, it can be broken into *manus* (hand) and *tenere* (to hold). Thus
the common French word for "now" derives from the idea of holding
something in the hand. If we allow the etymology to be read back into
the text of *Au moment voulu,* the act of writing ("eternally erasing the
eternal") prolongs the present moment by holding the pen in the hand.
Following this same etymological train of argument, we would read "la
fin" as a development from *finis.* "The end," then, is the border, the
outer limit. The hand which writes is always extending the outer limit
of the written line. Yet, somehow within the *récit* itself lurks a profound
"violence and passion of the end." The task of interpretation might be
the uncovering of the relationship of that end to the temporality of writing. To begin to execute that task we must go back to the moment
before the narration begins: to its title: "*Au moment voulu*" is nearly a
translation of "stirb zur rechten Zeit!," a slogan from *Also sprach Zarathustra.*[7] Actually, Blanchot gives us the exact translation in his essay
on Mallarmé's *Igitur* reprinted in *L'Espace littéraire:* "Meurs au moment
juste." Although no formula in *Zarathustra* precisely corresponds to the
phrase "au moment voulu," the Will is explicitly linked to the idea of
dying at the right time in the chapter "Vom freien Tode."[8]

The title *Au moment voulu* points back to Nietzsche's dictum, but the
issue of dying at the right time, at the willed time, is not directly relevant to Blanchot's tale. The death, or near death, of Judith which occurs between pages 131 and 137 sets up the occasion for a climactic
memory scene in which "le moment voulu" emerges as a shared experience:

> Claudia followed a bit after me. Everything was calm, I think
> she rested then. However, later, I saw *her* [*la*], looking at me through
> the open door of the hallway (I was opposite, in the studio). When
> I saw her again, she was sitting and, across the whole stretch, she
> seemed a bit lower to me, her body, half folded, her head droop-
> ing toward her knees. It has happened to me at another time, while
> I was living alone in the South,—then I was in my prime, during
> the day my strength was staggering, but there was a moment in
> the night where everything stopped, hope, possibility, the night;
> then I opened the door and calmly looked toward the base of the
> stairs: this was a totally calm and intentionless movement, purely
> nocturnal as they say. In this instant across the immense stretch,
> she gave me the impression of being seated, she herself, at the base
> of the stairs, on a large pivot-step; having opened the door, I was
> looking in her direction without her looking at me, and all the
> tranquility there had been in this so perfectly silent moment had

today the truth of this body gently bent in an attitude which wasn't that of expectation, nor of resignation, but of a deep and melancholy dignity. For myself, I could only look, with a view that expressed all the calm transparency of a final view, at this woman sitting near the wall, her head gently leaning toward her hands. Approach? Go down? I didn't want to, and she herself, in her illegitimate presence, accepted my gaze, but didn't ask for it. She never turned toward me and, after I saw her, I never forgot to withdraw calmly. This instant was never troubled, nor prolonged, nor put off, and perhaps she did not know me, and perhaps she was unknown to me, but it doesn't matter, because for one and the other this instant was actually the moment we had been waiting for [le moment voulu]. (*Au moment voulu*, pp. 137–39)

In this unanticipated paragraph an ambiguous scene from the past emerges. Most puzzling and shocking is the presence of Claudia in this spot in time. It is, in fact, such a shock that we may be tempted to ignore the referential sequence of the paragraph and make "*la*" refer to Judith.

Yet once the memory scene occurs the narrative of the Parisian sojourn ends—without a definitive terminus—and the monologue, situated in the time of writing, the time of the earlier intrusions of "maintenant" and "aujourd'hui," develops, gradually leaving off all references to either Claudia or Judith. In that monologue the coincidence of the image from the South with that in the Parisian apartment is the source of his inspiration and the subject of his meditation. The remaining twenty-seven pages reflect upon its meaning, but do not clarify the mystery of the italicized pronoun.

The Door: Opened and Closed

THE MODEL for this formal structure must be Proust's *Le Temps retrouvé* as described in "Le Chant des Sirènes."

To experience timelessness, to experience the lightning process through which two infinitely distanced moments (*bit by bit, yet all at once*) draw together and merge like two presences which, metamorphosed by desire, have become indistinguishable, is to experience the reality of time and in so doing to experience time as space and void—time untrammeled by the events that usually clutter it. Pure time devoid of events, mobile vacancy, active distance, living inner-space where time's ecstasies gather with enchanting simultaneity, what can this represent if not the time of narration, the time which is no *outer* time but experienced as *outer* as space, the imaginary space where art discovers and musters its resources?[9]

In the apartment a woman, *"la,"* Claudia or even Judith, if we press the ambiguity of the pronoun, was watching him through "la porte ouverte du couloir." That as well as her posture made the memory effortlessly emerge. In the very first sentence of the *récit*, the phrase, "la porte fut ouverte" sets the narrative in motion. To a large extent, *Au moment voulu* depends upon both the literal and the figurative opening of doors. As a metaphor Blanchot even uses the open door to describe the experience of Proust in the essay I have just cited.

It is indeed remarkable that the experience of *A la recherche* should be almost entirely reported here: the phenomenon of recall, the metamorphosis it heralds (transmutation of past to present), the impression that a door has just opened [qu'il y a là une porte ouverte] onto the peculiar realm of the imagination, and finally the decision to write under the influence of such moments in order that they may be elucidated.[10]

Everything that Blanchot writes of *Jean Santeuil* in that sentence is equally true of *Au moment voulu*. In fact, in both, events are essentially a structural pretext for the processes of recollection and elucidation.

Figure

LET US return for a moment to the opening of the *récit*. From the very first phase it operates under a minus sign. Beginning with the declaration of an absence, the narrator postpones Judith's name until the end of the sentence. Much later we shall learn that Judith is merely a nickname the narrator gave her, a name her friend did not know. The first instance of direct discourse in the text introduces a crucial and historically weighted term: "Mon Dieu! Encore une figure de connaissance!" At this stage we cannot suspect that the colloquial language hides a theological ambiguity. The French expression "figure de connaissance" means "a familiar face." Yet the phrase smuggles the term "figure"—figure, shape, form, trope, face—and "connaissance"—acquaintance, knowledge, consciousness—into the story at the very start.

To start the story, the narrator imagines a face-to-face encounter. He puts a face on the name Judith, which in turn bestows an illusionary credibility to the writing "I" by returning its imaginary gaze. This encounter is further ratified by the introduction of a fictional witness, Claudia. But if the tale proceeded seamlessly from this starting point there would be little point in introducing the rhetorical term. Of course, all the illusions collapse, the faces dissolve. We never learn the narrator's name; "Judith" turns out to be an invention for a character who never gets her own name; even Claudia disappears two-thirds of the way through the fiction.

We are deep in the story when we discover that the entire scenario was the preamble to an interior reflection, built around a maze of allusions in three languages. Behind the name of "Judith" we can hear Matthew's *sponsus,* Kierkegaard's Abraham, and the object of Leiris' erotic obsession. Judith names a figure for shifting literary references, which give weight to the ecstasies of the "I", writing through the paradoxes of literary time.

The movement of the *récit* from the familiar theater of representation to the anxious self-consciousness of a writing hand has its counterpart in the deployment of the word "figure," which is simultaneously descriptive and metalinguistic.[11] He tentatively concludes the penultimate paragraph of the book: "There where it sees me, there is perhaps a figure [il y a peut-être une figure] but enveloped, enclosed in the eternity of a reflection, if it is true that the shadow of things is the brilliant resemblance where they withdraw and which drives them back to the infinity of the like to the like."[12]

This emptying out of the substance of fiction is not the monopoly of modernism. However, it is characteristic of modernist texts to make an allegory of this negative moment. We saw it operating in Mallarmé's "Sonnet en yx." Blanchot had initiated his critical enterprise with a call for the Mallarméan novel. In *Au moment voulu* he meticulously withdrew the fictional momentum and much of the narrative logic from what appears to be a story of three persons. Like Mallarmé's sonnet, this route to depletion cannot complete itself because it has to cross over a moment or a series of moments in which the defacement of the "figures," as fictional masks, entails the resurgence of the figuration of literary genres, specifically, the parable and the philosophical tale.

In an essay on Kafka, published not long after *Au moment voulu,* Blanchot gives us an insight into his concept of "figuration":

> This demand for a premature dénouement is the principle of figuration [figuration]: it engenders the *image,* or, if you will, the idol, and the curse which attaches to it is that which attaches to

idolatry. Man wants unity right away; he wants it in separation itself. He represents it to himself, and this representation, the image of unity, immediately reconstitutes the element of dispersion where he loses himself more and more . . .

[. . .] all this powerful imagery does not represent [ne figure pas] the truth of a superior world, or even its transcendence. It represents [figure], rather, the favorable and unfavorable nature of figuration [figuration]—the bind in which the man of exile is caught, obliged as he is to make out of error a means of reaching truth and out of what deceives him indefinitely the ultimate possibility of grasping the infinite.[13]

Later, in the same volume, he speaks of "thought," "God," "absence," "language" (parole), and "death" as "figures of the ideal."

Reading the Italics

IF WE try to reconstruct a naive reading of *Au moment voulu,* looking for the turns that make this short text[14] so extraordinarily strange, we might note that there are oddities from the very beginning, but that they are slow to dominate the book. In the very first paragraph the narrator displays a tendency to be paradoxical: "Time had passed, and yet it was not past; that was a truth that I should not have wanted to place in my presence." Nevertheless, his continual resumption of the narrative seems to promise, for a while at least, that the events will clarify his state of mind.

However a pattern of deformation remains consistent until the first passage of extended dialogue:[15] each new paragraph reasserts the narrative only to drift into a more abstract, dialectical language in its concluding sentences. Again and again Blanchot repeats this movement with very slight variations. The acknowledgment of the narrator's severe physical illness provides the reader with a potential cause, within the story, for this tendency to veer away from the sequences of observations and events he seems eager to relate.

Only after the conclusion of the first exchange with Claudia, at night in the kitchen, does the plot lose any claim to the strictures of plausibility. Again, it is the opening of a door that sets up the metaphysical moment. The door to the kitchen opens so suddenly that the narrator leaps into Claudia's arms. Then, he tells us:

for her and for me, at that moment, what began to move, to open the door so silently, was nothing less terrible than a *thought* [*une pensée*], and no doubt it was quite different for each of us, but in that instant we at least had this much in common, that neither of us was capable or worthy of enduring it. (pp. 48–49)

We never find out more about this strangely italicized thought. There will be five other italicized phrases in the *récit*; three of them expressions in German or Latin; the ambiguous pronoun we have already encountered; and another set of phrases in French. I understand these orthographical exceptions to be one key to understanding the text. The hypostatization of the thought that can open a door marks the first breakdown of the rational narrative.

The other italics are distributed in close proximity to each other, four just before the middle of the book, and two on the same page in the final quarter.[16] These phrases generally occur when the narrator manages to abandon himself to his storytelling. They mark crises which project him into progressively more intense disassociations of perception and description. For instance, after the manifestation of the "thought," a series of metaphors indicate his isolation from the events he tries to narrate: everything appears behind a pane of glass, the visit becomes a timeless moment, the interactions of the three characters become a "tapestry."

Even when he denies that he is involved in a story which can have a continuation, the narrator continues his tale of daily life in the little apartment until the first of the next set of italics, an unidentified quotation from Schumann's *Dichterliebe*—(Claudia sings the phrase, "*Es fällt kein Strahl*")—catapults him into a brief crisis in which her "discretion" is personified and a purely linguistic barrier, "[n]othing but the phrase 'it's her'" becomes a "screen behind which she recedes" (p. 72). Then, shortly after this, a personified "shiver" takes hold of him, making him think of the German phrase "*zwischen Himmel und Erde.*" By virtue of their uniqueness in the text, these two German expressions seemed to be linked in a strangely italicized phrase meaning "There fell no ray . . . between heaven and earth." The first German phrase, and, indeed, all the songs in *Dichterliebe,* is by Heinrich Heine. Blanchot does a very clever job of turning it into a phrase which evokes the world of Hölderlin's hymns from this bitterly ironic and deeply subjective lyric.[17]

The Sirens' Song

HEINRICH HEINE also popularized the image of the beautiful Lorelei singing and combing her golden hair to lure lovestruck sailors to their death in his best known ballad. Blanchot alludes to this version of the siren myth when he describes the women of his story combing each other's hair; he makes the situation more complicated by making lesbianism part of the lure.[18] In "Le Chant des Sirènes," Blanchot will isolate the Sirens episode in Homer's *Odyssey* as the paradigm for the nature of all *récits*.

The narrator falls under the spell of Claudia and Judith as he watches them: "I saw them pass the comb and the brush, each through the other's hair, a ceremony with a thousand variations, which extended itself indefinitely. In this image, I recognized an antidote to the dissolving element of the snow, a cure, a game where time was played. Surely I had to take account of this view. Was I under the spell? Yes . . ." (p. 85). This scene takes place at a time when the narrator has fallen silent. His inability to speak arose from the inadequacy of his language. "I did not want to defile with truth what was even truer than it—and then, I am not a judge. Speech was not mine" (p. 83).

The silence, the spell, and the sudden interruption of the Lorelei vision by "le *mouvement brusque,* le *bond presque sauvage*" of Judith as her hair is accidentally pulled (the phrase appears twice in this passage, both times italicized) generates a crisis in which he suddenly utters "une sorte d'oracle." This Siren-like possession seizes the two women, or more precisely moves through them, as if from outside, but it becomes focused in an incident only when the violent, *"presque sauvage"* reaction of Judith breaks the spell.

Negating Hölderlin

WHEN WE turn to the passage in which *Es fällt kein Strahl* appears, we can see how Blanchot has encouraged a neglect of its poetical and musical sources:

> When I watched her approach, the impression of having already often heard that song—she sang a smooth and remote German—passed before me and this was, for both of us, a most intense light which coiled about and illuminated us from below. *Es fällt kein Strahl.* I had to realize in this instant that she didn't need to work that hard on such a tiny fragment, so classical. Her voice was marvelous, with an extraordinary restraint: she too had folded back her wings, and her flight, pulled back to the breast of a rarer element, went in search of the single happiness of singing, while she

herself waited, affirming, impassively, that the song would not begin. (pp. 70–71)

Here the German words, which are not even identified as part of a song, are removed from the figurative sense of "Es fällt kein Strahl in deines Herzens Nacht," to become part of a bilingual statement of a most intense light rising up as if from the earth. In this strange under-light the very beginning of the song is in question. That it is perpetually reserved is part of its fascination. In this context the avian metaphor is not as innocent as it might seem. The Sirens were part-bird and part-woman.

The second German phrase appears eight pages after the first; it too is in italics. At the climax of a fit of illness, the narrator had been seized by rage. This is the narrator's turn to be a speaker in tongues. Here he describes the effect on him:

> The impression, an effect of stupor, was that there was a lacuna there, but also, what was very depressing, that something was trapped: between heaven and earth, as they say. I thought these words in German, *zwischen Himmel und Erde*. I must have calmly lain down a little later. (p. 79)

I am on much less certain ground than before when I call *"zwischen Himmel und Erde"* a quotation. In "Wie wenn am Feiertage" Hölderlin wrote:

> Do you ask where they are? In song their spirit wafts
> When from the sun of day and from warm soil
> It grows, and storms that are in the air, and others
> That, more prepared in the depths of time,
> More full of meaning and more audible to us,
> Drift on between Heaven and Earth and amid the peoples.
> [Hinwandeln zwischen Himmel und Erd und unter den Völkern][19]

The rejoined German phrase directly reverses the sense of "Wie wenn am Feiertage"

In his early essay on the poet, Blanchot stresses the negative dimension of Hölderlin. For example, he writes:

> And that the holy Father himself, the pinnacle of light, was either abandoned to silence, or deprived of truth and life, that man, for his part, might become a mute shadow, isolated, without the warmth of true existence which is that of the heart: nature would

lose its essence . . . [T]he All made itself language in order to say: he who wants to encounter the obscure has to look for it in the day, look at the day, become day for himself.[20]

The dubiously concocted statement *"Es fällt kein Strahl zwischen Himmel und Erde"* links two moods of the narrator, joins his joyous pleasure in forgetfulness to his fevered anxiety of indetermination. The luminosity attending the sense of having already and often heard the song may be in direct contrast to the sudden darkness ("Cela fut soufflé comme une lumière" immediately precedes the impression of being between heaven and earth) and the urge to slam against the door (again) that generates his feeling of being trapped in midair. Yet both these moods together define the limits of an experience of time that has no place for the poetic "Jezt" (Now) as Heidegger interprets it, that is, as the "arrival of the Holy Ones . . . which alone engenders 'time.' "[21]

Nescio Vos

IN WHAT I have called the "death" scene, Claudia and the narrator open the door to the bedroom to see Judith rise from a rigidly prone position to shout two words in Latin, *Nescio vos,* and fall back on the bed. The narrator translates the phrase, "I do not know you [plural]" and adds that it must have been a grammatical example he once taught her. But this explanation hardly covers up the oddity of the Latin quotation. The German phrase *"zwischen Himmel und Erde"* could be contextualized as a free association in response to *"Es fällt kein Strahl,"* which is not at all odd once we understand that it was sung by a character represented as a professional singer. The text labors to disguise a Latin quotation; critics of the novel have been taken in by the narrator's guile or self-deception; for none of them note that it comes from the Gospel of Matthew.

It occurs in the parable of the ten virgins (chapter 25), which is itself one of a series of arguments about the coming of the day of judgment. Here is the entire parable with relevant passages from the Vulgate in brackets:

> Then shall the kingdom of heaven be likened unto ten virgins, who took their lamps, and went forth to meet the bridegroom. And five of them were foolish [Quinque autem ex eis erant fatuae], and five were wise. For the foolish, when they took their

lamps, took no oil with them; but the wise took oil in their vessels with their lamps. Now while the bridegroom tarried, they all slumbered and slept. But at midnight there is a cry, Behold, the bridegroom [Ecce sponsus venit]! Come ye forth to meet him. Then all those virgins arose and trimmed their lamps. And the foolish said unto the wise, Give us of your oil; for our lamps are going out. But the wise answered, saying, Peradventure there will not be enough for us and you: go ye rather to them that sell and buy for yourselves. And while they went away to buy, the bridegroom came; and they that were ready went in with him to the marriage feast: and the door was shut. Afterward came also the other virgins, saying, Lord, Lord, open to us. But he answered and said, Verily I say unto you, I know you not [Amen dico vobis, nescio vos]. Watch therefore, for ye know not the day nor the hour.

The *sponsus,* according to conventional interpretation, is Christ at the Second Coming. The final four lines of the parable have caused interpreters problems. Some have dismissed them as an invention of the Gospel writer. The brutality of the rejection, *nescio vos,* has bothered some. That is precisely what Blanchot needs from the parable: its brutality and its circumstance of utterance—through the door.

Parables are both simple allegorical illustrations and puzzlingly obscure narratives. In his *The Genesis of Secrecy: On the Interpretation of Narrative,* Frank Kermode lucidly discusses both faces of the New Testament parables.

> If we want to think about narratives that mean more and other than they seem to say, and mean different things to different people, with a particularly sharp distinction drawn between those who are outside and those who are inside, we can hardly do better than consider the parables . . .
> The sense of [Kafka's parable of the leopards] must be this: being an insider is only a more elaborate way of being kept outside. This interpretation maintains that interpretation, though a proper and interesting activity, is bound to fail . . . The opinion of Mark is quite similar: he says that the parables are about everybody's incapacity to penetrate their sense.[22]

In practice, Blanchot seems to be among those interpreters who read the parables as barriers to understanding, following Matthew 13.13:

"Therefore speak I to them in parables: because they seeing not, and hearing not, neither do they understand." Blanchot makes this much at least clear from his skewing of the parable of the foolish virgins, that his narrator misses the allusion, yet nevertheless he (and presumably the author as well) implicitly identifies with the excluded, the foolish and hasty readers who neither see nor hear. Blanchot's modernist transformation of theology into poetics invokes the parable, albeit obliquely, to underline the opacity of literary language.

The parable of the foolish virgins offers us a key to *Au moment voulu* which the commentators have missed, despite the fact that so many of them have quoted the Latin words. *Au moment voulu* is certainly not an allegory of the Second Coming. Nevertheless, "*Nescio vos*" institutes a game of allusions in which Judith and the narrator exchange roles as the *sponsus*. He repeats the story askew: he arrives, in the opening sentences, completely unannounced. Like a wise virgin, Judith is there to greet him. Claudia plays the role of the foolish virgin in this rehersal of the parable. Of course, Blanchot complicates the figuration by introducing the name of Judith, as if the *sponsus* were arriving at his own death trap. Later, when she shouts those words, both the narrator and Claudia become the *virgines fatuae* whom she refuses to take with her as she dies, if, indeed, she does die. Perhaps an equally important clue lies in the flexibility of the parable: like the expression "I do not know you," the whole parable can be shifted so that first the narrator, then Judith, plays the role of the awaited groom to the other's excluded virgin. Even later, when the narrator speaks of himself as little more than an image reflected in the empty space of his southern retreat, doors continue to slam (and windows open) around him: the lone first person voice, or hand holding a pen, becomes a vestigial *sponsus* to his own almost incorporeal *virgin*. The very instability of meaning within the ironies of literary quotation—here hyperbolically exaggerated by the contrast of sacred and secular contexts—operates in the passage from *Also sprach Zarathustra* from which Blanchot adapted the *récit*'s title:

> Verily, too early died that Hebrew whom the preachers of slow death honour: and to many hath it proved a calamity that he died too early.
>
> As yet had he known only tears, and the melancholy of the Hebrews, together with the hatred of the good and just—the Hebrew Jesus: then was he seized with the longing for death.
>
> Had he but remained in the wilderness, and far from the good and just! Then, perhaps, would he have learned to live, and love the earth—and laughter also![23]

According to Nietzsche, Christ died at the wrong time. His "Sehnsucht zum Tode" was not truly willed death.

The twenty-fourth and twenty-fifth chapters of Matthew's Gospel take up a very different embarrassment of timing. The early Church anticipated the return of Christ within the lifetime of the first generation of his followers. By the time the Gospel of Matthew was composed that expectation had long been relinquished. His sequence of parables, which includes that of the foolish virgins, stresses the uncertainty of the time of the return and tries to reorient the Church from a condition of expectation to one of preparedness.

Within the fiction, Judith becomes most vivid when she is disappearing. As such, she is a figure for the fictional genre itself, an exhausted and broken form of articulating time, which sustains its own ruins. On the lexical level, the word "maintenant" too survives as an adverbial ruin: the present participle of "maintenir" has come to designate a problematic extension of the present. If we permit a very late Blanchot text to gloss the *récit* of thirty years earlier—a dubious practice—the discussion of the Messiah in *L'Ecriture du désastre* shows us a link between the concept of "maintenant" and the promises of Messianic time at work in the parable of the foolish virgins:

> And if it happens that to the question "When will you come?" the Messiah answers, "Today [Pour aujourd'hui]," the answer is certainly impressive: so it is today! It is now and always now. [C'est maintenant et toujours maintenant.] There is no need to wait, although to wait is an obligation. And when is it now? When is the now which does not belong to ordinary time, which necessarily overturns it, does not maintain [ne le maintient pas] but destabilizes it? When?—especially if one remembers that this "now" which belongs to no text, but is the now of a severe, fictitious narrative [d'un récit de sévère fiction], refers to texts that make it once more dependent upon realizable-unrealizable conditions: "Now, if only you heed me, or if you are willing to listen to my voice." Finally, the Messiah—quite the opposite in this respect, for the Christian hypostasis—is by no means divine. He is a comforter, the most just of the just, but is not even sure that he is a person—that he is someone in particular [quelqu'un de singulier].[24]

When Judith cries *"Nescio vos,"* we cannot know what she intends, what she means. Nor is any of the development on the quotation, with its intricate qualifications, thematic in the *récit*. We can read her decree of nescience as a jealous reaction to the increasing intimacy, the growing respect within antagonism, between Claudia and the narrator. The narrator explicitly discounts Judith's self-consciousness in repeating these words which he claims he may have even taught her while illustrating some grammatical point. "It is true that even these words, they themselves, were an echo of another time, she really had to have learned them from someone (she knew almost nothing), but what had perhaps fallen from me as a grammatical truth, the immensity, after such a labor of shadows, she threw back in my face like the blessing and the curse of night" (p. 137). But through her, "l'immensité" or "la nuit" pronounces its blessing and curse. Thus the phrase itself, as a random Latin tag regurgitated in ignorance, suddenly and spontaneously comes back to him, so that simply as an act of speech it illustrates the very principle to which it is a literary allusion: since he has forgotten the conditions under which he taught her the expression and, furthermore, since he has also forgotten the source of the quotation, its utterance outside of his own voice catches him unprepared, like one of the foolish virgins. The mutedly religious language of "la bénédiction et la malédiction" is all he conserves of its theological import. The allusion to the delayed arrival of the *sponsus* marks the beginning of the book's end rather than the commencement of a final Judgment.[25]

The narrator cannot make the gesture of interpretive stoppage without elaborating another fiction, bringing into play a moment from the past when he made a grammatical point to "Judith," and at the same time trying to cut short another reading by asserting, for the first time, that she knew practically nothing. The *Nescio vos* functions in *Au moment voulu* like the "ptyx" in Mallarmé's sonnet, with this crucial difference: the presence of the narrator in the *récit* necessarily mediates the emergence of the ancient words. Matthew's Gospel resounds through Judith's fictive nescience to the narrator's anxious and occlusive recognition as he tries to persuade the reader that no echo exists.

Overwhelmed by the temporality of language, this narrator asserts his mastery of time by writing, holding the pen in his hand (maintenant). The discontinuous, allegorical equivalent of this paradoxical moment occurs whenever a reader holds the book. But upon opening the book, which is bound like a door, the familiar figure of Judith, the destroyer, images through the opening words.

In this precarious situation the repression of literary, and especially biblical, knowledge—or more precisely the obscuring of it—seems to be a necessary precondition for the literary genre—in this case, the parable—to emerge with renewed, modern force. The narration both describes and establishes a privileged moment when the emblematic confrontation takes place: Blanchot's emblem is not a visual allegory of sound, as the "ptyx" was in Mallarmé's sonnet, but a figuration of temporality; for the present opens up to disclose the historical waning of a genre which still offers a form for thinking about the nature of waiting and expectation.

Figural Names

IT TURNS out that "Judith" names a private relationship between the narrator and the woman to whom he gave the name. Unlike "Claudia," it is a name full of meaning. Etymologically, it means "the Jewish woman." In the apocryphal book of the Old Testament which bears her name, Judith saves the Hebrew nation from destruction by Nebuchadnezzar when she deviously presents herself before his general, Holofernes, as a traitor. Dazzled by her beauty, he invites her to a dinner in which she gets him drunk and then, when he has fallen asleep, cuts off his head. Blanchot does not mention this heroic and violent story, but he was certainly aware of the obsessive use Michel Leiris had made of it in his autobiography, *L'Age d'homme,* which he had reviewed in *Critique* No. 11, in 1947.

There is even a way in which *Au moment voulu* could be considered a reworking of *L'Age d'homme* on a highly abstract plane. In the autobiography Leiris represents himself as a Holofernes, fascinated by two images of female violence, the suicided Lucretia and the decapitating Judith. Furthermore, the chapter devoted to the presence of "Judiths" in his life is actually a fusion of memories of a distant relative, who was an opera singer, and of the roles she sang. In his review of *L'Age d'homme,* Blanchot finds the erotic confessions a pretext for an underlying encounter with the problematic relationship of a writing "I" to death: "*L'Age d'homme* is this lucid gaze through which the I in penetrating its 'interior obscurity,' discovers that what looks within him is no longer the I, 'the structure of the world,' but already the monumental statue, without gaze, without a face [figure] and without a name: the It of sovereign Death."[26]

During the first confrontation of Claudia and the narrator, at a moment when he had the first intimation of a rapport within their antagonism, she reacted with a cry: "But she promptly released herself and she hurled at me, in a half-voice: 'Judith'" (p. 35). At that point, Blanchot had not yet disclosed that the name was an invention of the narrator, and that Claudia did not know it. Therefore, it could only be read two ways: either as a call to her friend, or as in apposition to her

previous exclamation, "Mon amie!" which made the narrator understand that he had lost the right of seeking to qualify further the nature
of her relationship to her friend. In the light of what we later learn, it
turns out that Claudia, with equal likelihood, was calling *him* a dis-
tasteful name. The rapport he begins to feel strikes her as the treachery
of a Judith.

Two important aspects of *Au moment voulu* are illustrated in this case.
In the first place, we can see the deception of linear reading. Here, and
elsewhere in the book, events have to be read backwards. The circularity of understanding is thus dramatized. The second principle it demonstrates is the flexibility of references as Blanchot uses them. Like pronouns they shift their meaning as the speakers and the contexts change.
When Claudia calls the narrator "Judith!" she makes herself Holofernes;
but he does not assume the same role when he calls her friend that very
name. Similar problems occur with all the instances of biblical allusions
in the tale.

For example, the narrator compares Judith to Abraham. Blanchot's
revision of the story of Abraham and Isaac follows closely the first two
of Kierkegaard's four imaginary reconstructions of the episode. In the
first, Abraham tells his son that it is his own desire to kill him in order
to preserve Isaac's faith; in the second the event transforms Abraham's
way of seeing. This is most explicit in the journal entry JP III 3020,
where Kierkegaard imagines that he did sacrifice Isaac only to have him
restored, but in a way that he could no longer see him with joy.[27]

The parable, as Blanchot gives it, denudes Abraham of the moral
strength of Kierkegaard's Knight of Faith, and recasts him as the victim
of an ironical trap worthy of Kafka:

> I recognized this woman whom I have called Judith: she was not
> linked to me by a relation of friendship or enmity, happiness or
> distress; she was not disembodied for an instant, she was alive.
> However, as far as I can understand it, something happened to her
> which resembles the story of Abraham. When he came back from
> the land of Moria, he wasn't accompanied by his child, but by the
> image of a ram [image d'un bélier], and he had to live the rest of
> life with a ram. Others saw the son in Isaac, because they didn't
> know what happened on the mountain, but he saw the ram in his
> son, because he had made of his son a ram. Shocking story. I think
> that Judith had gone up the mountain, but freely [librement]. No
> one was more free, no one cared less for powers and concerned
> themselves less with the justified world. She would have been able
> to say, "There is a God who willed it," but for her that amounted

to saying—"It is I alone who did it." An order? Desire pierces through all orders." (pp. 147–48)

"Librement," more like Judith of Bethulia than the patriarch Abraham, she chose her fate and lived with the consequences of the principle of substitution represented by the scapegoat. In fact, we cannot wholly discount the possibility that she was the scapegoat herself; for, although the association of Judith and Abraham at first seems secure, the verbal construction does not prohibit her from taking the role of Isaac.

In "Kafka et l'exigence de l'oeuvre" (1952), which I have already quoted on the meaning of "figuration," Blanchot cites the story of Abraham and Isaac within the context of Kafka's and Kierkgaard's broken engagements. There he gives it a new explication.

> What is required of Abraham is not only to sacrifice his son but God: his son is God's future on earth, since time is none other than the Promised Land, the one and only dwelling place of the Chosen People, and of God through his people. Thus if Abraham immolates his only son he must immolate time; and immolated time [le temps sacrifié] will not be given back to him in the eternity of an afterlife [l'éternité de l'au-delà]—afterlife is the future, God's future in time. Afterlife is Isaac.[28]

In *Au moment voulu*, the narrator reads Judith as a willing Abraham (and/or Isaac). By replacing an order with a desire, by willing her own fate, she fulfills the commandment of Nietzsche's Zarathustra. If we push this further, reading analogies of Kafka's and Kierkegaard's aborted marriages into her story, we identify her as a *sponsus* who excludes even his own bride from the wedding feast. But the parable of the "image d'un bélier" suggests that there can be no sacrifice, and hence no redemption. Judith, parroting "Nescio vos" declares that the Kingdom will not come. She is the *sponsus* whose untimely arrival was calculated in order to declare "Nescio vos;" she is Abraham who knows the Promised Land is an illusion which she willingly sacrifices.

If we were to read Blanchot's parable as an instance of "figura," we would have to begin by recognizing the typological association of Abraham's sacrifice of Isaac to the Father's sacrifice of Christ. In this light, Blanchot's Judith can be said to display theological impatience; she "willingly" fulfills her "figurative" role in order to assure and hasten its denouement. Furthermore, when we turn back to the difficult statement on "figuration" in the Kafka essay, we see that for Blanchot it is precisely such an anxiety about time that motivates all figurative ty-

121

pology. All through *Au moment voulu* allusions to other texts turn into parables about time.

The Vanishing Beauty of Pure Time

AS THE tale nears its conclusion, the narrator conjoins the image of the "Strahl" [rayon] with the word, "maintenant":

> The fact that she was always most evident—there was her splendor; a threat directed against herself—announced that she was alive: yes, she took her flight, companion of a single moment. And now? Now, the evidence was shattered; the pillars of time, broken, hold up their ruins.
>
> "Now," strange ray. Now, furious force, pure truth without advice. It was actually then that we got along, but in the depths of now, there where passion means to love and not to be loved. Who loves is the magnificence of the end; who is loved, greedy care, obedience to the end. She was linked to me in that there radiated from her a joyous power in the light of which I rose precisely there, precisely now: coming into contact with her. I was linked to her, it being the day which made me touch its evidence. But if "this rapport was threatened," she became a sterile "I want it," and I, a cold and distant image. (pp. 148–49)

"Maintenant" is an "étrange rayon" precisely because it is not the *rayon* or *Strahl* which the gods send down from Heaven to Earth in a manifestation of Presence to which the poet can respond, like Hölderlin did, *Jezt aber tagt!*; nor is it the luminous underglow rising from below which the familiarity of song and the forgetfulness of words can induce. It has no content, no meaning, "Privée de conseil." But what then is the status of the "Maintenant?" The narrator cannot answer that without retelling his story. The second half of the paragraph, from "She was linked" on, does just that; it repeats the narrative in more abstract terms.

To learn more about this strange "Maintenant" let us turn back for the last time to "Le Chant des Sirènes." In the second part of the essay we find:

> Proust's experience of imaginary time could only occur in imaginary time and by turning he who undergoes it into an imagi-

nary being, an elusive image, present yet absent, motionless yet convulsed, like André Breton's definition of beauty. As a metamorphosis of time it starts by transforming the present in which it seems to occur, drawing it into the indefinite depths where the "present" re-enacts the "past," but where the past opens onto the future which it mirrors, so that what is about to happen reoccurs again and yet again. Doubtless the revelation occurs now, here, for the first time. But the image which is present here and for the first time is the presence of an "already other time," and what it reveals is that "now" [maintenant] is "another time" [jadis] and here is another place—a place always other, where he who thinks he can observe the metamorphosis without becoming involved can only turn it to his own advantage if he allows it to draw him out of himself and to involve him in the process where parts of himself, and primarily the hand that writes [main qui écrit], becomes almost imaginary.[29]

The cycles of repetition constitute the "temps pur" of the *récit*. In the eloquent concluding pages of *Au moment voulu,* Blanchot sustains his most powerful writing in exploring the contour of a narrative time from which events have been stringently removed. The lesson of the parable of the ten virgins is that one takes the side of the foolish five, eagerly awaiting, always missing, and being rejected by the Parousia, *das Heilige,* who belongs to the moment when the poet deludedly cries "Jezt aber tagt!"

Blanchot's distinction between *récit* and *roman* in "Le Chant des Sirènes," recalls Walter Benjamin's essay "The Storyteller: Reflections on the Work of Nicolai Leskov," which had appeared in the *Mercure de France* in July 1952. Pierre Klossowski had used those two terms to translate *Erzählung* and *Roman.* Benjamin saw the disappearance of the art of storytelling as part of the decline of *aura* in art which mechanical reproduction fostered. In his formulation the decline of storytelling is "only a concomitant symptom of the secular productive forces of history, a concomitant that has gradually removed narrative from the realm of living speech and at the same time making it possible to see a new beauty in what is vanishing."

"Living speech" and moral wisdom play no role in Blanchot's theory of the *récit* although they are central to Benjamin's concept of the *Erzählung.* Nevertheless, two passages from the essay call to mind Blanchot's thought in "Le Chant des Sirènes" and his practice in *Au moment voulu*:

The idea of eternity has ever had its strongest source in death. If this idea declines, so we reason, the face of death must have changed. It turns out that this change is identical with the one that has diminished the communicability of experience to the same extent as the art of storytelling [Kunst des Erzählens—l'art de narrer] has declined.

Actually there is no story [Erzählung—récit] for which the question as to how it continued would not be legitimate. The novel [roman] on the other hand, cannot hope to take the smallest step beyond that limit at which it invites the reader to a divinatory realization of the meaning of life by writing *Finis* at the bottom of the page.[30]

Blanchot's *récit,* in theory and in practice, corresponds to neither of Benjamin's antithetical forms. Instead, it is the form in which the art of narration—as the playing out in time of the tensions inherent in the "maintenant"—consciously considers the distinction between the narrative desire for continuation and the finality of meaning in the language of fiction. In Mallarméan terms, the modernity of the *récit* emerges when it becomes an allegory of itself; and like Benjamin and Blanchot's narrator, we can "see a new beauty in what is vanishing." This is what Blanchot reads in Balzac's *Le chef d'oeuvre inconnu:* the foot as an echo of the vanishing body, or reference and allusion stubbornly clinging to language, however abstract.

6

Saying "Nothing":
Persona as an Allegory of Psychoanalysis

INGMAR BERGMAN'S modernism has its sources in the same Nordic theatrical tradition from which Dreyer emerged, although it reached Bergman more directly: he was a stage director before and as long as he was a filmmaker; he wrote plays himself, and he staged at least nine different productions of Strindberg and five of Ibsen, in his prolonged encounter with the masters of Scandanavian modernism. Furthermore, since the release of *Persona* in 1966 critics have noted its affinity to Strindberg's one-act play "The Stronger," in which the encounter of two women, one utterly silent, forecasts the dramatic strategy of the film. Although I shall devote this chapter to *Persona*, I am not going to discuss the literary sources of Bergman's modernism, but instead consider the film as the filmmaker's exploration of the sources of his cinematic creativity, letting his own pattern of allusions guide my reading as Peterson's film did in my introductory remarks on *Mr. Frenhofer and the Minotaur*.

Within the narrative cinema the nearest correlative of Charles Olson's concept of the poem—as a field or region which is bounded by form for the purpose of discovering its own secret core—would be Bergman's *Persona*. The prologue of the film alludes elliptically to its genesis, but I shall extend that evidence to the published filmscript and to interviews by the filmmaker (which I am led to read skeptically) in hope of demonstrating the uniqueness of the film as a model for the poetics of modernist narrative cinema.

I want to argue that *Persona* covertly dramatizes a psychoanalysis from the point of view of a patient. Despite the apparent effort of the film-maker to camouflage this from the viewer, perhaps even from himself, critics of this central film in the Bergman canon have noted the startling analogy of the film's unfolding drama to psychoanalysis.[1] Of course, Bergman has treated psychiatry in his films; there is no reason to believe that he would not have depicted a psychoanalyst and patient if that was what he wanted to do. In fact, critics familiar with the film will immediately realize that there is indeed a psychiatrist in *Persona* who provides us with the background information about Elisabet Vogler's breakdown and even offers her own summer house for the patient's recovery with the help of her nurse Alma.

The Resistance to Allegory

IN ORDER to see the psychoanalytical drama embedded in the film we must recognize that the psychiatrist is a decoy, deflecting our understanding from the more central confrontation of Alma and Elisabet. But the psychiatrist is only the first of a series of obstacles which obscure the recognition of the psychoanalysis. The most blatant of these is the masterful *confusion of patient and doctor*. If we are to understand the details of *Persona* as a dramatized psychoanalysis, we must acknowledge that the nurse, Alma, is the neurotic patient, while the silent Elisabet represents the psychiatrist.[2] The greatest obstacle to such an interpretation, however, is the network of clues, some clearcut and many others highly ambiguous, the filmmaker offers us for sorting out scenes which take place in the nurse's imagination or dreams, and those which "really" take place within the fictive matrix of the film.

Originally entitled *Kinematography*, *Persona* projects an identity between the filmic experience and the agon fictively depicted within it. No other film by Bergman so unambiguously affirms the fragility of cinematic illusion. The film begins with the sparking of an arc light within a projector, and ends with its extinguishment; near the middle there is the catching and burning of a frame. Each of these three crucial moments is accompanied by a matrix of images which clearly situate these "events" outside of the world of the film's central fiction.

Bergman is an inconsistent and eclectic stylist. Although all of his films offer fascinating and innovative moments, he often articulates his cinematic dramas in the conventional visual rhetoric of a standard Hol-

lywood production. *Persona,* however, is his most systematically styl-
ized film. The meditation on the parameters of cinematography coincides in this special case with a thoroughly conscious and original use
of basic filmic structures. As we should expect, this is most obvious in
the handling of dialogue exchanges and shot–countershot. Since, by far
the greater part of the film describes the interaction of two isolated
women, an immense stress falls upon the ways in which the camera and
editing align these two people. In the superficially simple plot, a nurse,
Alma, reluctantly accepts charge of an actress, Elisabet, who refuses to
speak. They go to rest in the empty summer home of Elisabet's psychiatrist. After admiring and identifying with her patient, Alma grows
intensely hostile to her silence and passivity.

The dramatic climax of the film occurs when Alma confronts Elisabet with her analysis of her withdrawal into silence as a hysterical reaction to her barely concealed hatred of her son. Of course, we cannot
accept this "analysis" unanalytically. Still, for the moment, we can dwell
on the way in which it is represented on the screen. First of all, the
entire speech is repeated immediately after its initial utterance. The first
time, the camera remained fixed on Elisabet, the silent listener, at times
dissolving into progressively closer views of her face. The second time,
the same bold camera stare, the same series of dissolves to draw closer,
focuses upon Alma, her accuser. Conventional cinematography would
dictate the regular exchange of these two long takes (or pseudo-takes,
considering the dissolves). What Bergman gives us instead—the repetition of the speech—calls to mind the filmmaker's working materials,
as if they were two long takes from reversed angles of the same event,
filmed that way with the end of shot–countershot in mind. In the second of the "takes" to appear on the screen he even observed the convention of filming the speaker over the shoulder of the listener to reinforce the spatial continuity.

The Explosion of Shot–Countershot

INSTEAD OF intercutting the two perspectives back and forth while
maintaining the temporal unity of a single speech and thereby reassuring
his viewers of the spatial and temporal continuity of the event and,
therefore, of its "reality," the filmmaker meticulously superimposes Alma's face over Elisabet's. This is no standard superimposition. He has
prepared for the very special effect by filming both faces illuminated
from one lateral source—Elisabet's left, Alma's right—so that only the
opposite half of each face is lit during the two long "takes." Before the

superimposition occurs at the end of the second recital, this unusual highlighting seemed justified by the crepuscular light entering the house from a window beside the two women. But once the superimposition occurs, these images cease to appear as two half-lit faces, but as a single composite face fused from both women. Not only is the composite image a startling climax to this charged encounter, itself repeated twice and underlined the second time with a musical stress, but it is the sole visual link to the enigmatic images which begin, interrupt, and end the film.

In the framing episodes a boy, apparently awakened in a morgue, reaches out to touch a screen behind which the images of Elisabet and Alma are rapidly dissolving into each other. This attempt to make tangible contact with the image immediately precedes the film's titles—in fact, it even accounts for the film's title; for "persona" is the Latin word for "mask"—and it recurs just before the final cooling of the projector's arc lamp. In these shots, the backscreen projection and the pathetic failure to touch the face underscore its status as a mere image.

I take it as significant that the superimposition of the faces occurs within the fictive drama at the point where the spatial and temporal authority of shot–countershot collapses. The film begins after the pre-title sequence, with a marked suppression of shot–countershot. We see the nurse, Alma, being instructed about her new patient without seeing, at first, the doctor who is talking to her. When both figures in the exchange are later edited together, Bergman maintains his distance from the conventional montage by panning sharply from the back of Alma's head—and the talking doctor beyond her—to her hands clasped behind her back. We must wait a long time for the first undisturbed instance of shot–countershot, which occurs significantly when Alma reads Elisabet a letter from her husband; the countershot marks the moment when Elisabet snatches away the letter to suppress an explicit allusion to an erotic encounter. By suppressing shot–countershot when we should expect it, as in an early scene in which the offscreen psychiatrist asks Alma about her patient while only Alma is seen on the screen, and by tying reverse-angle cutting to the developing intimacy between the two women, Bergman inscribes meaning in this basic cinematic structure. It will correspond to Alma's growing comfort with her patient. That comfort, however, parallels the development of positive transference in psychoanalytical treatment. Therefore, the most extensive use of shot–countershot should occur, as it indeed does, during Alma's long autobiographical and confessional speeches soon after she and Elisabet move into the doctor's summer house.

Whose Perspective?

THE ALLEGORY of psychoanalysis proceeds quite efficiently in one respect. The stages of transference and transference neurosis proceed in a linear fashion and even constitute the highlights of the drama. In their first meeting, Alma gives a brief account of her history to Elisabet. As we subsequently learn, this introduction obfuscates the emotional tensions in her life. Immediately following that interview, Alma, alone in her room in the hospital where she works, turns straight toward the camera, as if it were a mirror, and thinks out loud about her new "patient." The first stage of her positive transference occurs as she reassures herself of the safety and solidity of her domestic life: "I'll marry Karl-Henrik and we'll have a couple of kids that I'll bring up. That's all decided, it's in me somewhere. I don't have to work things out at all, how they're going to be. That makes you feel safe." From this blinded soliloquy of self-assurance she immediately begins to speculate about Elisabet Vogler and falls to sleep repeating her name.

The next stage begins with a moment Bergman has claimed as the image which generated the whole film. Elisabet compares her hand to Alma's, who playfully resists, claiming it is bad luck. In the subsequent episode Alma reads to Elisabet from a book apparently about the psychology of religion. In our schematic account, these two scenes correspond to the patient's identification with the analyst and the subsequent desire to please and to understand psychological determinations. These two episodes prepare us for the long sequences of monologues which follow it in which the first painful material begins to emerge. For the moment, I shall pass over the content of these memories, to which I must naturally return, in order to bring more clearly into focus the shape of the transference. It is immediately after her expression of her erotic history that she imagines Elisabet seducing her. This is one of the cruxes at which Bergman is ambivalent about the status of what he shows us. We hear Elisabet speak briefly to Alma; we see her enter her room at night and caress her; yet the voice is so distant and the twilight so uncanny that we are induced to question whether we are watching an event just like the others we have seen or one located in Alma's imagination. Of course, from the perspective of the allegory of psychoanalysis this makes no difference at all. Everything in *Persona* reflects the perspective of the patient.

At this point one may object that what I am calling transference neurosis is equally true of intersubjective relationships outside of the psychoanalytical encounter. The strength of such an objection does not invalidate my approach. But it does demand that I carefully consider the *content* of the supposed psychoanalysis, not merely its dramatic form. This I shall do when I come to consider the relationship of the frame story to the agon of Alma and Elisabet. Before I come to this argument, I must describe the negative phase of the transference.

Alma becomes deeply upset and feels betrayed when she reads an unsealed letter Elisabet has written to her husband and given her to post. The letter describes in distant and somewhat amused tones Alma's confidence in her and the suspicion that she "is a little in love" with her. The letter itself is less significant than Alma's reaction to the impossibility of an erotic relationship with Elisabet. She deliberately leaves a large splinter of glass (which she accidentally broke) in Elisabet's path as she walks barefoot. This transformation of love into aggression climaxes in a shot–countershot exchange of glances which tacitly acknowledges Alma's role in the "accidental" injury. The shot–countershot is introduced by the opening of a veil-like curtain which had been so close to the camera that it was barely noticeable until Alma touched it. At this turning point, the "curtain raising" of negative transference, the will to break off the whole process manifests itself in the sudden catching and burning of the very frame of film on which Alma's bold stare is printed. Suddenly we are back in the material of the pre-title sequence. The film does get started again, after a delayed return to focus, as if the closeup *eye seen* in the interruption resisted focusing on the drama. The hostility between the protagonists continues. In the scenes that follow, Alma painfully "acts out" her aggression. For the most part, shot–countershot will be suppressed until the film's climax.

The accusation of coldness and mockery gives way to physical violence. By threatening to scald her face with boiling water, Alma elicits speech from Elisabet, who cries, "No, stop it!" From this point on, the transference neurosis plays its course. Alma manifests considerable ambivalence toward Elisabet: she aggressively analyzes her "illness," then begs forgiveness only to repudiate that plea. The stage is now set for a temporary displacement of the initial erotic transference. In a scene that distinctly parallels the episode following the long confession, Alma inverts that situation by wandering into the room of the sleeping Elisabet; instead of caressing her, she minutely catalogues her blemishes: "When you're asleep your face is all slack and your mouth is swollen and ugly . . ." Still, the erotic transference has not been negated, merely displaced. This scene merges into a sudden appearance of Elisabet's husband. Several details of this strange encounter will ultimately concern us. For the moment, it is enough to note that in making love to the husband both in front of Elisabet's face and behind her back (literally), Alma expresses, in a different form, her neurotic desire to participate in Elisabet's erotic life. Then, before a scene of regression in which Alma loses her control of syntax, she offers the analysis of Elisabet's hatred of her child which culminates in the compound image of both their faces.

The film diverges radically from the published script in its ending. Bergman had intended to bring back the doctor who would tell us that Elisabet broke her silence that winter and returned to her family and the theater. As we last see her, in the script, Alma has remained behind on the island and tries to write to Elisabet about a picture of a young boy held at gunpoint in the Warsaw ghetto which she has discovered in the house. In the film version, Elisabet has been seen fascinated by this picture.

The end of *Persona* is significantly more ambiguous than the script indicates. There is a final violent exchange between the two women in which Elisabet like a vampire, sucks the blood which comes from the nurse's wrist when she cuts herself with her fingernail. A sudden transition shows them back in the hospital where Alma coaches her patient to utter a single word: "Nothing." After this, the final shot—counter-shot exchange shows Alma peering through a door at Elisabet packing her belongings. When we are expecting a scene of Elisabet's departure, we see, instead, Alma closing up the summer house, and, eventually, getting on a bus. Of course, upon reflection, we realize that in an off-screen passage of the drama, Elisabet must have departed first, leaving Alma to close up the house. But the mild shock of the sequence, as Bergman depicts it, corresponds to the ambiguity of the termination of psychoanalysis, necessarily an anticlimax: a mutual, perhaps tacit, agreement between patient and analyst, in which the patient finds herself alone, performing her duties. In the midst of this conclusion there is a dramatic closeup of a statue which had appeared in the background in an earlier shot. In *The Touch,* in which it reappears, it is identified as a medieval Madonna. This will be relevant to the interpretation of the crucifixion imagery, later in this chapter.

By overlooking a large array of details, I have tried to bring to the foreground a schema in which the dramatic events of *Persona* can be seen as representative of the stages of psychoanalysis: a referral (the meeting with the psychiatrist who sends Alma to Elisabet), the initial interview, the preparation for transference, the acceleration of transference in the confessional disclosures of the patient, transference love, the development of negative transference which leads to the projection of the traumatic source of the neurosis on the analyst, and the termination.

131

The strongest objection I have to consider to this allegory is nothing less than its very starting point: Elisabet's silence. It is this silence and willingness to let Alma work through her trauma that makes her identification with the analyst so immediately apparent. In the final analysis she is too silent. No objective account of a classical Freudian psychoanalysis—or any other for that matter—could account for a rigidly mute doctor. To get beyond this crux, we must examine the peculiarity of the allegory I have outlined.

Hostility to Psychoanalysis

THE FIRST question it poses is: Why would a filmmaker operate in this way? Psychoanalytical critics would assume that neurotic complexes can and do determine the infrastructures of films. But why should psychoanalysis itself be so disguised? Bergman could have made a film about psychiatry if that is what he wanted to do. The interesting fact is that he did make such a film a decade after *Persona*. *Face to Face* (1974) dramatizes the mental collapse of a psychiatrist, again played by Liv Ullman (although I do not find that to be very important, since she has played so many diverse roles in Bergman films). The filmmaker's hostility to psychoanalysis—and his interest in it—are quite transparent in this later film, where we hear Dr. Wankel, the Ullman character's hospital superior, say, "Twenty years ago I realized the inconceivable brutality of our methods and the complete bankruptcy of psychoanalysis." The disreputable psychiatrists in *Thirst* (1949) and in *The Lives of Marionettes* (1980) are yet further examples of Bergman's hostility to the process.

I assume this very hostility can tell us something about the genesis of *Persona*. The film not only recreates the dynamics and tensions of psychoanalysis; it massively defends itself against it. The most blatant form of that defence would be the presence of the psychiatrist at the beginning of the film (and at the conclusion as well, in the script). She is an ogre who attacks Elisabet with metaphysical banalities before sending her off to her summer home. In the script Bergman's fury at this creature is barely disguised. Her final "analytical" speech ends, "Personally I would say you have to be fairly infantile to cope with being an artist in an age like ours." The filmmaker adds these remarks: "The doctor is very pleased with what she has said, particularly the last bit."

Her very presence in the film is a decoy to divert systematic viewer/readers from the psychoanalytical relationship between Elisabet and Alma. That she is female may be another displacement. The world of *Persona* is radically feminized. The weak and perhaps even blind husband of Elisabet makes an appearance which can easily be read as a fantasy or dream. If Bergman had an experience in psychoanalysis (which has not been confirmed) and draws upon it in this film, then the substitution of a woman for a man parallels the reversal of the roles of nurse and patient. In fact, if we include the doctor, we can see the defensive displacement of a situation involving either two men or one man and one woman (the analyst) into a fiction of three women. While preparing the script for *The Silence* (1963) Bergman told Vilgot Sjöman that he would translate his dream of two men into a story about two women; "he was afraid that the part was too close to himself." [3]

Furthermore, the very suppression of the interpretive work of the analyst (Elisabet in the allegory) might emerge from the same hostility. In that case we must look elsewhere for the interpretive moments. Certainly, the letter would be one, in that case; for it dramatizes both the patient's desire to see the doctor's private notes and to read his mind; the resistance to the doctor's professional insight is merely a typical neurotic syndrome which can be treated clinically (amounting to a denial of the transference love that the patient wants). Other reflections of interpretative moments (as constructed from the hostile viewpoint of a patient) would be the doctor's banal speech, the reading of the psychology textbook (intercut with the barren stones of the island), and Elisabet's two speeches: "No, stop it!" and "Nothing." From this negative viewpoint, a psychoanalyst is someone who *says nothing,* or, more luridly, who sucks the patient's blood. The fact that we can so easily accept Elisabet's first speech as a fantasy of Alma's underlines the repression of analytical interventions. In *Face to Face* Dr. Wankel's bitter speech about psychoanalysis concluded: "I don't think we can really cure a single human being. One or two get well despite our efforts." It is perhaps useful to note (keeping in mind that associations between films made a decade apart are of dubious value) that *Face to Face* begins with a dramatization of ambivalent transference love as the patient, Maria, begs the doctor, played by Ullman, to make love to her after a long aggressive speech in which she tells the doctor she is sure she would be a poor lover.

Primal Scene

READERS GENEROUS enough to accept my account of the displacement of the interpretive work of the analyst from the central allegory of the analysis as a function of the defensive resistance to the overt dramatization of the psychiatric event, may yet raise another, still more cogent, objection to my thesis. Psychoanalysis is not simply a formal agon between patient and analyst; it must have a specific content, and furthermore, that content determines the nature and character of the transference. Until now, I have skirted this fundamental point. I can no longer avoid it.

To get at the content of the analysis, the neurotic problem, we must resign efforts to distinguish between reality and fantasy or dream in the central story of the film and we must simultaneously grant an equal "psychological" status to the interruptive frame story. Everything, then, that appears on the *screen* in *Persona* will become material for analysis. With this in mind, I want to bring into evidence some of the filmmaker's statements about the film. In the interview volume, *Bergman on Bergman,* we find:

> Shall we talk a moment about the boy in the film? Well, while I was working on *Persona,* I had it in my head to make a poem, not in words but in images, about the situation in which *Persona* had originated. I reflected on what was important, and began with the projector and my desire to set it in motion. But when the projector was running, nothing came out of it but old ideas, the spider, God's lamb, all that dull old stuff. My life just then consisted of dead people, brick walls, and a few dismal trees out in the park.
>
> In hospital, one has a strong sense of corpses floating up through the bedstead. Besides which I had a view of the morgue, people marching in and out with little coffins, in and out.
>
> So I made believe I was a little boy who'd died, yet who wasn't allowed to be really dead, because he kept on being woken up by telephone calls from the Royal Dramatic Theatre. Finally he became so impatient he lay down and read a book. All that stuff about *The Hero of our Time* struck me as rather typical—the overstrained official lying on his sickbed. Well, all this is trival. But that's how it works—and suddenly two faces are floating into one another. And that's where the film begins. As for the interpretation, you can interpret it any way you like. As with any poem. Images mean different things to different people.[4]

Bergman's description of the genesis of *Persona* encourages speculation about the frailty of his creative powers as he imagined it during that crisis. But even without the help of his comments, several patterns would support the allegory of psychoanalysis as a key to this film. They are 1) the recurrent representations of an onlooker; 2) the fantasies of an unwanted or aborted child which accompany every mention of sexuality; 3) the "free association" of images from Bergman's history as a filmmaker which parallel the narrative; and 4) the unusual reservation of shot–countershot to underline the important moments in the drama I have identified with the structure of transference.

Many critics of the film have pointed out that the boy in the frame episode seems to correspond to Elisabet's son. If one remains strictly within the narrative evidence of the film, this would be unjustified. The photograph of the son, which we see only briefly on the screen, appears to be a different boy. But if one accepts that the displacements and condensations I have maintained are at work on all levels in the film, this association of the two boys is more than justified. It is the key to the enigma of the film. We recognize its importance only when we are ready to concede that both Alma and Elisabet are "masks" for a very different drama than the one we seem to be witnessing during most of the film. Up until this point I have traced an allegory of a psychoanalytic encounter in which Alma plays the role of the patient and Elisabet that of the analyst. Now I am about to make an argument for the identity of Alma and the boy out of the frame episode. In other words, the entire film reflects the perspective of a patient in psychoanalysis for whom the adolescent boy is a crucial screen memory.

Extreme care is required in the identification of the boy. Bergman offers us an enormous boost when he says that he "made believe he was a little boy who'd died." Why then, we must ask, did he not find an appropriate actor to play this boy? Why did he turn instead to the very figure he had used in his penultimate film, *The Silence?* To make the identification complete he shows him reading the same book in both films, Lermontov's *A Hero of Our Time.* Perhaps most revealing of all is the error Bergman makes in describing the book. There is no "overstrained official lying on his sickbed" in Lermontov's novel. The novel's place in the earlier film can easily be accounted for. *The Silence* shows the same boy, along with his aunt and mother, passing through a foreign country (the language of which none of them know) which seems about to go to war, if it has not already done so. Lermontov's novella takes the form of travel notes about a fascinating romantic figure in an exotic Caucasian landscape. The parrallelism between the subject of the book and the reader in *The Silence* does not carry over to *Persona.* In place of it, Bergman erroneously attributes his own condition at the time of the film's genesis, "an overstrained official"—Director of the Royal Dramatic Theatre which, in the same interview book, he called "purgatory," adding, "Nothing worse can happen to me for the rest of my life"—"lying on his sickbed." At the time of the creation of the first script of *Persona* Bergman was hospitalized with an infection that impaired his sense of balance.

The Lermontov book carries over to *Persona* to reinforce the fact that this boy brings with him all of his associations from the earlier film. Bergman's error underlines the personal identification he had with the boy in both films. This leads us directly to a consideration of *The Silence,* a much less obscure film than *Persona.* In it, the boy is a figure of ambivalent maturity. He reads beyond his years, but he can behave with immaturity, as when he urinates in the corridor of the hotel (where most of the film transpires) immediately after a company of dwarfs dress him up as a little girl. This ambivalence suggests that the adolescent is a screen for an infantile trauma. In *The Silence* the boy's preoccupation with the primal scene is a thematic concern: he is fascinated by a painting of a satyr and faun; he reports to his aunt about the lovemaking he listens to in his mother's room as she makes him wait in the corridor. In fact, the only time we ever see the book in *The Silence* is at the very moment that the boy looks up from reading to tell about his voyeuristic spying.

The primal scene trauma lies at the core of *Persona.* This, above all, accounts for the incorporation of the figure from *The Silence.* Before further discussion of the film, I shall turn to Henry Edelheit's essay "Crucifixion Fantasies and their Relation to the Primal Scene." Here is his definition of "the primal scene schema":

> I do not maintain that every image of an erotic encounter is a primal scene representation, but I believe that such images may (and in the cited instances do) have specifiable traits which label them as "primal scene material." First among these traits is the characteristic double identification, which may be either simultaneous or alternating (the depicted roles are readily reversible). The sensory modality most often represented is the visual (which puts emphasis on the polarity viewer/exhibitor), and the setting is often a theatre or an arena. A libidinal-aggressive encounter is represented (often a combat, a contest or a ritual sacrifice) in which the observer is implicated.
>
> The double identification itself results in typical ambiguities. These can be summarized in the following questions: (1) What is happening? (2) To whom is it happening? Who is the victim and who the aggressor? (3) How many people are involved? One? Two? Several? Or is it one composite creature? (4) What is the anatomy of the scene? If it is made up of more than one individual, which

one has the penis? (5) Where am I (the observer)? Am I partici-
pating or am I excluded?

These ambiguities arise from the pattern of double identifica-
tions which I call *the primal scene schema.*[5]

When I first read Edelheit's article, I was instantly struck by how his
five questions summarized my experience of *Persona.* I trust that many
readers who have not developed concrete interpretations of the film on
their own will share my reaction. At this point, I am prepared to argue
that what is true of the film as a whole is true of its most obscure images. In fact, *Persona,* as a film about primal scene disturbances and the
psychoanalytical revelation of them, not only defensively obscures its
true theme, it also compulsively projects upon its viewers a repetition
of that "libidinal–aggressive encounter."

Fragments of an Autobiography

WHAT BERGMAN calls "a poem . . . in images" represents his free
association of moments in the history of his genesis and development
as a filmmaker. They also turn out to be the very images Edelheit catalogues in his article. Only one, however, is a direct quotation from an
earlier Bergman film. The speeded up farce in which a skeleton figure
pops up and chases a frightened man in a nightgown comes from *Prison*
(1949, also called *The Devil's Wanton*), the first film Bergman both wrote
and directed himself. It is framed by a story about the making of a film.
The farce is a film the protagonist finds in an attic, a souvenir of his
childhood; it symbolically recapitulates the events which are leading him
into psychosis. These frames of films-within-the-film stress the psychological validity of symbolic action. There is even a little boy in the
film who hides in a cellar so that his parents will fear he is dead—the
forerunner of the filmmaker's fantasy that he was "a little boy who
died." Furthermore, Bergman tells us, again in the interview book, that
the farce is "a reconstruction of one little scrap of film I bought" when
he had a primitive projection apparatus for the "toy theatre" with which
he played as a ten or eleven year old child.

I do not know the origin of the cartoon which first appears in the
projector gate after the Academy leader. It suggests a childhood memory of the cinema. The fragment from *Prison* follows it, after a return
of the shot of film rushing through the projector gate and a flash of a
child's hands. We do not see enough of the farce to know what is going

on, yet it is significant that it takes place in a bedroom, where the haunted man dives under the covers to escape what pursues him. Psychoanalysts would call this multiplication of reasons for the relevance of the fragment "overdetermination"; for it condenses the origin of Bergman's cinematic experiences with his first filmmaking efforts while alluding covertly to primal scene experiences.

The next two images of the opening "poem" are more displaced references to his earlier films. We see a spider, then several shots of a lamb being fleeced and butchered. In *Through a Glass Darkly*, the mentally disturbed heroine, Karin, tells of her hallucination, which we do not see, in which God attacks her as a lusty spider. In the farce as it appears in *Prison*, the sleeper is awakened by a spider over his head. The lamb seems to be an even further displaced allusion ("God's lamb," Bergman calls it) to the apocalyptic background of *The Seventh Seal*. The climax of this series of images, in terms of violence reinforced by the soundtrack, is the next shot of a nail being driven into a hand, clearly a representation of the crucifixion. At this point, we can profit from turning back to Edelheit's article, which centers upon crucifixion fantasies. "In crucifixion fantasies (which may be either conscious or unconscious) the figure of Christ nailed to the cross represents the combined image of the parents and *at the same time,* by way of the double identification with the parents, it represents the helpless, observing child."[6] Edelheit bases these conclusions on his own clinical experience as well as diverse analyses of literary and psychoanalytical sources. In "Mythopoesis and the Primal Scene," he presented a more elaborate argument for interpreting compound mythological beasts (centaurs, etc.) as figures of the same double identification with the parents, which is consistent with the psychoanalytical discussion of Picasso's Minotaur series, as noted in the Introduction, and which opens up possibilities for a psychoanalytical reading of *Mr. Frenhofer and the Minotaur*.[7] One persistent feature of such figures is the multiplication of legs. The image of the spider, filmed from below, perhaps through a glass, would be just such a displacement for the legs of the parents engaged in lovemaking.

The collage of images referring to earlier Bergman films quickly gives way to the representation of a morgue, but only after a series of transitional images: a blank brick wall, a forest, a fence of iron spikes. The vertical of the forest trees and the fence suggest the bars of a crib, as indeed does the ironwork of the bed in the farce fragment. This may be significant because the adolescent boy "wakes up" in the morgue to witness the "two faces floating into one another" just as an infant might awake in his crib to discover the parents "floating into one another."

The sequence ends with a dramatic presentation of reverse-angle cutting. The boy wakes up, tries to read his book, cannot, looks around and becomes fascinated by the camera; he reaches out as if to caress it. This is the moment when Bergman first reverses the angle showing the boy from behind, reaching out to caress the image of the dissolving faces, or, more literally, the screen from behind which they are projected. This first instance of shot–countershot in the film calls attention to itself in two ways: first, by having the boy look directly into the camera, and reach out as if to touch it, the filmmaker brings into play the only locus of offscreen space that would not be automatically absorbed into the fictive space that all other pivots of shot–countershot generate. Second, the reversed shot does nothing to hide the fact that the boy is confronting a screen. The unified spatial "event" that he thus depicts has been drained of its fictional authority. Nowhere else in the prologue does montage elaborate coherent spatial relationships.

After a brilliant title sequence in which images from the film to come flash between the stark credits, the filmmaker repeats a version of the shot–countershot with which the prologue ended. After the white screen dissolves into the white door of a hospital office, Alma enters and stares attentively toward the camera while the offscreen voice of the doctor instructs her about her patient. Only after several different shots of Alma listening, the angles reverse but the focus is set on Alma's back, not on the blurred doctor in the far background. This self-conscious articulation of narrative space deliberately differentiates itself from the "poetic" montage of the prologue and the credits. In no other film by Bergman does the mechanics of narration demand so much attention. This emphasis on narration is reflected on the sound track as well by the long erotic story which Alma tells Elisabet.

The Work of Analysis

I BELIEVE the peculiar temporality of the psychoanalytical encounter can clarify this formal distinction in cinematic modes between the poetic and the narrative. The psychoanalytic process, represented in *Persona* by the story of the two women, and punctuated by the restrained and systematic deployment of shot–countershot to distinguish the critical stages of the process, takes the special temporal and dramatic form I have outlined in the first pages of the chapter, regardless of the nature (or content) of the disturbance it seeks to uproot. But by structuring so clearcut a frame around the film, and by dramatically interrupting the center of the narrative with material from that frame, Bergman presents us with an alternative to the narrative mode. Within the story itself there are two episodes within conceptual brackets, and both, significantly, show us Elisabet when she is alone. She is horrified by the telecast of a burning bonze in Vietnam and fascinated by the image of the boy in the Warsaw ghetto. On one level, the distinction between documentary and fictive images corresponds to the discrimination between narrative and poetic modes of representation. But we must not forget that Elisabet gives her attention in both cases to mediated events and furthermore that the mediations occur at the outer boundaries of cinematography, television and photography. In addition to that, both have been doctored, or transformed by editing. The apparently "direct" transmission of the newsreel from Vietnam turns out to be a subtle montage when we listen to the muted soundtrack carefully. The English-speaking newscaster is describing a battle while we are looking at the monk burning himself to death. Only the mention of "flame-throwers" connects, as if in free association, the commentary to the imagery. Correspondingly, the fracturing of the photograph into details, and the temporalization of those details as montage, recovers its crude reality for cinema.*

*This effort to animate a still photograph automatically brings us face to face with the difference between photography and cinema. Bergman is not original in his technique here. In fact, he may have been influenced by a remarkably successful short film which exploited this principle: Chris Marker's *La Jetée* which had been released four years before *Persona*. I am struck by the possibility of a profound influence not because the technique of reframing details of a single photograph for dramatic emphasis is common to both films—for that had not been original with Marker—but by the thematic, or rather psychoanalytical, similarity of the two films. A primal scene disturbance is represented more obviously in the Marker film which narrates the story of a man who had been a young boy when atomic bombs destroyed Paris in the sudden beginning of a Third World War. In an allegory of psychoanalysis, similar to that of *Persona*, a team of doctors work with the now grown man to explore the imagery of his repressed memory. The chief doctor is at first frightening, then benign, and finally diabolical as the stages of transference are refracted through the story.

The painful journey into the past becomes the narrative of his love affair. But the woman he loved in this fiction of interpenetrating times was none other than the woman he watched as he stood by the criblike railing of the airport on the day of the traumatic bombing. At the end of the film the doctors succeed in making him realize that the man he saw killed on the jetty, just before the massive destruction, was himself as he rushed to the woman. The splitting of the character into lover and observing child characterizes the primal scene structure.

The brilliance of this short film devolves from Marker's ingenious association of still photography with the discontinuities of memory; his imitation of shot–countershot, reframing, and elliptical montage within the limitation of the still format; his identification of the initiation of a sexual relationship with the one instance of actual cinematography in the film—after a series of dissolves on the face of the sleeping woman, closing-in on a calculus of diminishing time gaps, she opens her eyes in conventional film time, implicitly acknowledging with her glance her lover and confirming in the same gesture the Orphic theme of the film—and his situating the penultimate meeting (the most elaborate in terms of montage) of the lovers in a natural history museum, where the static stuffed animals they are inspecting metaphorically correspond to the snapshots through which we imagine the lives of these characters.

The primal scene schema and the allegory of psychoanalytical therapy is sufficiently disguised by the science fiction narrative of *La Jetée*—the critical literature shows no notice of it—for it to have been an unconscious influence on Bergman. It is significant that, like Marker, he shows us a young boy on the verge of confronting a violent trauma, and perhaps even more significant that Bergman's Jewish boy (somewhat older than Marker's and therefore closer to the figure of the prologue) is the *real* victim of a historical war. This establishes a distance from Marker's film and reinforces the function of the film-within-a-film as a form of reality testing.

In the allegory of psychoanalysis these scenes represent the analyst, or rather the patient's fantasy of the analyst, reacting to and puzzling over evidence. The sociopolitical nature of the images, as well as their appearance as films within the larger film indicate that the issue of reality is emerging within the fictional matrix.[8] Yet, at the very moment when reality-testing becomes an issue, Bergman, as a filmmaker conscious of his art, confesses that the violence of political reality escapes that art, but undercuts that confession by mediating both the newsreel and the photograph through montage.

In the story of the two women, the primal scene disturbance embedded in the poetic prologue emerges in the persistent association of sexual voyeurism and rejection of a child. Alma's long erotic story, which marks the success of the transference, is a tale of the stimulation of watching others make love and being watched. It ends, significantly, in abortion. This form of the positive transference leads immediately to a fantasy in which the patient (through Alma, his surrogate) makes love to the doctor. In the negative transference, the patient imagines the doctor watching, ambivalently, while his surrogate makes love to the doctor's lover. This scene entails the corresponding hysterical affirmation of affection for the child. After this reversal has run its course, the patient projects upon the doctor the full force of the obsession. In the repeated scene, which I have already described, the patient elaborates a fantasy of parental rejection and painfully realizes that the actual subject of the fantasy is not the doctor but herself.

The evidence of the film cannot take us further into the infantile development of the Oedipal trauma than this. The ambiguous age of the boy at the beginning of the film is an indication of this barrier. As a figure of late childhood, or early adolescence, he screens out the crib memory of the primal scene which the prologue enacts. He is decidedly younger than the two boys who are described in Alma's erotic confession. Their youth, of course, is central to that episode. It provides another reason for the ambiguous age of the boy. If the reader can accept my postulate that the psychoanalytical subject of the film is a male adult who projects an image of himself as the infant/adolescent, the association of the primal scene schema and the story of the two boys initiated should not be difficult. From the perspective of this hypothetical subject the primal scene experience has exacerbated his adolescent sexuality at the end of the latency period. Furthermore, his desire to replace the father as the mother's lover seems to have left an unconscious residue of guilt which has manifested itself in the defensive idea that the mother wished to destroy or reject the child.

Persona is replete with parallels and echoes on the visual, dramatic, and aural levels. One of the latter provides an important link between the primal scene schema and the transference. The morgue in the prologue is represented through a series of unconnected details, to the accompaniment of the sound of dripping water. That same sound recurs as Alma reads Elisabet's letter about her. The film covers up this connection by situating the letter episode during a heavy rainstorm. Alma sets off to post the letters during a downpour but by the time she comes to read the "report" on her, the storm has diminished to the steady dripping which we had first heard during the prologue. This auditory repetition dramatizes the association between the primal scene memory and the turning point of the transference. This remains unconscious for the patient and, if we can judge from the silence of the critical literature on this point, the filmmaker has subtly projected this unconsciousness onto his viewers.[9]

Ancient Dramas

THE DRAMATIC parallels are more overt, and subject to traditional literary analysis. The radio soap opera, in which the plea for forgiveness had provoked a fit of laughter from Elisabet, matches the radio fragment Alma hears the night of her violent fight. This time it urges the defensive withdrawal into silence we associated with Elisabet: "—don't speak, don't listen, cannot comprehend—What means are we—us to persuade—to listen. Practically—excluded. These continuous calls up —." That is all the script gives us. Even in its elliptical incoherence it constitutes the bridge between the situation of Elisabet ("don't speak") and the complementary speech about Elisabet's son. Not only the dissolution of syntax but the concatenation of pronouns ("are we—us to persuade") forecasts the later regression: ". . . the incomprehensible disgust and pain and then all the many words. I, me, we, us, no, what is it? Where is closest, where can I get a grip?"

In terms of cinematic construction, the meeting with Elisabet's husband reflects the initial presentation of the doctor. The camera remains a long time on Alma as she listens to his offscreen voice while trying to tell him she is not Elisabet. Like the doctor also, his speech is impervious to the particularity of the person he addresses. This solipsism coincides with the ambivalence of his appearance. When we do finally see him, he takes off his dark glasses but does not acknowledge that Alma is not Elisabet or that there are two women before him. The way in which he stares and his gesture with the glasses creates a disturbing ambiguity in which the viewer does not know if he can see or if he is blind.

The very suggestion of blindness marks him as an Oedipal figure, in his weakened, self-defeated stage. This direct hint of the myth of Oedipus merely reinforces the overt mythological reference that Bergman gives us, twice. We are told, and we see in an insert, that Elisabet broke down during the last performance of *Electra*. The insert, near the beginning and at the end of the film, shows her in that persona. In psychoanalytical mythology, Electra corresponds to Oedipus. The female version is consistent with the transposition of sexual identities throughout the film. Had Bergman made the film about two men, one a nurse and the other an actor who fell silent while performing the principal role of *Oedipus Tyrannos,* the psychoanalytical allegory would have been blatant to the point of caricature. In the corpus of surviving Greek tragedies there are two plays entitled *Electra,* one by Sophocles and one by Euripides. Bergman, whose knowledge and experience of theater is as extensive as his of cinema, does not tell us which *Electra* Elisabet was performing when she first broke down. It would hardly have mattered; for the difference between the plays has no relevance for *Persona.* On the other hand, the fact that he left this point undefined may have a meaning. There is no other instance of two surviving Greek plays called by the same title. "Electra" as a title, then, represents a loss or confusion of authorship and, furthermore, suggests the common denominator of the mythic persona—the female counterpart to Oedipus—as more important than the poet who dramatized it.

Much of *Persona* can be seen as a defense against the threat to creativity an artist imagines that psychoanalysis poses. The internal allusions to *Prison, Through a Glass Darkly, The Seventh Seal,* and *The Silence* suggest that Bergman is both questioning and seeking assurance from his achievement as an artist. The allusion to the films he projected as a child reinforces this suggestion and leads to speculation about the relationship of that creativity to his childhood fantasies. In these terms, becoming a filmmaker would be the fulfillment of a fantasy in which the child, as a passive viewer of films, becomes their engendering agent, while defending himself against the obsessive fantasy of being an unwanted, potentially aborted, child. In general, the sense of threat to creativity would have been confirmed by the conclusion of the smug hospital psychiatrist, had Bergman not removed it from the script.

The comparison of the script with the finished film reveals the degree to which the shooting and editing of *Persona* was a process of discovering its "secret center." The double confrontation over the torn picture seems to have been invented after the film was shot; likewise the composite face. It is reasonable to assume that the pretitle sequence was made after the composite face appeared in the editing of the confrontation. Finally, even though Bergman indicates in the script that he would like the film to break in the middle, the images of the interruption have no place in the script and are derived from the pretitle sequence. Yet, nowhere is the intimacy between the frame story and the central drama so explicit as in the interruption of the burning frame which follows the first outbreak of violence between Alma and Elisabet. Again the crucifixion and the haunted sleeper reappear from the opening. But this time the sequence ends not with the boy reaching out, as in the first shot–countershot to touch the image, but in a closeup of an eye, itself a synecdoche for the boy and a metaphor for his voyeuristic obsession. From the eye Bergman cuts back to the cottage where Elisabet is convalescing, but the image is very slow to regain focus, as if it were seen by that traumatized and fascinated eye from the interruption. The entire film defensively asserts that the repression of free association, analysis, and reflection on one's own achievement, is essential to keep the fictional story in focus, to keep the work going. In this the most obscure of Bergman's films a suppressed allegory of psychoanalysis is a modernist reflection on the sources of cinematic creativity.

At the beginning of chapter 3 I invoked the classical tricotomy of dramatic, epic (narrative), and lyrical modes to set up a preliminary set of distinctions among the films of Dreyer, Bresson, and Bergman that I had chosen for detailed examination. Perhaps it would be justified to conclude that as films inflected by theater, *Ordet* and *Gertrud* build to climactic and far from obvious conclusions; one, in which a visionary learns how to be a vehicle for resurrection; the other, in which a woman learns to say farewell to her visionary goal. *Pickpocket,* most clearly of Bresson's adaptations of fiction, describes both the ironic failure of the cinematic *Bildungsroman* to delineate the stages of an education that would prepare the protagonist for a decisive moment of vision, and at the very same time, it describes the contradictory formation of a sensibility that can receive the grace to leap from an ironic to a redemptive mode of figuration. *Mouchette* illustrates how problematic the rupture between those contradictory modes can be. Finally, *Persona* can be assimilated to the lyrical, rather than dramatic or narrative, mode only insofar as its real "subject" lies—almost—outside the film. I call the narrative which this "subject" witnesses an allegory, but I must distinguish it from the allegories of Dovzhenko, by distinguishing between their implied viewers. Dovzhenko hints to his viewers that they have the choice of two roles: they can be either bloodthirsty decadents who require thrills of anticipated violence, suspense, and perhaps last minute rescues, or students of mathematical engineering, who are learning the applications of an abstract calculus for the melioration of the human environment. Bergman's viewer is a version of the film's author, metonymically represented by fragments of his earlier inventions and obsessions. By skillfully diverting our attention from the framing and interrupting images to the psychological drama which the imaginary eyes within his film witness, Bergman stresses the film's narrative rather than lyrical dimension. Had the emphasis been on the former, it would have been appropriate to call the film's genre autobiography, which is a fusion of lyrical and narrative modes.[10]

7

The Sentiment of Doing Nothing:
Stein's Autobiographies

A POETICS centered on the ambiguity of the pun is common to Charles Olson and Gertrude Stein. In both cases, Emerson's definition of "The Poet" and of language as "fossil poetry" overshadows their theories. But whereas Olson sought a language haunted by both historically and personally charged images, Stein directed her astounding energies to the opposite—and impossible—task of forging a language purified of historical and psychic phantasmagoria.

When Gertrude Stein wrote that America was the oldest country in the twentieth century, she was suggesting, among other things, that American modernism predates that of Europe. Charles Feidelson Jr., Roy Harvey Pearce, and recently Carolyn Porter have identified, from very different perspectives, the Emersonian and central tradition of American literature as a native version of modernism.[1] In the remaining chapters of this book, I shall concentrate on aspects of modernism in American literature and avant-garde cinema, expanding on the idea I suggested in the introduction that the Emersonian heritage is our aesthetics of radical Protestantism devoid of a deity, unless it would be an aspect of the self. The most impressive resistance to visual representation in modernist literature is the astonishingly fecund writing of Gertrude Stein from *Tender Buttons* (1911, published 1913) until 1932, when she wrote her most accessible book, *The Autobiography of Alice B. Tok-*

las. Yet, although her language during those two decades was remarkably opaque, she claims to have written from visual stimulation: "I write with my eyes, not with my ears or mouth . . . A writer should write with his eyes, and a painter paint with his ears." For her "writing with [her] eyes" did not mean reproducing sights through language but seeing words on the page and disengaging the auditory imagination. Even when she comments on *Tender Buttons* as if they were a series of still lifes or "realistic pictures," she can criticize as obscure a text as "A Piece of Coffee" for making "too much appeal to the eye."[2]

Stein never believed that writing could escape meaning: "I made innumerable efforts to make words write without sense and found it impossible. Any human being putting down words had to make sense out of them."[3] But sense and representation were not synonomous for her. For writing to be exciting, it had to be autonomous.

Such radical personalization would find its justification in the Emersonian aesthetics to which Stein fully subscribed. In "History" he had written: " 'What is history,' said Napoleon, 'but a fable agreed upon?' This life of ours is stuck round with Egypt, Greece, Gaul, England, War, Colonization, Church, Court and Commerce, as with so many flowers and wild ornaments grave and gay. I will not make more account of them. I believe in Eternity. I can find Greece, Asia, Italy, Spain, and the Islands,—the genius and creative principle of each and of all eras, in my own mind."[4] Stein is an Emersonian to the extent that she asserts the creative autonomy of the mind as the basis for her modernity. In fact, all of the American writers and filmmakers I discuss in this book share with Emerson a Protestant vision of an artistic calling as an election, even when they are most critical of Emerson.

If a single paragraph in the work of one powerful writer could set the tone for the entire career of another, later writer, I would suggest that Gertrude Stein's prolific and prodigious literary project expands from the following well-known passage in Ralph Waldo Emerson's "Self-Reliance":

> These roses under my window make no reference to former roses or to better ones; they are for what they are; they exist with God to-day. There is no time to them. There is simply the rose; it is perfect in every moment of its existence. Before the leaf-bud has burst, its whole life acts; in the full-blown flower there is no more; in the leafless root there is no less. Its nature is satisfied and it satisfies nature in all its moments alike. But man postpones or remembers; he does not live in the present, but with reverted eye

laments the past, or, heedless of the riches that surround him, stands on tiptoe to foresee the future. He cannot be happy and strong until he too lives with nature in the present above time.[5]

It is not only that Stein's emblem, the poem "Rose is a rose is a rose is a rose" printed in a circle, attempts to reenact the autonomy of the roses under Emerson's window; or that the insistent happiness of her several styles implies that she has succeeded in living in the present, above time; but, most significantly, her antipathy to what she called "human nature" was her recognition of the place of postponement and memory in the autobiographical writings which brought her fame along with a crisis of identity: to her, the inability to say with Descartes "I think, I am" became the nursery rhyme phrase, "I am I because my little dog knows me."

For Stein the articulation of a theory of literature coincided with the writing of autobiography. As early as 1926 she had written and delivered "Composition as Explanation," a lecture on her early writing, for audiences at Oxford and Cambridge. But it was not until the unexpected success of *The Autobiography of Alice B. Toklas* (1933) that the fifty-eight year old author began the theoretical endeavor which resulted in *Lectures in America* (1935), *Narration* (1935), *The Geographical History of America or the Relation of Human Nature to the Human Mind* (1936), and *What are Master-pieces* (1940). During this final period of her career she supplements the first autobiography with *Everybody's Autobiography* (1937), *Paris, France* (1940), and *Wars I Have Seen* (1945).

She consistently distinguished the autobiographical texts and theoretical lectures from her other writing—which she called novels, poetry, and plays although she frequently violated generic norms—because they were written for an "audience." The writers and painters who were "creating modern composition authentically"[6] did so without calling upon "memory," without consideration of anything outside themselves, and without concern for money. When Stein described her own genius as the ability to talk and listen at the same time, she meant that writing was, for her, the most intense form of this simultaneity. In *What are Master-pieces* she declared flatly: "The minute your memory functions while you are doing anything it may be very popular but actually it is dull. And that is what a master-piece is not, it may be unwelcome but it is never dull. . . . This is what makes secondary writing, it is remembering, it is very curious you begin to write something and suddenly you remember something and if you continue to remember your writing gets very confused" (p. 152).

The opposition of memory to authentic writing reappears when she discriminates between human nature and the human mind and between identity and entity. For an entity there can be no repetition: "There is only repetition when there are descriptions being given of these things not when the things themselves are actually existing and this is therefore how my portrait writing began" (p. 102).

The Portrait

IN "PORTRAITS and Repetition" Stein invokes a theoretical model for portraiture from the illusionary structure of the cinema and its use of the principle of persistence of vision. "Funnily enough the cinema has offered a solution of this thing. By a continuously moving picture of any one there is no memory or any other thing and there is that thing existing, it is in a way if you like one portrait of anything not a number of them . . . I of course did not think of it in terms of the cinema, in fact I doubt whether at that time [before 1907] I had ever seen a cinema but, and I cannot repeat this too often any one is of one's period and this our period was undoubtedly the period of the cinema and series production. And each of us in our own way are bound to express what the world in which we are living is doing . . . In a cinema picture no two pictures are exactly alike each one is just that much different from the one before, and so in those early portraits there was as I am sure you will realize as I read them to you also as there was in *The Making of Americans* no repetition" (pp. 105–6).

Stein does not tell us how in 1934 she came to think of the mechanical principle of cinematic illusion as an analogy for her writing. She may have derived her knowledge of this principle from Hugo Munsterberg's *The Photoplay* (1915). Munsterberg had been one of her mentors when she was a student of psychology at Radcliffe in the early 1890s, just before the invention of cinema. Certainly she would have had a chance to read Munsterberg's book before 1923, when the first indirect allusion to the relationship of cinema and her portraiture occurs. Approximately one fourth of the way through "If I Told Him: A Completed Portrait of Picasso," we find the following paragraph:

> Shutters shut and open so do queens. Shutters shut and shutters and so shutters shut and shutters and so and so shutters and so shutters shut and so shutters shut and shutters and so. And so shutters shut and so and also. And also and so and so and also. (p. 230)

This portrait will be of further interest to us shortly, as a complex example of Stein's allegorization of the portrait genre. I shall return to it after considering the status of vision in Stein's work.

The cinematic model is not specifically visual for her, although she does acknowledge in the companion lecture, "Plays," that the transition in cinema from silence to sound might have provided her with "a new way of understanding sight and sound in relation to emotion and time" which she was working out through the writing of plays. When she came to feel the need for extending her portraiture by including her sense of sight along with talking and listening, painting became her theoretical model:

> And so I began again to do portraits but this time it was not portraits of men and women and children, it was portraits of anything and so I made portraits of rooms and food and everything because there I could avoid this difficulty of suggesting remembering more easily while including looking with listening and talking than if I were to describe human beings . . . The painters naturally were looking, that was their occupation and they had too to be certain that looking was not confusing itself with remembering . . . I began to wonder at at about this time just what one saw when one looked at anything really looked at anything. Did one see sound, and what was the relation between color and sound, did it make itself by description by a word that meant it or did it make itself by a word in itself . . . I became more and more excited about how words which were the words that made whatever I looked at look like itself were not the words that had in them any quality of description. (pp. 113–15)
> In "Portraits and Repetition" Stein describes a further phase in which melody became the basis of her portraits before abandoning the genre to write *The Autobiography of Alice B. Toklas*.

I take the significance of Stein's reflections on the turn to incorporating optical stimuli in her portraiture to be that it was the occasion for her to "concentrate on melody." She admits "this melody for a little while after rather got the better of me."

Pictures and Resemblance

STEIN'S OBSCURITY is not a function of citations or of verbal coinage. In *The Autobiography of Alice B. Toklas,* she has "Alice" tell us:

"She experimented with everything in trying to describe. She tried a bit inventing words but she soon gave that up . . . The use of fabricated words offended her, it was an escape into imitative emotionalism."[7] The distinction between "a word that meant it" and "a word in itself" provides a key to her eccentric theory of the visual image. "A word that meant it" must be a word that refers to some object or aspect of the phenomenal field. What, then, would "a word in itself" mean? To a very great extent Stein repeats in very original terms the principle of Symbolist poetics: The "word in itself" suggests Mallarmé's definition of poetic magic: "la merveille de transposer un fait de nature en sa presque disparition vibratoire selon le jeu de la parole" ("The wonder of transposing a natural fact in its almost vibratory disappearance according to the play of the word").[8] Much of the lecture "Poetry and Grammar" describes how she came to generate her poetry by replacing the denotation of nouns with modes of connotation. However, when we compare examples of her poetic practice, even the examples she quotes in her lectures, the status of vision in her work is far from evident. Of course, a difference between her early participial style with its emphasis on abstract diction and the language of *Tender Buttons* (and the works of the decade following it) is obvious. In her early portrait of Picasso (1909) we read:

> This one was working and something was coming then, something was coming out of this one then. This one was one and always there was something coming out of this one and always there had been something coming out of this one. This one had never been one not having something coming out of this one. This one was one having something coming out of this one. This one had been one whom some were following. This one was one whom some were following. This one was being one whom some were following. This one was one who was working.[9]

In a sort of verbal slow-motion Stein dwells on the prolific and protean nature of Picasso's creative energy. The portrait of him she "completed" fourteen years later, "If I Told Him," may invoke the impression of the artist's personality or "entity" through its shifting rhythms, but instead of participles and adjectives which in the earlier portrait seem to derive from the observation of the painter and his works, the vocabulary of representation and its limitations dominates the later portrait.

"Exact resemblance to exact resemblance the exact resemblance as exact as a resemblance, exactly as resembling" is the most explicit Steinian passage in which the very nature of portraiture finds its definition. Yet, even here the pun dominates: the difference between the adjective "exact," the adverb "exactly," and the verb "to exact" guides us into the problematic core of the poem: the exactitude of the literary portrait has to be erected on the slippery ground of conjunctions, prepositions, adverbs, and pronouns. The overlapping repetitions of the vatic incantation bring to the fore inexact relational terms: if, I, him, would, now, not, as, full, so, also, actively, who, first, presently, he, proportions, there, father, whether, fairly, well. Out of the negative superlative "not at all" she extracts a new positive superlative "at all" which cannot quite shake off its negative connotations. In fact, if we allow the rhyme pattern of the penultimate passage its full power, the sequence "note . . . float . . . dote . . . denote . . . ," it can drive us to read "connote" into the intercalated word "cannot."

The only proper noun within the portrait is "Napoleon," which is repeated frequently within the first third of the text. It would be satisfying to be able to read the final line ("Let me recite what history teaches. History teaches.") as a conclusion about the one historical figure named in the portrait—or two if we include Picasso, or three, if we add Stein as "I." But that final line denies what, at first, it seems to say, when the lesson of history becomes a tautological echo, remotely a poetological reminder of the Narcissus story from Ovid's *Metamorphoses*.

The lecture "Pictures" provides what may be a very personal gloss on the name Napoleon. Stein begins her autobiographical reflection on the importance of paintings in her life with a recollection of the first painting that interested her as a child: a panorama of the Battle of Waterloo. More than a historical illustration it too was an exciting tautology for her: ". . . I knew a good deal about it already because I always read historical novels and history . . . but though all that was exciting the thing that was exciting me was the oil painting . . . It the oil painting showed it as an oil painting. This is what an oil painting is."[10]

From 1911 until 1932 such private references mingle freely with the intense anatomy of the language of representation in Stein's writings. Then a major transformation of her style occured. It began as a lark. While Alice B. Toklas was typing "Stanzas in Meditation," Stein's longest poem, a book-length text of massive difficulty, Stein herself began to ventriloquize her companion's autobiography. The result, *The Autobiography of Alice B. Toklas,* told Stein's life as if observed and recounted by Toklas. It was an unexpected success. In the United States it became a best seller. When Stein returned to America to lecture in the wake of its popularity, she shrewdly observed that the attention she received was more a result of the writing that no one understood than the one book everyone did.

Between Two Photographs

SHE HERSELF understood autobiography as a form of publicity. It could not escape irony. Not only the structural irony through which she attempted to envision herself in Toklas' eyes and tell her life in Toklas' dry narrative style, but an epistemological irony, which she called "identity," generates autobiographical discourse as she understood it and practiced it. The frontispiece of the first edition exemplifies her irony: a photograph of a dim interior shows Stein's profile, deep in shadows, as she sits writing at a table in the right foreground of the image; to the left, Toklas, in brighter light can be seen through a door she has just opened as if she were about to interrupt the writer. The caption does not name Stein: "Alice B. Toklas at the door, photograph by May Ray." The final page of the volume is a plate illustrating a holograph of the first page, entitled "First page of manuscript of this book." Perhaps the opening photograph must be reinterpreted: Toklas could be leaving the room, about to close the door after her so that Stein may be left to write "her" story. Or she could be posing, modeling for Stein and/or photographer Man Ray.

The final paragraph of the text faces the manuscript illustration:

> About six weeks ago Gertrude Stein said, it does not look to me as if you were ever going to write that autobiography. You know what I am going to do. I am going to write it for you. I am going to write it as simply as Defoe did the autobiography of Robinson Crusoe. And she has and this is it.

That final demonstrative pronoun refers simultaneously to the book one has just read and to the illustration on the opposite page. The paragraph could also be read as an extended caption to Man Ray's photograph, providing the text of the conversation between the writer and her subject which the mute image cannot capture. The gestures toward a circularity of form suggest the example of Proust's monumental novel, which Stein reluctantly admired. Finally, the mention of Defoe crystalizes the irony. Where we might have expected Boswell, she mentions instead a work of fiction.

In a sense, *The Autobiography of Alice B. Toklas* has been framed between two photographs, situated as it were, in the fraction of a second that would mark the change of two cinematic shots. The first gives us the master shot of the two women; the second cuts to a closeup of the page on the writing desk, an insert shot. Neither image presents us with crucial or even pertinent information (as the photographs illustrating Stein, her family, and her friends interspersed within the text do), but together the two framing photographs delineate a temporal shift of viewpoint within which the entire autobiographical narrative, with its own involuted temporality, transpires.

For Stein, autobiography entails seeing oneself rather than being oneself. Fiction and photography make claims for an objective, stable universe where things can be identified. She came to think of *The Autobiography of Alice B. Toklas* as a narrative of what "had happened," after she had written most of *Everybody's Autobiography,* her 1937 account of the consequences of her success. It is to that volume that I wish to turn my attention now; for it is there that the question of autobiography and its ironies become thematic.

Never Mind the Ridicule

BETWEEN THESE two autobiographies Stein did most of her work as a theorist of literature. *Everybody's Autobiography* depicts the visit to America during which the texts of *Lectures in America* and *Narration* were delivered; it also describes briefly the tour of England during which she lectures on "What are Master-pieces and Why Are There So Few of Them." Finally, *The Geographical History of America* was written during the same three-year span.

Everybody's Autobiography and the theoretical books constructed from her lectures reflect the most profound artistic crisis of Stein's forty-year-long career as a writer. Writing *The Autobiography of Alice B. Toklas* gave her the freedom to indulge in a colloquial style she had not employed since *Three Lives.* She could gossip, drop the names of famous and powerful people, flatter herself by extolling her "genius" hyperbolically, and suggest guidelines for reading her largely unread books, all through the mask of Alice. However, she was not prepared for the enormous success she received even though she had craved it for years. It lead to a massive writing block and a perilous obsession with her "identity." *Everybody's Autobiography* responded to that crisis; to a limited degree, it enacted the overcoming of it. In an unusually candid short statement, "And Now," published in *Vanity Fair* in 1934, she admitted that her new autobiography would be "rather sad":

When the success began and it was a success I got completely lost. You know the nursery rhyme, I am I because my little dog knows me. Well you see I did not know myself, I lost my personality . . . and for the first time since I had begun to write I could not write and what was worse I could not worry about not writing and what was also worse I began to think about how my writing would sound to others, how I could make them understand, I who had always lived within myself and my writing.

Her new writing, she proceeds to inform her enlarged audience, will be like *The Making of Americans* in that it will no longer reflect her interest in the relationship of diction to seeing:

now everything that is happening is once more happening inside, there is no use in the outside, if you see the outside you see just what you look at and that is no longer interesting, everybody says so or at least everybody acts so and they are right because now there is no use in looking at anything.

In this "Introduction" which precedes the five, chronologically sequential chapters of *Everybody's Autobiography,* Stein suggests that the narrative follows free association rather than chronology. The studied movement forward and backward in time which structured the Toklas autobiography (chapters consecrated to Toklas' childhood, her arrival in Paris in 1907, Stein in Paris from 1903–07, Stein's childhood, and three chapters of their life together from 1907–32) has no equivalent in the second autobiography. In the final chapter she tentatively declares its aesthetic advantage over the earlier work:

And now I almost think I have [simply said what was happening] the first autobiography was not that, it was a description and a creation of something that having happened was in a way happening not again but as it had been which is history which is newspaper which is illustration but is not a simple narrative of what is happening not as if it had happened not as if it is happening but as if it is existing simply that thing.[11]

Whereas the literary conceit that molds *The Autobiography of Alice B. Toklas* is a fictional exposition of the subject's temperament, talents, and fascination with Gertrude Stein, with subtle echoes of Mark Twain's ironic ventriloquism, *Everybody's Autobiography* portrays the author's apperception of her reputation, reception, and experience of her dramatized works. In a sense she travels to the United States to see her own text of *Four Saints in Three Acts* performed, and to perform herself as a lecturer. That too precipitates a crisis when she finds herself listening to her own voice. Throughout the book there are significant allusions to the role of interviews, photographs, and even a film clip of her in manufacturing her "identity."

The fascination and devotion of the putative author, Toklas, to the actual author, Stein, in the earlier book, gives way to the more problematic relationship of Stein to her image, her writing, the sound of her own voice, and the meaning of her success, in the sequel. Emblematic of the newly discovered distance of self to self are the geographical tropes prompted by her return to America after thirty years in France. National and personal identities reflect each other asymmetrically.

The sadness of *Everybody's Autobiography* is not obvious. Stein sustains her cheerful tone even as she mixes allusions to her loss of a sense of "entity" with accounts of her domestic life and public acclaim. Even in the final lines of the book she proclaims her satisfaction despite the seemingly permanent rupture in her selfhood: "perhaps I am not I even if my little dog knows me but anyway I like what I have and now is today (p. 318)." Her optimism is as Emersonian as her language which echoes the climax of his masterpiece, "Experience," in which he writes of overcoming his grief at the shattering loss of his young son.

If we look at the final paragraph of the second autobiography as a unit, we can see the Emersonian declaration interwoven with an allusion to the end of Wordsworth's *The Prelude:*

> And I like being in London and I like having a ballet in London and I like everything they did to the ballet in London and I like the way they liked the ballet in London and then we went back again to Paris and going back I saw the only thing I have ever seen from an airplane that was frightening, a wide layer of fog close to the water that went right down the middle of the Channel, but the large part near the shore was clear I do not know why but it was frightening and there we gathered everything together and left for Bilignin. That is a natural thing, perhaps I am not I even if my little dog knows me but anyway I like what I have and now is today. (p. 318)

Wordsworth's final natural image for the Imagination in his autobiography comes from his description of a climb of Mt. Snowden. A fog blocks his view of the sea at dawn. There was "a fracture in the vapour/ . . . Through which the homeless voice of waters rose,/ that

Fig. 1 Pablo Picasso, "Minotauromachie" (1935). Museum of Modern Art.

FIGS. 2-6 SIDNEY PETERSON, *MR. FRENHOFER AND MINOTAUR* (1949).
Fig. 2 Consecutive frames from the opening of the film.

Fig. 3 Consecutive
        Frames.

Fig. 4

Fig. 5 Consecutive
frames.

Fig. 6

Figs. 7-8 Marcel Duchamp,
Anémic Cinéma (1925).

Fig. 9 Man Ray, *L'Etoile de mer* (1928).

FIGS. 10-14 ALEXANDR DOVZHENKO, *ZVENIGORA* (1928).
Figs. 10-11 Timosh's demonstration and students in countershot.

Fig. 10

Fig. 11

FIGS. 12–14 PAVLO'S
LECTURE AND REACTIONS
IN COUNTERSHOTS.

Fig. 12

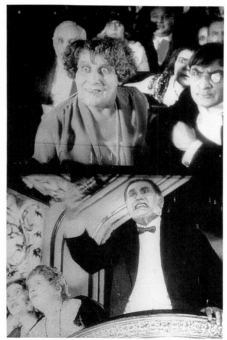

Fig. 13 Consecutive
frames.

Fig. 14

Fig. 15 Carl Dreyer, *Ordet* (1955).
Johannes sees the Man with the Scythe.

Fig. 16

Fig. 17

Figs. 16-17 Carl Dreyer,
Gertrud (1964).
Gertrud's poem.

Fig. 18 Robert Bresson, *Pickpocket* (1959).
Consecutive frames of Michel spoting a pickpocket on the metro.

FIGS. 19-24 ROBERT BRESSON, *MOUCHETTE* (1967).
Figs. 19-21 Start, middle, and end of one shot.

Fig. 19

Fig. 20

Fig. 21

Figs. 22-24 Three shots, Mouchette gives her father her pay; a stranger buys a token for a bumper car ride, and gives it to Mouchette.

Fig. 22

Fig. 23

Fig. 24

FIGS. 25-26 INGMAR BERGMAN, *PERSONA* (1966).
Figs. 25 Consecutive frames from pretitle sequence.

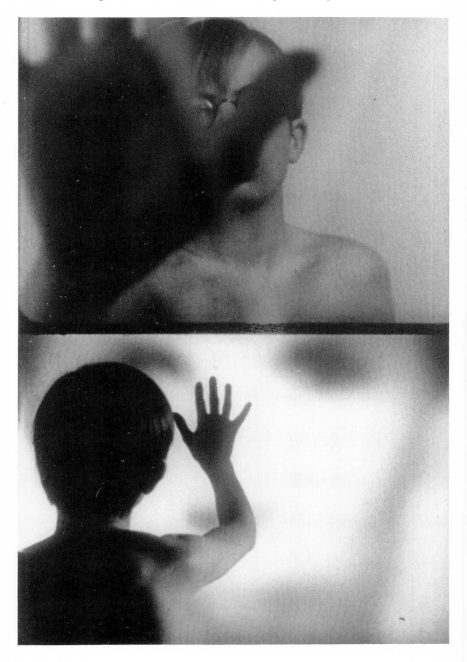

Fig. 26 Consecutive frames after Elisabet steps on shard of glass; she stares at Alma in countershot.

Figs. 27-28 The title page and last page of Gertrude Stein's *The Auto-biography of Alice B. Toklas* (1933).

THE

Autobiography

OF

ALICE B. TOKLAS

ILLUSTRATED

Harcourt, Brace and Company

NEW YORK

Fig. 27   Alice B. Toklas at the door, photograph by Man Ray

THE AUTOBIOGRAPHY OF ALICE B. TOKLAS

and a pretty good editor and a pretty good vet for dogs and I have to do them all at once and I found it difficult to add being a pretty good author.

About six weeks ago Gertrude Stein said, it does not look to me as if you were ever going to write that autobiography. You know what I am going to do. I am going to write it for you. I am going to write it as simply as Defoe did the autobiography of Robinson Crusoe. And she has and this is it.

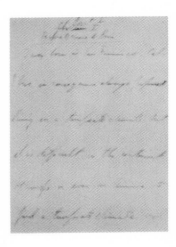

First page of manuscript of this book

Fig. 28

Figs. 29-31 Jean-Marie Straub and Danielle Huillet, *Moses und Aron* (1975). Start, middle, and end of the opening shot of the film.

Fig. 29

Fig. 30

Fig. 31

Fig. 32

Figs. 32–33 Stan Brakhage,
Blue Moses (1963).

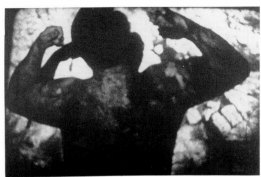

Fig. 33

Fig. 34 George Landow, *Wide
Angle Saxon* (1975).
Consecutive frames of the
film, *Regretable Redding
Condescension* and the Wide
Angle Saxon applauding.

dark, deep thoroughfare had nature lodg'd/ The Soul, the Imagination of the whole." Like Wordsworth, another English-speaking sojourner in France, Stein records her recovery from a period when the power of vision threatened to tyrannize her sensibility, but she is even more like the Emerson of "Experience" when he writes: "Nature, as we know her, is no saint . . . We must set up the strong present tense against all the rumors of wrath, past, or to come . . . Life is a series of surprises and would not be worth taking or keeping if it were not." Here is his conclusion, which she seems to have set as her model throughout *Everybody's Autobiography*:

> We must be very suspicious of the deceptions of the element of time. It takes a good deal of time to eat or to sleep, or to earn a hundred dollars, and very little time to entertain a hope and an insight which becomes the light of our life. We dress our garden, eat our dinners, discuss the household with our wives, and these things make no impression, are forgotten next week; but, in the solitude to which every man is always returning, he has a sanity and revelations which in his passage into new worlds he will carry with him. Never mind the ridicule, never mind the defeat; up again, old heart!—it seems to say,—there is victory yet for all justice; and the true romance which the world exists to realize will be the transformation of genius into practical power.[12]

In both autobiographies Stein works hard not to "mind the ridicule" or the "defeat." In the later one she tropes defeat into success, the ridicule in "publicity."

Stein was as sensitive to the ridicule in which she was held as she was to the enormous success of her literary and artistic discoveries: Picasso, Braque, Matisse, Hemingway, Fitzgerald, Wilder, etc. She knew, of course, the fragility of her claims on their fame. In *Everybody's Autobiography* she acknowledges that the publicity generated by the Toklas autobiography gave her both an entrée to the famous and an attractive aura of mystery to them.

The Decline of the Male Hero

SETTING IN motion several motives for the work, the introduction to *Everybody's Autobiography* points to its climactic moment, a party for Stein in Beverly Hills in which she would meet Charlie Chaplin and Dashiell Hammett. In fact, the gist of her conversation with Hammett occurs in the introduction—on page 5 rather than on pages 282 and 283 where Chaplin assumes the foreground; it is not mentioned when she gets around to describing the party.

This displacement is no accident or sloppiness. Stein brings her discussion with Hammett to the front of the book to apologize for its genre. In effect, she tells us she has turned to writing autobiography because the novel is no longer a viable form. The claim is couched in what appears to be a casual stream of associations. She tells us that she is most eager to meet Chaplin and Hammett of all the people in the United States to whom her new celebrity has given her access. It is with Hammett that she raises the question of the novel; she does it in terms of gender. Why is it, she coyly inquires, that unlike the nineteenth century when "women could never invent women they always made the women be themselves seen splendidly or sadly or heroically or beautifully or despairingly or gently," while men "did invent all kinds and a great number of men (p. 5);" why in the twentieth century can men only write about themselves? Hammett, implicitly agreeing with her, attributes this phenomenon to a lack of confidence men have in themselves. Stein does not argue here that women have assumed the power of fictive invention. In fact, like most of the anecdotes in this book, this one appears without authorial comment or conclusion. The point, subtly implied, is that fictive invention itself is an archaic vestige that Charlotte Brontë and George Eliot (her two examples) began to discard, and that she, as their heir, has rejected in her autobiographical writings.

Cinema's Contrived Plots

BEFORE I turn to the crucial evocation of her meeting with Chaplin, I would like to examine Chaplin's own account of the encounter as evidence of the ridicule that Stein had to endure repeatedly. She did not live to read Chaplin's *My Autobiography* (1964). The tone of his remarks may have been colored by the insightful way she had described him two years after their meeting.

First Chaplin:

> Back in Beverly Hills, I had received an invitation to meet Gertrude Stein at the house of a friend of mine. When I arrived, Miss Stein was seated on a chair in the center of the drawing room, dressed in brown, wearing a lace collar, her hands on her lap. For some reason she looked like Van Gogh's portrait of Madame Rou-

lin, only instead of red hair with a bun on top Gertrude had short-cropped brown hair.

The guests stood around at a respectful distance, forming a circle. A lady-in-waiting whispered something to Gertrude, then came to me. "Miss Gertrude Stein would like to meet you." I hopped forward. There was little opportunity to talk at that moment because others were arriving and waiting to be introduced.

At lunch the hostess placed me next to her and in some way or other we got on to the subject of art. I believe it started by my admiring the view from the dining-room window. But Gertrude showed little enthusiasm. "Nature," she said, "is commonplace; imitation is more interesting." She enlarged on this thesis, stating that imitation marble looked more beautiful than the real thing, and that a Turner sunset was lovlier than any real sky. Although these pronouncements were rather derivative, I politely agreed with her.

She theorized about cinema plots: "They are too hackneyed, complicated and contrived." She would like to see me in a movie just walking up the street and turning a corner, then another corner, and another. I thought of saying that her idea was a paraphrase of that mystic emphasis of hers: "Rose is a rose is a rose"—but an instinct stopped me.

The luncheon was served on a beautiful Belgian lace tablecloth, which evoked several compliments from the guests. During our confab, coffee was served in very light lacquer cups and mine was placed too near my sleeve, so that when I slightly moved my hand I upset my coffee over the tablecloth. I was mortified! In the middle of my profuse apologies to my hostess, Gertrude did exactly the same thing, upsetting her coffee. I was inwardly relieved, for now I was not alone in my embarrassment. But Gertrude never dropped a spangle. Said she: "It's all right, it didn't spill on my dress." [13]

Here is Stein's account:

We were to go to dinner in Beverly Hills which is the same as Hollywood this I have said we were to meet Dashiell Hammett and Charlie Chaplin and Anita Loos and her husband and Mamoulian who was directing everything and we did. Of course I liked Charlie Chaplin he is a gentle person like any Spanish gypsy bull-fighter he is very like my favorite one Gallo who could not kill a bull but he could make him move better than any one ever could and he himself not having any grace in person could move as no one else ever did, and Charlie Chaplin was like Gallo. Gypsies are intelligent I do not think Charlie Chaplin is one perhaps not but he might have been, anyway we naturally talked about the cinema, and he explained something. He said naturally it was disappointing, he had known the silent films and in that they could do something that the theatre had not done they could change the rhythm but if you had a voice accompanying naturally after that you could never change the rhythm you were always held by the rhythm that the voice gave them. We talked a little about the Four Saints and what my idea had been, I said that what was most exciting was when nothing was happening, I said that saints could naturally do nothing if you were a saint that was enough and a saint existing was everything, if you made them do anything then there was nothing to it they were just like anyone so I wanted to write a drama where no one did anything where there was no action and I had and it was the Four Saints and it was exciting, he said yes he could understand that, I said the films would become like the newspapers just a daily habit and not at all exciting or interesting, after all the business of an artist is to be really exciting and he is only exciting, when nothing is happening, if anything happens then it is like any other one, after all Hamlet Shakespeare's most interesting play has really nothing happening except they live and die but it is not that that is interesting and I said I was sure that it is true that an interesting thing is when there is nothing happening, I said that the moon excited dogs because it did nothing, lights coming and going do not excite them and now that they have seen so many of them the poor things can no longer see the moon and so no lights can excite them, well we did not say all this but that is what we meant, he wanted the sentiment of movement invented by himself and I wanted the sentiment of doing nothing invented by myself, anyway we both like talking but each one had to stop to be polite and let the other one say something. (pp. 282–83)

Chaplin makes a large implicit claim for the power of his visual and verbal memory, as he writes this anecdote thirty years after it occured. It is the very kind of writing Stein repudiated with her rejection of "memory" in her theoretical writings of the thirties. The visual details, as well as the comparison of Stein's posture to that of a seated figure in a painting, runs counter to her doctrines of the separation of vision and language and of the radical autonomy of writing and painting.

The most interesting part of Chaplin's recollection of Stein concerns her concept of the cinema. She seems to be elaborating on a trope from Fernand Léger's *Le ballet mécanique* (1924): the film opens with an homage to Chaplin in the form of a cubist abstraction of him coming apart in an animated dance. It also contains the first instance of loop printing to my knowledge: a woman carrying laundry ascends a long flight of steps by the river. The shot of her climbing two or three steps recurs many times in succession, so that her movement becomes mechanical; the gesture of her gathering the folds of her skirt to climb comes to resemble the many levers and flywheels in the film.

We should remember that when Stein and Chaplin met he had completed his first sound film, *City Lights* (1931), with a complicated, sentimental plot framing his antics. For ten years, he had been making feature-length films mixing maudlin romance with energetic comedy. We may take Stein's comments, if they are recorded in good faith, to reflect the cubist enthusiasm for the short films that made Chaplin an international star at the time of the First World War.

Stein's version of the conversation holds our attention, both for what it asserts and for what it means in her book. Chaplin provided her with the opportunity to articulate an antithesis between two "inventions," "the sentiment of movement invented by himself . . . and the sentiment of doing nothing invented by myself." "Sentiment" is Stein's complex word in this formulation; it covers both a cast of mind and an emotional response to an action. It links her to Chaplin; they are both artists who are "really exciting" in their abilities to invent emotive casts of mind.

It may help to bear in mind that Stein was fully aware that films achieve the illusion of movement through a process of repetition with slight variations; she had lectured on that process before meeting Chaplin. The hackneyed, complicated, and contrived films Stein seems to decry would be the sound films that restrict the flexibility of rhythm. She finds herself agreeing with Chaplin, suggesting an imaginary film constituted by rhythm alone and the sentiment of movement, but he takes her suggestion as pontification. The repetition she fancies would emphasize what she takes to be the most original aspect of his work; it sounds to him like a version of the modernism which earned her ridicule.

Her aspiration to create a literature of "entity" which would embody the sentiment of doing nothing required not only repetition but the dissolving of fictional characters, discussed that same afternoon with Hammett, but placed 277 pages earlier in the book. In such a literature there would be no place for the conventions, complications, and contrivances of plot.

The common cause variously espoused by Mallarmé, Blanchot, Olson, and Stein would be the suspension of the visualizing power of literary language. The strategies of negation are more direct in the French tradition than in the American; for Mallarmé and Blanchot were both avid readers of Hegel, while Stein and Olson, superficially sharing an enthusiasm for the philosophy of Alfred North Whitehead (Toklas calls him one of the three geniuses she has known, along with Stein and Picasso), ultimately derive their sense of dialectics from the "optative mood" of Emerson.

Thus Stein and Olson repeatedly make use of the binary opposites, inside and outside, in their poetics. Their work aspire to be monads, reflecting history from within by means of etymology or literary allusion one moment, attempting to banish it the next. For Stein these binary terms can shift to "human mind" and "human nature," deftly enclosing a traditional mind/nature dichotomy within an aesthetic anthropology; Olson raids Whitehead's definition of a "region" and Emerson's use of "boundary" to parallel effect.

Unlike Rousseau, and even Montaigne before him, Stein cannot assert the equation, I am my book. For her, autobiographical writing is necessarily publicity or a covert apology for "the realest poetry." Therefore, the valorization of self-discovery implicit in Olson's oneiric poetics has no resonance in her work. Her paradoxical task was to drive autobiography in the direction of the monadic, "the realest poetry." She acknowledged the impossibility of this task by claiming they were the autobiographies of others: Alice B. Toklas or Everybody.

But at her strongest and most obscure Stein is most Emersonian, affirming her radical newness and disowning generic links to past art. "[I]t is people who generally smell of the museums who are accepted, and it is the new who are not accepted . . . That is why James Joyce was accepted and I was not. He leaned toward the past, in my work the newness and difference is fundamental." However, she shared with Joyce a descent from Flaubert,[14] whose unfulfilled desire to write a novel "about nothing . . . held together by the strength of its style" (to Louise Colet, Jan. 16, 1852) may be a source for her "sentiment of doing nothing."

For the most part, Stein's writing resists the opening up to the archaic past which characterizes most of the modernist texts and films discussed in this book. Furthermore, her rejection of religious speculation, starting most emphatically with her own Judaism, would seem to leave little room for the theologizing of the work of art I maintain is so central to modernist thought.

Nevertheless, her models for autonomous beings who radiate the sentiment of doing nothing are Catholic saints in *Four Saints in Three Acts*. Even more significantly, she resorts to a theological trope when trying to define the nature of reading, when the literary rather than communicative function of language was at stake. In *Narration,* she lectured on the transmission of emotion through writing: "That is what mysticism is, that is what the Trinity is, that is what marriage is, the absolute conviction that in spite of knowing anything about everything about how any one is never really feeling what any other one is really feeling that after all three are one and two are one. One is not one because one is always two that is one is always coming to a recognition of what the one who is one is writing that is telling."[15]

The mystic marriage of writer and reader here expands to a trinity which would include the empirical self, the perceiving and remembering body. For the reader of the literature of "entity," which Stein wrote when she had no audience in mind, only an act of faith links the words of the text to an empirical reality. The problems of representation and history are, in turn, tied to the more conventional literature of identity, of which *The Autobiography of Alice B. Toklas* was her first mature effort.

Finally, Stein's imaginary cinema is not essentially a mode of visual representation but a rhythm capable of articulating the temporal duration of an entity. The aesthetic excitement generated by a literary expression of such an entity becomes a function of the opacity and the self-reliance of the text as it reflects, allegorically, the condition of a natural object.

8

Out Via Nothing:
Olson's Genealogy of the Proper Poem

MALLARMÉ'S SONNET form and Blanchot's obscure parables underline generic continuities which link modernist texts to the poetic and narrative traditions of antiquity. Olson's counter-paradigm emphasizes a break with generic conventions, but ends up aping the still older Hesiodic and Lucretian forms. Olson's "projective" verse is as indebted to the poetics of Walt Whitman as Mallarmé's sonnets or Blanchot's tales are to their traditions. In turn, Whitman's apparent freedom from the constraints of form was a reflex of his seizure of Emerson's oratorical mode as a lyrical model. Olson, like Whitman and Stein, is an Emersonian. Like Whitman he allows the play of associations, in which dreaming plays a vital role, to mold his poems from within.

The Poetic Region

THE ATTRACTION of Charles Olson's theoretical writing derives from the urgency of his tone. It is willfully eccentric, elliptical, and yet familiar. It establishes the authority of the teacher and appeals to a fantasy of academic life. Utopian educational schemes are central to Olson's vision, and he first attracted attention in the literary world as the Rector of Black Mountain College. This posture as an eccentric didactician is clearly indebted to the cranky and aggressive tone of Ezra Pound's essays. Perhaps some elements of the notorious seminar style of Perry Miller, a central figure at Harvard when Olson was doing graduate work in American civilization, found their way into the student's later essays. Olson used the printed page, at times, like the blackboard of an over-excited professor; chiastic lines, arrows, angular inserts, and immense brackets—more often than not unclosed—appear in his most puzzling and most rewarding collection of essays, *Proprioception*.

Our familiarity with his stance and style is a measure of how solidly entrenched he was in the Emersonian tradition that dominates American poetics. The dialogue between the lecturer of *Nature* and the voice Emerson calls "my Orphic poet," in that short book, is the ultimate model for Olson's vatic didacticism. Yet, whenever he mentions Emerson, he is dismissive and superficial; he consciously and avidly took over Melville's troubled relationship to Emerson, as many other American artists have.

The eccentricity and urgency of Olson's prose style suggests the autodidact. He was far from that, however, having studied literature at Wesleyan, Yale, and Harvard. Yet he hides this training with his prophetic boisterousness. Olson's jeremiad can entail the bundling and banishing of centuries, even millennia. But, in his wild speculations on the history of language and consciousness can be seen an eagerness to recast conceptions of time, and its relation to the self, that are wholly Emersonian.

Charles Olson assured himself that he was going back to the root meaning of *historein* [ἰστορεῖν], "to investigate and discover for oneself" as used by Herodotus, in his poetic project because he did not want to acknowledge his indebtedness to Emerson. But the paradox of Emerson's pervasiveness is that every American who insists that he is starting out from scratch, making a genre and a tradition all his own, and perhaps even a theoretical apparatus to support it, is adhering to Emerson's tradition, often using *his* favored genres and even parroting *his* theories.

The volume most often consulted by visitors to the Special Collections in the library of the University of Connecticut is Olson's copy of Alfred North Whitehead's *Process and Reality*.[1] From the time Olson first read the book, around 1953, it became a crucial text for him. By and large, his marginalia suggest ways of construing Whitehead's cosmology as a poetics. At the end of "Extensive Connection" (chapter 2, part 4), one finds the longest and most coherent gloss in the volume. The beginning of the statement which reads "The inside of a poem, its volume" promises the reader an articulation of the poetics Olson was deriving from his reading. In deciphering it, I could not, however, make out several words in the pencil note until I read through the Whitehead passage on the same page. There one finds:

> The inside of a region, its volume, has a complete boundedness denied to the extensive potentiality external to it. The boundedness applies both to the spatial and the temporal aspects of extension. Wherever there is ambiguity as to the contrast of boundedness between inside and outside, there is no proper region.[2]

In the note I had been struggling with, Olson had written out Whitehead's three sentences word for word, changing only the term "region" into "poem." His definition of poetic enclosure begins "the inside of a poem" and continues with Whitehead's words until the conclusion that an ambiguity between inside and outside means "there is no proper poem." Trying out Whitehead's language as his own, in the privacy of his library, Olson was testing the limits of repetition and the powers of transformation. The phrase "a proper poem" would have a resonance for Olson that "a proper region" would lack for Whitehead. In Olson's theoretical writings the adjective "proper" always has its etymological force, coming from *proprius,* meaning "one's own." By changing "region" to "poem," Olson appropriated Whitehead's philosophical discrimination; yet he attempted to make the passage his own. Here the gesture is as blatant as it is casual. The appropriations and transformations of poetic, philosophical, and psychological texts play an important role in Olson's essays.

In "The Poet," Emerson had made a proclamation of the naming function of the poet and the etymologist which corresponds to Olson's peculiar use of the word "proper," and to his adaptation of Whitehead's description of boundedness:

> [T]he poet is the Namer or Language-maker, naming things sometimes after their appearance, sometimes after their essence, and giving to every one *its own name* and not another's, thereby rejoicing the intellect, which delights in detachment or *boundary.* (Emphasis mine.)

Image as Vector

I SHALL briefly examine one of Olson's most elusive essays in order to illustrate how he has inflected Emerson's concept of the precise name, by way of Whitehead, into his own theory of the image. In 1958 Olson wrote to Cid Corman that he was thinking of writing a supplement (about "rhyme and pun") to his most famous polemical essay, "Projective Verse." On April 22, 1959, Elaine Feinstein wrote a note to Olson inquiring about his attitude toward the poetic image: "Orient me: what emphasis do you give to the use of the Image . . .?" The "Letter to Elaine Feinstein" which he published along with "Projective Verse" in 1959 and 1960 is dated May 1959. It is one of Olson's most important and puzzling theoretical texts. He defines the image in a virtually hermetic code:

> Image, therefore, is vector. It carries the trinity via the double to the single form which one makes oneself able, if so, to issue from the "content" (multiplicity: originally, and repetitively, chaos— Tiamat: wot the Hindo-Europeans knocked out by giving the Old Man (Juice himself) all the lightning.[3]

Olson called the dense, elliptical, and allusive letter to Elaine Feinstein "this swirl—a bit like Crab Nebula." It puts a heavy burden of interpretation, even of decoding, on the sympathetic reader. Following the model of Whitehead's revision of Descartes, in which the thinker is created by "vectors" of thought (rather than the subject generating thoughts), Olson describes the form and content of a poem emerging from the principles he calls "the trinity" and "the double." Before attempting an interpretation of these obscure terms, we have to compare this passage to other instances of Olson's use of that poetic shorthand. The trinity must be "the basic trio: topos/typos/tropos, 3 in 1" which he had mentioned earlier in the letter. Later in the same text he will come to the concept of the Image's double: "The other part is certainly 'landscape'—the other part of the double of Image to 'noun.' By Landscape I mean what 'narrative'; scene; event; climax; crisis; hero; development; posture; all that *meant*—all the substantive of what we call literary."

The Double reappears as a graph that resembles a fraction:

> The Double, then, (the "home"/heartland/of the post-
> Mesopotamians the AND the post-Hindo Eees:
> At the moment it comes out   the Muse ("world"
>   ————————————
>   the Psyche (the "life"

> You wld know already I'm buggy on say the Proper Noun, so much so I wld take it Pun is Rime, all from tope/type/trope, that built in is the connection, in each of us, to Cosmos, and if one

taps, via psyche, plus a "true" adherence of Muse, one does reveal "Form."[4]

An unpublished chart, actually a true "swirl" of notes all over a page, which is numbered 59 among Olson's miscellaneous papers, contains the note "Image Pt. II of P.V." Near that is written:

Psyche and Muse
(self   (word
this life   home
_____   vicinity

Topos, Typos, Tropos

THE SAME page contains an allusion to the concept of the trope:

line as verse
to turn (trope
. . . "plough"
ones own furrow
proper furrow

Olson made abundant use of the far-ranging and often speculative etymologies in *Webster's International Dictionary*. So, the movement from the "trinity via the double" to the "single form" in the passage quoted above involves foraging in the dictionary. I believe that even the motto Olson gave himself, when he wrote in "The Present Is Prologue," "I am an archaeologist of morning" (which his editors chose for the title of his collected poems), actually hides an etymological figure.[5] *Webster's* links the roots of "form" and "morn." In these terms Olson would be calling himself "the speaker of the origin of form." In the "Letter to Elaine Feinstein" he performs a similar gesture when he elaborates on the word "Form."

in other words the "right" (wahr-) proper noun, however apparently idiosyncratic, if "tested" by one's own experience (out plus in) ought to yield along this phylo-line (as the speech thing, above) because—*decently* what one oneself can know, as well as what the word *means*—ontogenetic.[6]

Here Olson subscribes to Haeckel's law that ontogeny recapitulates phylogeny. By the phylogeny of "Muse" he probably means language itself. Not just his native English or American speech, but language as a palimpsest of historical changes. Olson was enthralled with etymology and he paid particular attention to theories of Mediterranean linguistic exchange between Semitic and Indo-European speakers. He also dabbled in linguistic anthropology, as his references to the work of Whorf and Malinowski indicate.

By being "buggy" on "the Proper Noun" he seems to mean that his passion for etymology reveals unexpected "puns." The very alliteration of the Greek triad, topos/typos/tropos, suggests an intimate interconnection of functions of the poetic act, fusing his own obsessive concerns with geography, mythology, and poetic history into a triune first principle.

Obviously, the theological overtones of the "trinity" and of Yahweh's identification of himself did not escape Olson, when he scribbled in the margin of his copy of *Process and Reality*: "demonstrative here/I am the 4th of topos, *typism,* tropism and the great blow of Nature [like God but *not* God]." In paraphrase, we might say that the poetic act emerges from a sense of place [topos], both in the world and on the page; takes a turn [tropos] with the creation of the "proper" noun, so that both the authorial persona and the typographical materiality [typos] of the poem come into being. The persona has a double nature because it is the locus of the intersection of the poet's language with his "proper" psyche.

This constitutes a denial of the autonomy of the poetic images as his two declared mentors, Pound and Williams, conceived it. To Olson imagery remains an ineluctible reflex of the poetic projection of language: it "issues forth" like the Minotaur in its labyrinth ("The Librarian") or looms like statues unexpectedly encountered ("The Distances") from the charged conjunction of place, etymology, and trope, as suddenly and as elusively as the sense of poetic selfhood seizes the inspired poet. Thus images in Olson's sense arise from the urgencies of poetic composition: they are peripheral but inescapable visions.

Oneiric Landscape

DREAMS PLAY a large role in Olson's poetry. "The Librarian" seems to be the transcription of a nightmare. The poem anticipates the thinking which resulted in the "Letter to Elaine Feinstein." In fact, Olson describes writing the poem in the very letter to Corman on the envelope of which he announces that the supplement to "Projective Verse" is finished.

The opening repetition of the poem declares that the theme will be "The landscape (the landscape!)" which is a term for a complex cluster of thoughts in the theoretical texts. Before the sentence can complete itself, the poet takes on the role of the Double (another central concept in the "Letter to Elaine Feinstein"). The guidance of the theoretical essays should urge us to look for the rhyme of a pun. It is to be found in the trope of the city of Gloucester as the metonymy for the poet. In his dream poem he is both seer and seen, Maximus and Gloucester. The "shore one of me is" finds its double in "(from offshore, I, Maximus)." Gloucester is literally a shorn edge of land and figuratively the shore or prop with which the poet tropes and creates himself in the poem. The gloss on *Landscape* in "Postscript to Proprioception & Logography" is "to bring the land into the eye's view." The Doubling of the self, "shore" and "offshore," focuses the oneiric landscape.

The poem is a rapid movement of condensations and displacements which Olson calls "combinations/(new mixtures)." The first figure to emerge besides the doubled dreamer is his father. He has usurped the poet's paraphernalia, books and manuscripts, but he appears as their agent rather than their author. In the most curious twist of the poem, the dreamer, in one of his double roles, scans his father's merchandise as a source for the poem of his persona, Maximus.

In an autobiographical note for the 1955 edition of *Twentieth Century Authors,* Olson wrote, "I am still, at 40 [the text was probably written several years before its publication] hugely engaged with my parents, in fact more engaged with them now than with that I spent so much time on in my 20s and 30s: society, and other persons. . . . But what strikes me (and I now suspect has much more governed the nature of my seven years of writing than I knew) is, the depth to which the parents who live in us (they are not the same) are our definers."[7] In 1948 Olson wrote three prose memoirs of his father, who had died in 1935 estranged from his son over a trivial issue. Several of the best poems in *The Distances* refer to the death of the poet's mother on Christmas Day, 1950. There were no other children in the family. Yet it is important for my discussion of "The Librarian" to know that a male child, a year older than the poet, had died at birth. The only evidence of this in print is line 19 of "JUST AS MORNING TWILIGHT AND THE GULLS, GLOUCESTER, MAY 1966 THE FULL FLOWER MOON" in *The Maximus Poems, Volume Three*: ". . . a brother died at birth a year before myself was born—." Equally obscure are the conditions of Olson's second marriage. Butterick lists his meeting of Constance Wilock in May 1940, but he gives no date for marriage or divorce. Their daughter, Katherine Mary, was born in October 1951. The same ambiguity surrounds the description of Elizabeth Kaiser, Olson's second wife, in Butterick's chronology. They met in 1954 at Black Mountain College where she was a student. Their son, Charles Peter, was born the following year.[8]

Fathers and Brothers

THE TENSIONS of Olson's domestic upheaval are inscribed in "The Librarian" written less than two years after his son's birth. I quote it in its entirety:

> The landscape (the landscape!) again: Gloucester,
> the shore one of me is (duplicates), and from which
> (from offshore, I, Maximus) am removed, observe.
>
> In this night I moved on the territory with combinations
> (new mixtures) of old and known personages: the leader,
> my father, in an old guise, here selling books and manuscripts.
>
> My thought was, as I looked in the window of his shop
> there should be materials here for Maximus, when, then,
> I saw he was the young musician has been there (been before me)
>
> before. It turned out it wasn't a shop, it was a loft (wharf-
> house, in which, as he walked me around, a year ago
> came back (I had been there before, with my wife and son,
>
> I didn't remember, he presented me insinuations via
> himself and his girl) both of whom I had known for years
> But never in Gloucester. I had moved them in, to my country.
>
> His previous appearance had been in my parents' bedroom where
>   I
> found him intimate with my former wife: this boy
> was now the Librarian of Gloucester, Massachusetts!
>
>> Black space,
>> old fish-house.
>> Motions
>> of Ghosts.
>> I,
>>   dogging
>>   his steps.

       He
       (not my father,
       by name himself
       with his face
       twisted
       at birth)
       possessed of knowledge
       pretentious
       giving me
       what in the instant
       I knew better of.

       But the somber
       place, the flooring
       crude like a wharf's
       and a barn's
       space

I was struck by the fact I was in Gloucester, and that my daughter
was there—that I would see her! She was over the Cut. I
hadn't even connected her with my being there, that she was

here. That she was there (in the Promised Land—the Cut!
But there was this business, of poets, that all my Jews
were in the fish-house too, that the Librarian had made a party

I was to read. They were. There were many of them, slumped
around. It was not for me. I was outside. It was the Fort.
The Fort was in East Gloucester—Old Gorton's Wharf, where
                                        the Library

was. It was a region of coal houses, bins. In one a gang
was beating someone to death, in a corner of the labyrinth
of fences. I could see their arms and shoulders whacking

down. But not the victim. I got out of there. But cops
tailed me along the Fort beach toward the Tavern

       The places still
       half-dark, mud,
       coal-dust.
       There is no light
       east
       of the Bridge

Only on the headland
toward the harbor
from Cressy's

I have seen it (once
when my daughter ran
out on a spit of sand

isn't even there.) Where
is Bristow? when does I-A
get me home? I am caught

In Gloucester. (What's buried
behind Lufkin's
Diner? Who is

Frank Moore?

The loaded word "insinuations" in the thirteenth line turns the composite figure of the old father and young musician into the objectionable character who will turn out to be the "Librarian of Gloucester, Massachusetts!" and therefore a custodian of books and manuscripts crucial to the development of Maximus as a Herodotean historian, seeking evidence for himself. The insinuations of the Librarian never emerge thematically in the poem. Yet Olson follows that turning point with insinuations of his own in the sixth stanza.

The metrical shift which occurs after this dramatic climax indicates that Olson is working with two different rhythms derived from the lyrics of William Carlos Williams.[9] The long lines recall the sinuous, eccentrically accented, and often abruptly shifting metrics of "The Yachts." Furthermore, Williams' fine poem also depends upon an oneiric turn. In the final three stanzas the waves are personified as if they were drowning sailors overrun by the yachts which skillfully cut through them. In fact, the very image with which Williams achieves his startling transition repeats itself in "The Librarian."

Arms with hands grasping seek to clutch at the prows.
Bodies thrown recklessly in the way are cut aside.
It is a sea of faces about them in agony, in despair . . .

Those synecdoches of violence enter Olson's poem when he returns to the rhythm of "The Yachts" in his own fourteenth stanza. The other rhythm is the more familiar short line of Williams which extends its syntax vertically, as in the dream poem "Perpetuum Mobile: The City":

173

> For two hours
> > they worked—
> > until
> he coiled
> > the thick
> knot upon
> that whorish
> > head—
>
> Dragged
> > insensible
> upon his face
> by the lines—

Olson uses his short lines to halt the metamorphoses of the poem's opening, and even to attempt to sort out the figures in transformation in the eighth stanza. The phrase "by name himself" almost translates *nomen proprium,* the proper noun. It is the poet who bears his father's name: they were both Charles Joseph Olson. Another name comes to the consciousness of the dreamer, a name he does not disclose at this point in the poem, but which would be that of a man "with his face/ twisted/at birth."

There is only one full proper name in the poem. The enigmatic final lines are "Who is/Frank Moore?" As is often the case in Olson's poetry, the final volume of *The Maximus Poems* glosses this problem. On page 201 near the end of "I am going to hate to leave this Earthly Paradise" we read: "pushed-in left-side face like/Frank Moore's birth face forceps/bent." Butterick provides the useful gloss that Frank Moore was a composer with whom Olson was friendly during his political period in Washington before he determined to live as a writer. This accounts for the transformation of the father into a young musician.

The Primal Scene

"THE LIBRARIAN" presents the reader with an intensely personal series of shifting moods which are meticulously orchestrated. Even though the first person narrator is bifurcated in the second line, it is not until the word "insinuations" appears in the fifth tercet that the sinister dimension of his subjective split begins to control the mood. The dreamer's recognition that "I had moved them in, to my country" reasserts his domination over the phantasmagoria while it provides a foil for the dramatic sixth tercet which casts him into the gloom of the three stanzas of short lines. The "But" which begins the last of them is not syntactical. It rhetorically enlarges the scene of the action, "Black space . . . the somber/place," while dismissing the fluid events which seem to occur within it. The problem of naming the "He" is lessened by the superiority of the narrator over his "pretentious" antagonist. Yet the place teases him. As he struggles with bringing it into focus and definition, a sudden recovery seems to occur. The anticipation of seeing the young daughter of his first marriage leads him enthusiastically to a biblical hyperbole. He compares the other side of the Blynman Canal in Gloucester ("the Cut") to "the Promised Land." Yet no sooner does that metaphor occur than its negative associations take over the poem. In the extension of the analogy to Moses, the poet cannot cross over into the Promised Land. He is detained by a poetry reading. As the leader of Gloucester's few published poets, Olson implies he is a Moses and calls them "all my Jews."

The first two sentences of line 48 mark a crucial turning point: "I was to read. They were." The repetition of the infinitive "to read" is necessary to complete the sense. The poet was to be diminished to the role of one among many Gloucester poets. By leaving off the infinitive in the second sentence he reduces the rivals to mere being. This negative turn is not sudden. The word "business" and the phrase "the Librarian had made a party" prepare the tawdry scene. The violent fight he glimpses, when he rejects the reading, brings the poem to its most terrifying moment. Not only is he the helpless witness to the murder—a situation which naturally induces a feeling of cowardice—but he becomes a guilty suspect. The guilt is reinforced by the reciprocal inversion of "But cops/tailed me" to the earlier "I,/dogging/his step."

The daughter, who is near but unapproachable, returns in the poem as an even younger child, suddenly threatened with drowning, in a suppressed episode which leaves only the residue of the father's guilt. The vantage point from which "I, Maximus) am removed, observe" is not simply one of cool detachment but a fascination tied to the threatening disappearance of the sandbar and the guilt toward his daughter. In psychoanalytical discourse such fascination can be a manifestation of the Primal Scene.

The very duplication of the dreamer into a removed observer and a participant in the action of the poem suggests the classical fantasy of observing the parents's intercourse. The sequence of tercets which opens the poem are further evidence of this process. The window of the father's bookshop allows him to observe at a remove. The ambiguous "insinuations" occur right after the mention of the poet as a husband

and parent and in a context ("via") of the musician "and his girl." But the most important point in this chain of fantasies is that the adultery with the dreamer's former wife was discovered in his parents' bedroom.

The witnessed intercourse has been displaced onto the most frightening moment in the poem. It is the gang murder of which he can only see "their arms and shoulders whacking/down." The guilt and suspicion which falls upon the dreamer as he moves along the beach immediately after glimpsing that scene underscores the displacement. He both wants to watch and participate in the act which scares him. Henry Edelheit has observed that the primal scene schema "can be either simultaneous or alternating, with both principals in a sadomasochistically conceived sexual act. The sensory modality most often represented is the visual, and the setting is often a theater or arena. A libidinal-aggressive encounter is represented in which the observer is implicated. The nature of the encounter (often a combat, a contest, or a sacrifice) is characteristically enigmatic."[10] Olson's metaphor for the murder scene is "in a corner of the labyrinth/of fences." The labyrinth, as Olson well knew, was the prison of just such a mythological creature, the minotaur, the illicit offspring of Pasiphae and a bull. The other mythological reference in the poem, the Pisgah vision of Moses, entails an allusion to the injunction of Jahweh at the end of Deuteronomy that Moses might see but not enter the Promised Land. Olson had read Freud's *Moses and Monotheism* and used it in preparing a chapter of *Call Me Ishmael* which I shall cite later in this chapter. Freud attributes the formation of the Mosaic Father-religion, and the creation of Moses as a powerful paternal figure, to primal scene reactions.[11] He views Moses as a dual personality and as a father in the shadow of a greater father and former wife on the one hand and his children on the other. We should remember that Olson's Mosaic analogy is not fulfilled. Unlike the prophet of Deuteronomy, the dreamer leaves his "Jews," the other poets, and he never *sees* his daughter or the Promised Land in the poem. He is suspended in the "half-dark."

The Double's Proper Name

THIS ELABORATION of the primal scene in "The Librarian" prepares a reading of the strange questions which end the poem. Maximus, as a historian in the Herodotean sense, is a researcher of "what isn't even there" anymore. A sandbar erased by shifting ocean patterns would be the very material of his "finding out for himself." Bristow would be another. One of the heroes of *The Maximus Poems,* Captain John Smith, indicated a settlement called Bristow, a seventeenth-century spelling of Bristol, just south of Gloucester on his 1614 map.[12] The site "isn't even there" today. Olson would have passed through the region where Smith located it when he drove to or from Gloucester along highway I-A. With the mention of the old road, another ambiguity enters the poem. If Olson is approaching Gloucester, he is very near when he enters the region of Smith's Bristow. But if he is trying to return to Black Mountain College in North Carolina, he is still within the immediate periphery of Gloucester. The suspension of the sentence "I am caught/in Gloucester" across a stanza break underscores the ambiguity about the direction of his movement. By the time Olson wrote "The Librarian"—late 1956 is a guess—he had published the first twenty-two poems in the Maximus series and had written many more. He is caught in his role as Maximus and that is the source of his anxiety at this point in the poem. It may be that the thematic confrontation with that anxiety in the coda to the poem is just what takes "The Librarian" out of that series. Olson referred to "The Librarian" in 1966 as "the best poem I ever wrote." He explained, "It's all [about] Frank Moore —describing him as my brother, the brother that got born misshapen, and all that." He also called Moore his "doppelgänger," adding "he's like a part of me that I won't keep acquainted with."[13]

Jacob Arlow's psychoanalytical study "The Only Child" illuminates the primal scene fantasy in which Moore, a disfigured man, plays the role of the poet's brother. Arlow concludes his four case studies as follows:

> However, regardless of what he learns, the only child blames himself for the fact that there were no other children. His specific fantasy consists of the thought that he had destroyed potential rivals by devouring them when he was inside the mother's body. This fantasy was observed in all my cases, without exception. Claustral fantasies, as well as some claustrophobic symptoms, usually very mild, were also common. The specific fear was the danger of retaliation from the embryos that had been destroyed. What the only child unconsciously fears is an encounter with these adversaries in the claustrum and being devoured from within by the rivals whom he had devoured and incorporated.[14]

Two of the four cases contain instructive examples. In the first "the patient . . . [felt] both guilt for destroying siblings and fear that the siblings in the form of the foetus or cancer would retaliate and destroy her."[15] I have already pointed out that anxiety toward his son, and especially his daughter estranged by divorce, operates in this poem. In all four cases claustral fear plays a large role. Following Arlow's lead, we may conclude that the black, barn-like space which frightens the dreamer more than the noisome librarian, because it contains the "Motions/ of ghosts," is the scene of a uterine fantasy.

I believe a further step may be taken in the analysis of this poem by considering the fusion of psychoanalytical method and poetic history proposed by Harold Bloom.[16] In "The Librarian" the poets of Gloucester are alternately the people Olson, like Moses, leads into the Promised Land and the siblings he fears he had murdered. But there are at least two rivals who haunt the poem, threatening to "kill" the poet. They are Williams, whose rhythms Olson has adopted, and, even more potently, Whitman. Whitman had dominated the earlier poem, "As The Dead Prey Upon Us," with which Olson continually associated "The Librarian." That poem about his mother's ghost is a diminished version of Whitman's great nocturnal fantasy "The Sleepers."[17] The precariousness of "the business of poets" remained a crucial issue in Olson's best poems.

Up Against the Lord

IN THE letter to Corman (January 2, 1958) written when he was working out the topos, tropos, typos schema, he elaborates a "hunch":

> That the holdup is the difficulty of the barrier reached in the Non-Euclidean Shove (my old cry abt the "univ. of discourse"—that the ghost of Plato still furthers; & we ain't getting through the wall, fast as we can travel, because we ain't quiet enough to make the sound *proper* to a wrap-around (instead of an objective) space.
>
> To which adheres the humanist biz: all the Zen etc/habit etc/ hip queer queen hipster are right to go it back to the p-poor self, but you can't scream society. One is up against the Lord, as Clement of Alexandria was the last to inform the boys right on.
>
> The rumble is an old one: the soul, yes? And man in vacuum (meaning, without motor parts), in order to have his speed & not go apart, heeds CARE (itas) 1st him *self* (Him-self)—& lawd, it do take doin.
>
> > Love
> > O

Olson's mother, an Irish Catholic, had raised him in her religion. He was lapsed, although he did occasionally attend Mass with his son. It is most likely that he read Clement for his description, albeit negative, of Greek cultic religion. *Prostreptikos pros Hellenas* ("Exhortation to the Greeks") draws an unbridgeable distinction where Olson read a pleonasm with the words λόγος and μῦθος. For Clement the *Logos,* as the person of Christ, stood in direct opposition to the empty legends μῦθοι κενοί of the Greek tradition. "The boys" in Olson's letter to Corman must be poets. That would mean that the mythopoeic poet faces the impossible challenge of countering the dominant mythology of Christianity. In his first book, *Call Me Ishmael,* Olson had argued that Melville did precisely that in *Moby Dick* and then succumbed to a form of Christianity which ruined all of his later books.

Olson's position on Melville's turn to Christianity is most emphatic in the fragment from the first version of *Call Me Ishmael*: "In Adullam's Lair." At that time Olson was as preoccupied by Dostoevsky as he was by Melville. He understood their different relationships to the *Logos* and to mythopoeia in the following terms:

> A Dostoyevsky can create a Christ in his own image, and make Jesus palpable. He accepted what Melville denied, the crucifixion of his own flesh and being.[18]

In the same draft we find the source for an important passage in the later book:

> Paternity for Pierre lay behind portrait, face, presence, day; it lay in Rome, Greece, Egypt, with contemporaries—Enceladus, Memnon, Cyclops, Pharoah. Beneath "the Switzerland of his soul," an immensity of Alp and Rocky and Andes Mountain, lay "ten million things . . . as yet uncovered to Pierre." This Pierre, the uncreated, the Ahab who kinged and captained no world because his creator had foresworn his Imagination for Christ, this man had a backward and downward in him like a pyramid: "The old mummy lies buried in cloth on cloth; it takes time to unwrap this Egyptian king." Melville denied him. (p. 5)

In the chapter called "Moses" in *Call Me Ishmael,* Olson transferred the agony of paternity to Melville himself:

> Melville was agonized over paternity. He suffered as a son. He had lost the source. He demanded to know the father.

Kronos, in order to become god, armed himself with a sickle and castrated his father Uranus. Saturn used a pruning knife. Kronos and Saturn in turn were overthrown by their sons banded together in a brother horde. The new gods of Jupiter were, in their turn, attacked by other sons. These sons—they were the "Giants"— lost. They are described as more akin to men.

Enceladus was among them. He is a constant image in Melville. Melville saw his likeness in defeated and exiled heroes, not in successful sons, who, by their triumph, become the fathers.[19]

The phrase "One is up against the Lord" in the letter to Corman, describes the situation of modernist Titanomachia. Clement's *Prostreptikos* polemically narrates the defeat of the Greek pantheon by the triumphant *Logos*. Although Olson identifies himself with the defeated sons, he suggests a new strategy based on a multilingual pun. "CARE(itas)" injects the element of meticulous attention into the Latin *caritas*, meaning "love," or "affection." This is not a head–on rejection of Christianity but a dialectical recovery of some of the love and truth which the Church fathers monopolized in Christ. The seventh chapter of Clement's book calls upon the degraded testimony of poetry to convict pagan theogony.

In the perpetual war between poetry and philosophy or theology, Olson was always prepared for battle. His extraordinary excitement over *Preface to Plato,* which even astonished Eric Havelock, its author, grew out of the thesis that *The Republic* was essentially written to counteract the power of poetry. The position of poetry long after the death of the Greek gods is a typical Romantic theme. In "The Distances" Olson evokes the power of "CARE(itas)" in a context that fuses his identification with Melville and Whitman in his vision of pagan antiquity.

Distance Avails Not

JOHN HAYS Hammond Jr., an affluent inventor of nautical instruments, built a castle as his home in Gloucester. He lived in it with Harry Martin. Olson was a frequent visitor in the castle. There are two classical statues in the tower of the castle, which, according to the poet Robert Kelly had been identified as Zeus and Augustus Caesar.[20] He added that it was commonly held although never published, that the poem addressed the relationship of Hammond and Martin. In the poem another inventor takes Hammond's place. Paul Christensen, in his book

Charles Olson: Call Him Ishmael, has unearthed useful information about the "German inventor":

> The allusion is to Karl Tanzer, an eighty-three-year-old x-ray technician, who fell in love with a sickly young Cuban girl. After her death he removed her body from the grave and preserved it in paraffin; he then kept it in his house for eight years, during which time he was forced to replace parts of her body with plaster casts. According to local newspaper reports, he serenaded her each night on a homemade pipe organ. When the police arrested him in 1952, they found the corpse dressed for bed and her hair decked in fresh flowers. He told the court at his hearing that he was building a plane and that as soon as she returned to life, he planned to fly with her back to Germany.[21]

Olson incorporated aspects of this bizarre story into his poem as a repetition of the myth of Pygmalion.

THE DISTANCES

So the distances are Galatea
                       and one does fall in love and desires
mastery

           Old Zeus—young Augustus

Love knows no distance, no place
                  is that far away or heat changes
into signals, and control

           Old Zeus—young Augustus

Death is a loving matter, then, a horror
                    we cannot bide, and avoid
by greedy life

           we think all living things are precious
           —Pygmalions

                     a German inventor in Key West
who had a Cuban girl, and kept her, after her death
in his bed

after her family retrieved her
he stole the body again from the vault

Torso on torso in either direction,
                    young Augustus
                                    out via nothing where messages
are
        or in, down La Cluny's steps to the old man sitting
a god throned on torsoes,

                    old Zeus

Sons go there hopefully as though there was a secret, the object
to undo distance?
                                    They huddle there, at the bottom
of the shaft, against one young bum
                                    or two loving cheeks

                Augustus?

You can teach the young nothing
                                    all of them go away, Aphrodite
tricks it out,
                    Old Zeus—young Augustus

You have love, and no object
                                or you have all pressed to your nose
which is too close,

                    old Zeus hiding in your chin your young
                    Galatea

the girl who makes you weep and you keep the corpse live by all
your arts
                    whose cheek do you stroke when you stroke the stone face
                    of young Augustus, made for bed in a military camp,
                    o Caesar?

O love who places all where each is, as they are, for every moment,
yield
                    to this man
                                    that the impossible distance
be healed,

that young Augustus
and old Zeus

be enclosed

"I wake you,
stone. Love this man."

The stories of Pygmalion and Tanzer demonstrate that, in Whitman's words, "distance avails not."[22]

Olson cannot accede to Whitman's sublime optimism. Perhaps some of his skepticism comes from what we know of Whitman's difficult homoeroticism. But it is Melville's troubled sexuality that comes into the poem through the teasingly obscure allusion of "La Cluny's steps."

Olson, of course, was fully aware of the unhappy homoerotic component of Melville's adoration of Hawthorne. In "The Distances," the "Sons" who descend the stairs at the Hôtel de Cluny in Paris are first Melville and Whitman, then the inventors Tanzer and Hammond, followed by Olson himself.

On December 5, 1849, Melville visited the Musée des Thermes in the Hôtel de Cluny in Paris. The statue he encountered at those preserved Roman baths was undoubtedly not of Zeus. But whatever it was, it made a deep impression on him and it provided a metaphor for the terrors of the unconscious in the forty-first chapter of *Moby Dick*. The entire paragraph in which Melville probes Ahab's submerged madness has relevance to Olson's poem:

> This is much; yet Ahab's larger, darker, deeper part remains unhinted. But vain to popularize profundities, and all truth is profound. Winding far down from within the very heart of this spiked Hotel de Cluny where we here stand—however grand and wonderful, now quit it;—and take your way, ye nobler, sadder souls, to those vast Roman halls of Thermes; where far beneath the fantastic towers of man's upper earth, his root of grandeur, his whole awful essence sits in bearded state; an antique buried beneath antiquities, and throned on torsoes! So with a broken throne, the great gods mock that captive king; so like a Caryatid, he patient sits, upholding on his frozen brow the piled entablatures of ages. Wind ye down there, ye prouder, sadder souls! question that proud, sad King! A family likeness! aye, he did beget ye, ye young exiled royalties; and from your grin sire only will the old State-secret come.[23]

183

The text of "In Adullam's Lair" is nearly as elliptical as "The Distances." The same episode turns up there without clarification:

> Ahab was the reach of Melville's life, but in Ahab he died. He went an extraordinary *distance* down beneath the Hotel de Cluny in his Captain. There he stopped, sad fool of shaken self. He knew a dearth and feared death. (p. 2; emphasis mine)

Ancient Voices

THE "CAPTIVE king" that Melville describes would be a version of Kronos, Zeus' father, whom he overthrew and imprisoned in Tartarus. The dreadful repetitions of the violence of shifting generations permeate the allusions of the poem. Even Pygmalion and Galatea are subjected to that dire economy. Of course, the identification of the statue which Pygmalion made and loved with the sea nymph Galatea is a modern invention. It has no classical source. When Ovid narrates the story of Pygmalion in Book Ten of the *Metamophoses* it is amid illustrations of how Venus shows "sua numinus ira." Pygmalion had rejected the love of women after seeing the prostitutions of the Propoetides, but he was "tricked out," to use Olson's phrase, by Venus-Aphrodite into doubting the inanimate nature of the statue he created. Although Venus answered the prayer of Pygmalion and turned the statue to flesh, the family that Pygmalion and Galatea engendered, as Ovid immediately relates, ended in the disastrous incest between their grandson, Cinyras, and their great-granddaughter, Myrrha.

With his mythological allusions and his American poetic history, Olson situates "love" in the field of generational revolt and Titanomachia. Two of the distances which "are Galatea" can be gauged by the dialectic of repulsion and power in the erotic temperament of Pygmalion.[24] The poem collapses these tensions into the opposition of "old Zeus—young Augustus."

The line "Old Zeus—young Augustus" operates as an oxymoron with historical and literary justification. The distance between Greece and Rome, immortal and mortal, god and man, had been bridged by the deification of the emperor and by his manifestation as *Zeus Aineiadas*.

Olson probably knew a translation of the poem from the ninth book of *The Greek Anthology,* which would read, in my approximate rendering: "Daphne who once rejected Phoibus now makes a dark-flowered shoot rise from the altar of Caesar. [Fleeing] from a god she found a greater god; after hating the son of Leto, she desires Zeus from the line of Aeneas. As for her root, she did not establish it in mother earth, but in stone. Not to give birth for Caesar, even for a rock, is impossible."[25]

In this lyric Caesar is clearly Augustus in his role of *Zeus Aineiadas*. Olson may have been aware of the rumor recorded in Suetonius that *Divus Augustus* was the homosexual lover of his uncle, Julius Caesar: "adoptionem avunculi stupro meritum."[26] That could account for the curiously anachronistic image Olson presents of the elder Caesar caressing the statue of his nephew. If it is true that Olson chose the "proper" names of Zeus and Augustus from the metonymic displacement of the statues in Hammond's castle, the mediation of sculpture—its transformation of the two ancient figures into stone—underlines at once their substantial identity and their frozen distance from each other.

"The Distances" is actually an ode to the Emersonian divinity Eros and a reversal of Melville's negative version of that divinity, "Amor Threatening."[27] Even the initial catachresis, "So the distances are Galatea," has its resonance in American literary history. In Theocritus' eleventh Idyll she is λευκὰ Γαλάτεια [white Galatea].[28] "White Galatea" is almost a pleonasm; for her name means "milky whiteness." If we stretch this etymological figure, in a manner that is sanctioned by Olson's dictionary rummaging, her name becomes the "proper noun" for "whiteness." Thus she is not only the white Parian marble that Pygmalion made and loved, but also "the whiteness . . . that above all things appalled" Melville's Ishmael, and even "the ruin of the blank that we see when we look at Nature," which Emerson insists, "is in our own eye."

The blank white distances which are Galatea confront the poet initially as the empty white page on which he must write his poem. In that act of writing, the "proper" bounded poem has to establish a range of visibility between the blank that is in our own eye and the blankness beyond the horizon of sight. This is the difficult task for love or CARE(itas).

These two limits of visibility repeat what Olson called "The Double" in his "Letter to Elaine Feinstein." In fact, the parenthetical formula "(out plus in)" reappears in a crucial axis around which "The Distances" pivots:

> out via nothing where messages
> are
>   or in, down La Cluny's steps to the old man sitting
> a god throned on torsoes,

The outer limit, or the "Muse," is language itself, while the inner domain, or the "Psyche," contains the sculpted vestiges of Titanomachia.

The work of CARE(itas) is to place the object of love within a negotiable distance, one in which the transmission of "heat" is possible. The ambiguous term "object" at the line break repeats the placement of the same term ten lines above: "a secret, the object/to undo distance?" In both instances the meaning shifts from the "object" as a thing to the "object" as a goal.

Blank Vision

THE OPTICAL vertigo of the opening catachresis extends to the dizzy sequence of pronouns that are inflected in the unraveling of the poem. The chain runs from "one" to "we," "you," and "I." The only stable references are to "he," "her," and "they," in the middle of the poem. The pronouns shape the poem. The "we" of the opening section are defined in the thirteenth line "—Pygmalions." Pygmalions are poets, and inventors, who have turned away in an erotic revulsion from the unexamined desires of the natural world and its genetic cycle. As such, Olson counts himself with Melville and Whitman.

He distances himself from the other Pygmalions, first by introducing the grizzly story of Karl Tanzer whom he associates with Polyphemus,[29] and then by bringing to the foreground the homoerotic components of the relationship he obliquely subsumes under the formula, "old Zeus —young Augustus."[30] The shift of the pronoun, "you," from the colloquial generalization ("You can teach the young nothing") to the specific address ("whose cheek do you stroke") reinforces the distancing. When the separation is complete, the poet can offer his prayer to the divinity of love, which in the final lines allows him to speak as the Orphic poet and to utter the Word of transformation:

> "I wake you,
> stone. Love this man."

In order to be granted the gift of the Word that can transform stone, the poet addresses a formal prayer to Love which catalogues the divine attributes as the power over topos/tropos/typos.

If "The Distances" was indeed born of a visit to the tower of Hammond's castle where the two statues occupy niches on different landings of the staircase, Olson troped that unstated topos into the thermal baths below the Cluny museum. Perhaps the confining space of the tower was a factor in exciting the uterine fantasy of the claustrophobic poet. In any case, he is clearly identifying with Melville at that moment of the poem's genesis. Hammond and his environment have no thematic place in the poem because Olson merely uses the visit to generate a prayer for himself, and perhaps for his young son. The "impossible distance" which separated him from his father threatens the psychic life of the son he has "created." Although the poem despairs of teaching the lesson of his experience to "the young," the experience, troped through the intricate allusions of poetic history, yields a poem that will give the title to his most widely distributed collection of non-Maximus lyrics. It may be the finest of his meditations on paternity as he prays for an awakening of yet another Charles Olson, one whose middle name, Peter, puns on stone.

9

Whoever Sees God Dies:
Cinematic Epiphanies

I become a transparent eyeball; I am nothing; I see all; the currents of the Universal Being circulate through me; I am part or particle of God.

—Emerson, Nature.

MOSES' UNGRANTED desire to see Yahweh in Exodus 33 has been a paradigm for the limits of the visible to several modernist writers and filmmakers. In this chapter, I shall contrast two American versions of that encounter with two European allegorizations of it. The passage is:

> And the Lord said to Moses: This word also, which thou has spoken, will I do. For thou hast found grace before me: and thee I have known by name.
> And he said: Shew me thy glory.
> He answered: I will shew thee all good, and I will proclaim in the name of the Lord before thee: And I will have mercy on whom I will: and I will be merciful to whom it shall please me.
> And again he said: Thou canst not see my face: for man shall not see me and live.
> And again he said: Behold there is a place with me, and thou shalt stand upon the rock.
> And when my glory shall pass, I will set thee in a hole of the rock, and protect thee with my right hand, till I pass.
> And I will take away my hand, and thou shalt see my back parts: but my face thou canst not see.

This sublime scene, the most powerful metaphor of vision in our tradition, describes the fatality and impossibility of seeing God of the Old Testament. Nothing in the Hellenic tradition matches it. Homer's gods were often dangerous when they manifested themselves before men, but the greatest heroes could penetrate their disguises and meet them face to face. Virgil further divested them of their perilous numen. At the end of the *Gospel of John,* when Jesus is first called "God"—by Thomas—he is not only seen with impunity, but his wounds are touched.

In a theoretical text written shortly before *Au moment voulu,* the eloquent "Literature and the Right to Death," Blanchot aligns Hegel's statement on the Life of the Spirit, from *The Phenomenology of the Spirit* (that it "endures Death" and "maintains itself in it") with the theory of literary language he has extracted from his reading of Mallarmé, Hölderlin, and Francis Ponge. Again, it is a biblical allusion that attracts my attention:

> Whoever sees God dies [Qui voit Dieu meurt.] In speech what dies is what gives life to speech; speech is the life of that death, it is "the life that endures death and maintains itself in it." What wonderful power. But something was there and is no longer there. Something has disappeared. How can I recover it, how can I turn around and look at what exists *before,* if all my power consists in making it into what can exist *after?* The language of literature is a search for this moment which precedes literature.[1]

Genesis, the starting point of our literary tradition, had begun in the dark. The first speech, the *Fiat lux,* does not occur until the third verse. The narrator of Genesis makes the emergence of light coincide with the initial mimesis of God's language, but he also finds words for that moment which preceded the possibility of sight. In Exodus, God speaks to Moses, but he denies him the sight of his Glory, which Blanchot interprets as the moment before language.

The acknowledgment of a sublime invisibility at the core of literary language links Blanchot's modernism to that of Mallarmé. Furthermore, the allusion to the denial of Moses' request to look upon God—contained in the citation of the divine warning "Whoever sees God dies"—can also be found in the poetry of Charles Olson and the cinema of Stan Brakhage and of Jean-Marie Straub and Danielle Huillet. In each of these cases, the refusal of apotheosis constitutes a paradigm for the problem of visibility in modernist art.

Against Hierarchies

WHEN CHARLES Olson lectured the students at Black Mountain College that "[reality] is unfinished business," he was reassuring himself of the continuity and urgency of the poetic tradition. He stressed the relationship between reality and narrative:

> The original & greater reality still governs the present & the stories of that reality have two *uses:* (1) to give men *motives* for their acts in respect to that reality (obviously, they have to acknowledge its existence, *first*) & (2) *directions* for the performance of their acts.[2]

In this lecture, "The Science of Mythology," from the series he called *The Chiasma,* he insists that repetition is the basis of continuity. While the philosophical tradition seeks to "explain" and thereby conclude an argument, the primitive and essential human impulse is to narrate. He underlined this point in the notes in his lectures: *"to tell about it, and to tell about it as others have told it,* is *one* act, simply, that the reality itself is one, now." *"Mythological,"* meaning *"what is said,"* comes to be "the one true word to cover reality."[3]

Literature, for Olson, unlike Blanchot, was a term to be avoided. In the isolated community at Black Mountain College, with sometimes less than ten students, he maintained an intellectual tyranny, vigorously opposed to the dominant literary taste of the 1950s. After the collapse of the college in 1956, Olson moved back to Gloucester, Massachusetts, where he lived a life almost as isolated, and, in fact, surrounded occasionally by many of the same people, until he accepted a professorship at SUNY/Buffalo in 1963. Throughout the 1950s and into the early 1960s, he explored a poetics and a poetry that would be the energetic equivalent of the impressive renewal of the avant-garde arts of painting, sculpture, dance, music, and film that was then taking place in the United States, and which would play a powerful role internationally during the next decade and a half. It is significant that, despite its tininess and poverty, Black Mountain attracted John Cage, Merce Cunningham, Willem De Kooning, Theodore Stamos, David Tudor, Lou Harrison, and Franz Kline to its faculty.

Clement Greenberg, who briefly taught art history there, wrote about Abstract Expressionist painting in a manner that reflects Olson's poetics:

The "all-over" may answer the feeling that all hierarchical distinctions have been, literally, exhausted and invalidated; that no area or order of experience is intrinsically superior, on any final scale of values, to any other area or order of experience. It may express a monist naturalism for which there are neither first nor last things, and which recognizes as the only ultimate distinction that between the immediate and the unimmediate.[4]

This passage from Greenberg concerns the rejection of representational space and the centerless use of the total surface of the canvas ("the 'all-over' " effect) in American avant-garde painting after the Second World War. Yet it also addresses the fear of hierarchies and the lust for immediacy which dominates Olson's poetics. In *The Maximum Poems,* "Maximus, at Tyre and Boston," Olson repeats his rejection of hierarchies:

> we who throw down hierarchy,
> who say the history of weeds
> is a history of man,
>
> do not fail to keep
> a sort of company: all
>
> is how the splendor is worn . . .

Olson's rejection of hierarchies and his insistence on the repetition of mythopoesis are typical late Romantic gestures aimed at shifting the center of poetic inspiration away from the persistence of solipsism.

Cognition and Vision

"MAXIMUS, TO Gloucester, Letter 19 (A Pastoral Letter [sic]" presents an arrogant version of the Exodus episode in an attack on conventional religion. I shall quote the whole poem:

> Maximus, to Gloucester, Letter 19 (A Pastoral
> Letter
>
> relating
> to the care of souls,
> it says)

He had smiled at us,
each time we were in town, inquired
how the baby was, had two cents
for the weather, wore
(besides his automobile)
good clothes.
                    And a pink face.

It was yesterday
it all came out. The gambit
(as he crossed the street,
after us): "I don't believe
I know your name." Given.
How do you do,
how do you do. And then:
"Pardon me, but
what church
do you belong to,
may I ask?"

And the whole street, the town, the cities, the nation
blinked, in the afternoon sun, at the gun
was held at them. And I wavered
in the thought.

I sd, you may, sir.
He sd, what, sir.
I sd, none,
sir.

And the light was back.

For I am no merchant.
Nor so young I need to take a stance
to a loaded
smile.

I have known the face
of God.
And turned away,
turned,
as He did,
his backside

2

And now it is noon
of a cloudy sunday.
And a bird sings
loudly

And my daughter, naked
on the porch, sings
as best she can, and loudly,
back

> She wears her own face
> as we do not,
> until we cease to wear
> the clouds
> of all confusion,
>
> of all confusers
> who wear the false face
> He never wore, Whose
> is terrible. Is
> perfection

This poem was written in May 1953, the year Olson first read Alfred North Whitehead's *Process and Reality,* which deeply influenced his thought and poetic diction. The mode of apprehension of "the face/ of God" may have shifted from "seeing" to "knowing" under the influence of that reading. In the chapter "God and the World," Olson had marked the sentence: "Conceptual experience can be infinite, but it belongs to the nature of physical experience that it is finite." Beside the word "infinite" he drew a line to his marginal note "GNA?" He also connected "finite" to "VID?" The question marks indicate that he was testing, as he often did, the usefulness of Whitehead's text as a confirmation of his own poetics. He thought that these two Indo-European roots would reveal the source of many poetic and epistemological problems.

From Indo-European *Gna, we get the words "know," "notion," "cognition," "gnosis," and "physiognomy," as well as Old Norse *kenna,* which means "to name" (especially, in poetic kenning), Latin *nota,* which is a sign or cipher, and *Narrare,* meaning "to relate." *Vid gives us Latin *videre,* "to see," and "vision," "view," and "evidence," among other sight words. Through the related Greek form comes "idea," "history," and "story."

In his 1956 booklet, *Proprioception,* he makes the following distinction:

> *Notional* (GNA—know it
> instantly
> "Carrying a full meaning of its own"
>
> The *other* knowing of NOUN, proper (proprius)
> noun—that which belongs to the self
> . . .
>
> VID—vision of
> Self: you I some other
> God[5]

The "face/ of God" can be known but not seen, for knowing is an instantaneous act of creation by naming, narrating, and writing down in signs, according to Olson's derivations.

The poet covertly alludes to the Sinai scene by way of Melville, whose work was the subject of his first book. In the chapter of *Moby Dick* devoted to "The Tail" of the whale, we find:

> Dissect him how I may, then, I but go skin deep; I know him not, and never will. But if I know not even the tail of this whale, how understand his head? much more, how comprehend his face, when face he has none? Thou shalt see my back parts, my tail, he seems to say, but my face shall not be seen. But I cannot completely make out his back parts; and hint what he will about his face, I say again he has no face.[6]

Olson's God is neither the Yahweh of Moses nor Melville's sublime nature, the destroyer. The poet, as Emerson's liberating god, tropes the Divine Presence. Olson's innovation of the Sinai scene puns on the meaning of "trope." In knowing the divine, he "turned away,/turned,/ as He did, his backside." In his lecture series, *The Chiasma,* he described the compulsion to tell which is at the center of all experience as "this tropism, I believe it must properly be called, that out of the organism of our life, our life turns to tale."[7] Olson's God is the terrible perfection against which the poet turns and enters time.

In Blanchot's version, the same scene is initially temporal. When he asks, "how can I turn around and look at what exists *before,*" he acknowledges that the desire for immediacy is visual precisely to the extent that the act of seeing, or retaining in sight, is a measurement of the abiding "now." In literary language, that "now" is always para-doxical, according to Blanchot.

The last six lines of the first part of "Letter 19" demonstrate the repetition and the troping which Olson takes to be the essence of my-thology. He reinvents the scene on Sinai to accommodate his severe treatment of the local minister. The second part of the poem offers the innocence of his baby daughter as a mediation for "the face/ of God." Her echoing song reflects a long tradition of religious poetry stemming from the Nineteenth Psalm. Still, there is a nagging solipsism in the poet's turning from "the face/ of God" which carries over into his read-ing of the child and her song. Not the naked girl herself, but what the poet would make of her, calls to mind William Carlos Williams' won-derful lyric "Danse Russe," in which we see the poet

> danced naked, grotesquely
> before my mirror
> waving my shirt round my head
> and singing softly to myself:
> "I am lonely, lonely.
> I was born to be lonely,
> I am best so!"[8]

In "Letter 19," as elsewhere in Olson's poems, it is difficult not to suspect that "the face/ of God" has not been mediated by the face of another poet. Perhaps it is Whitman chanting to the water, the sun, and to the future readers of "Crossing Brooklyn Ferry," "I watch you, face to face." When Olson declares, as he does in "Letter 19," that he be-longs to a church of one, he means he belongs to the congregation of American poets pastored by Emerson, Whitman, and as far as he is concerned, Williams and Pound as well.

Olson freely tropes upon Exodus because he does not find its nar-rative more sacred than the Greek texts with which he often works. Victor Bérard, whom he read in translation, was Olson's guide to the etymological and chartographical functions of ancient literature. In *Did Homer Live?* he suggested that the events of Genesis and Exodus may follow the same pattern of origin he believed he had discovered in Ho-mer's *Odyssey*. He wrote: "Each episode in the *Odyssey* could give us other instances: the explanation of proper names by means of an ad-venture, or rather the creation of an adventure to explain a proper name is one of the constant features of the Poem."[9] That declaration, which informs the crux of Olson's poetics, follows an analysis of the episode of the Sirens. Bérard maintains the eccentric thesis that Odysseus' adventures translate the Semitic place-names which the Phoenicians gave the navigational landmarks of the Mediterranean. He derives *Siren* from the Hebraic *sir* ("song, canticle") and the pan-Semitic *en* ("to fasten, to hold in, to bind by evil arts"). Bérard uses this etymology to account for both the bewitching fascination of the Sirens' song and the hero's protective "binding" to the mast of his ship.

He also makes the point that a related derivation of *en* in Semitic yields the word for "cloud" and that the same double meaning attaches to the Latin noun *fascia,* which means both "a bond" and "a cloud." Something similar occurs in the second part of "Letter 19." The "cloudy sunday" becomes "the clouds/ of all confusion." If Bérard's etymology actually operates in this poem, it points to a Homeric Moses, a Moses *polytropos,* who adventures perilously close to the God of Sinai but safely turns away to trope the encounter into a narrative.

The Elimination of All Fear Is in Sight

THE TABERNACLE encounter of Moses and Yahweh also motivates Brakhage's film *Blue Moses* (1962), an exercise in negative polemics directed against European "art films" of the early sixties (especially those of Bergman, Antonioni, and Resnais) and dialectically related to the achievement of Maya Deren in the forties. It may well have been Brakhage's belief—as it was that of Jonas Mekas in his *Village Voice* "Movie Journal" of the period—that the "art film's" discontinuities in narrative and in montage which were hailed as innovations by many American film critics at that time had been more radically explored by Maya Deren twenty years earlier.

The most obvious distinction of Blue Moses among the works of Brakhage's maturity is its sound track. Since 1957 less than ten of his more than one hundred films have had sound at all; this remains his only experiment in synchronous speech. He has argued that any sound distracts from the subtlety of the image and deforms the rhythms of the montage. Maya Deren, too, had held a modified version of this position, at least from 1943 until 1947, when she made her first four silent films. Furthermore, the making of *Blue Moses* coincided with the completion of his first, and most polemical, theoretical book, *Metaphors on Vision,* in which he maintained that one primary task of the film-maker was to spare his film from preconceived symbolism and especially from letting language guide and determine its sights. Like Baudelaire he proposed the child as the type of the artist, adding, in contradistinction to Baudelaire, that the infant's advantage was that he was prelinguistic. The opening paragraphs of his book *Metaphors on Vision* couples the negative power of language with the culture of the Book, especially the Christian *Logos:*

> Imagine an eye unruled by man-made laws of perspective, an eye unprejudiced by compositional logic, an eye which does not respond to the name of everything but which must know each object encountered in life through an adventure of perception. How many colors are there in a field of grass to the crawling baby unaware of "Green?" How many rainbows can light create for the untutored eye? How aware of variations in heat waves can that eye be? Imagine a world alive with incomprehensible objects and shimmering with an endless variety of movement and innumerable gradations of color. Imagine a world before "the beginning was the word."
>
> To see is to retain—to behold. Elimination of all fear is in sight—which must be aimed for. Once vision may have been given—that which seems inherent in the infant's eye, an eye which reflects the loss of innocence more eloquently than any other human feature, an eye which soon learns to classify sights, an eye which mirrors the movement of the individual toward death by its increasing inability to see.[10]

His singling out the color-word "green" for opprobrium should make us aware of the irony of the title *Blue Moses.* In the first place, the film is in black and white. The figurative and colloquial meanings of "blue" exemplify the filmmaker's suspicion of the power of language to move away from sensual immediacy by a linguistic principle of mythologizing the psyche and society. As a descriptive term, "blue" generalizes a variety of color phenomena, glossing over even such crude distinctions as between the sea and the sky; but as a figurative term, it comes to mean melancholy through the now faded concept "blue devils," suffering in hell-fire. Then, through other figurative leaps it suggests what is morally severe (as in "blue laws"), aristocratic ("blue blood"), gloomy, and speedy ("a blue streak"). Of all the color words in English it has the widest range of colloquial meanings. In Brakhage's title it is itself a figure for the power of figuration to generate meanings through catachresis. Within the verbal text of the film, the pronoun "you" holds a comparable position of inverse privilege. In his lectures at that period, Brakhage repeatedly spoke of "the hooker's 'you'" as the principle of engagement, through sex, mystery, or suspense, by which the attention of a member of the audience is seized; and as the film prolongs itself by withholding what he wants or fears to see, the visual texture of the film becomes irrelevant.

The English "you" syncretizes singular and plural, but more importantly for Brakhage, it both institutes a linguistic relationship of the self to all others, and forms the basis of religious reverence. At the time Brakhage made this film, he linked his cinematic enterprise, in conversations, to that of Wittgenstein's critique of metaphysics in *Philosophical Investigations*. After 1955 he had repudiated the use of actors in film as an error and a mark of cinema's historical thralldom to drama. In 1957 he enacted a personal drama himself, in *Flesh of Morning*. Since then, with minor exceptions in his prolific oeuvre, he has limited the human events in his films to what he *sees* in his daily life, occasionally ceding the camera to his wife or a companion for images of himself and, more rarely, working with found footage. Along with the rejection of acting, Brakhage would deny the aesthetic validity of any prestructured plot, of supports such as tripods and mounts which eliminate the bodily presence of the cameraman, and, most startlingly, as I have indicated, of sound.

Blue Moses grew out of the filmmaker's conversations on some of these issues with Robert Benson, who had acted in a few of his earliest films. In the resulting film Benson appears as both a prophet and an actor. Brakhage's Emersonianism is so radical that he identifies these two roles, finding them parallel forms of a failure of "self-reliance" which he would base upon what one sees for oneself. In this direction his thinking was reinforced by his dedicated reading of two reluctant Emersonians: Olson and Zukofsky. For instance, he admitted that he took Olson's *Proprioception* as his guide when in *Metaphors on Vision* he writes:

I would say I grew very quickly as a film artist once I got rid of drama as prime source of inspiration. I began to feel that all history, all life, all that I would have as material with which to work, would have to come from the inside of me out rather than as some form imposed from the outside in. I had the concept of everything radiating out of me, and that the more personal or egocentric I would become, the deeper I would reach and the more I could touch those universal concerns which would involve all man.

But one looks in vain in *Proprioception* for a passage closer to Brakhage's rhetoric than one finds in Emerson's early lecture "The American Scholar":

The poet, in utter solitude remembering his spontaneous thoughts and recording them, is found to have recorded that which men in crowded cities find true for them also. The orator distrusts at first the fitness of his frank confessions, his want of knowledge of the persons he addresses, until he finds that he is the complement of his hearers;—that they drink his words because he fulfills for them their own nature; the deeper he dives into the privatest, secretest presentiment, to his wonder he finds this is the most acceptable, most public, and universally true.[11]

Brakhage also invokes the doctrine of "Necessity," fundamental to the late Emerson of *The Conduct of Life,* as the controlling force in his artistic decisions, abjuring all considerations of the effect of a sequence or a film upon the audience. Any direct consideration of manipulating the emotions or expectations of the audience would evoke the condemnation of "the hooker's 'you.'" Thus the initial speech of the actor of *Blue Moses,* who couches a truth central to Brakhage's theory of cinema in the language of a merchant of fear is significant. He begins by assuring the audience: "Ladies and gentlemen . . . don't be afraid . . . we're not alone . . . there's a filmmaker in back of every scene . . . or was . . . once."

Footprints as Indices of Time

HE INTRODUCES the issue of fear at the very start with the negative imperative. In the course of the film, this prophet will work himself up over footprints he has found in the wilderness, alluding elliptically to a man and a woman who had seen them and wondered "What would anyone be running to . . . or from . . . here." The footprints are always called "tracks," a pun on the sound track, and more distantly a reference to the visual imprint of the cinematic image on the sensitive chemical emulsion.

In *Metaphors on Vision* the filmmaker had written, "The elimination of all fear is in sight." With his diction and his mode of exposition the melancholy Moses strives to induce fear by withholding insight, showing where the tracks had been ("They're hopelessly obscure now"), and continuing sentences across shot changes in which the actor's costumes, and even painted-on or stuck-on beards, change. He asks repeatedly, "Do you see what I mean by all this?"

The story of running footprints, which Brakhage has said comes from an uncanny experience he and his first wife once had while walking in the mountains near their Colorado home, could be a parody of the unresolved disappearance of a woman in the middle of Antonioni's *L'Avventura* or the ambiguous plot of Resnais' *L'Année derniere à Marienbad*. These spoofs, funny at the time of the film's release, cover-up an older and more crucial cinematic allusion: Maya Deren's earliest films had been models for Brakhage's first efforts at filmmaking, just as they had been for several filmmakers who preceded his 1952 debut. The first film she made on her own, *At Land* (1944), was a psychodrama in which she acted as well as directed and edited. Washed up by the sea in the opening, reverse-motion shots, she wanders through a number of landscapes, across a lively banquet table, flirts with a succession of men and caresses two women's heads; but the people she meets barely acknowledge her existence, if at all. The montage of the film uses shot–countershot to develop the mysterious subjectivity of the heroine. When the camera is turned upon her, the image is quite often composed so that the movement into and out of the frame in one place, say, the beach, can be matched to that in another, such as the banquet table, so that it appears that she moves from one space to the other in a single step or gesture. In the final moments of the film, after she had seized a chess piece from one of the women she caressed, we follow her running in a montage that retraces backwards the episodes of the film. To mark this regression the camera is almost always placed in a position that would have been the countershot of her glance earlier, e.g., if she had looked up at the tower before, now she is filmed from that tower. This inverse recapitulation dramatizes the nature of shot–countershot and explodes its fiction of the absence of the camera. In the final image of the film we see her running along the beach; the camera records her first footprints, then pans upward to see that she had run farther than would be possible in the time of the camera movement, leaving a line of tracks behind her. Of course, this effect was achieved easily by stopping the camera after the first steps and restarting it when she was far down the beach. That final image is a metaphor for the indexical nature of the filmic image, a trace on the photosensitive strip, which does not have to obey the laws of time as we conventionally experience it. It is, actually, another representation of the principle of the trick film and animation.

Deren had been the first theoretician of the American avant-garde cinema. *Blue Moses* was made two years after her death. Her last theoretical article "Cinematography: The Creative Use of Reality," which had appeared in *Daedalus* in 1960, contained a condemnation of the turn

Brakhage had taken away from her position with his coming to maturity as a filmmaker:

> While the [photographic] process permits some intrusion by the artist as a modifier of that image, the limits of its tolerance can be defined as that point at which the original reality becomes unrecognizable or is irrelevant (as when a red reflection in a pond is used for its shape and color only and without contextual concern for the water or the pond).
>
> In such cases the camera itself has been conceived of as the artist, with distorting lenses, multiple superimpositions, etc., used to simulate the creative action of the eye, the memory, etc. Such well-intentioned efforts to use the medium creatively, by forcibly inserting the creative act in the position it traditionally occupies in the visual arts, accomplish, instead, the destruction of the photographic image as reality.[12]

Blue Moses is as much a response to Deren as a parody of the fashionable European films of the early sixties. The changes of costume and scene and the film's circular structure recall *At Land,* as does the prophet's final cry: "The woman . . . his wife, so to speak . . . the tracks . . . THOSE DAMN TRAAACKS! . . . You see . . . You see . . . You SEEEE."

Deren accepted the conventionally manufactured camera and lenses ("attuned to Renaissance perspective" in Brakhage's deconstructive polemic) as tools by which reality automatically reproduces itself. But she insisted upon the priority of montage as a means of creating a uniquely cinematic time and space. Her theory tacitly assumed the centrality of the performer and of shot–countershot structures. In fact, most of her films feature dancers. In *Meshes of the Afternoon, At Land,* and *Ritual in Transfigured Time* shot–countershot dominates the montage.

By speaking into the camera, the actor of *Blue Moses* forecloses on the possibility of conventional shot–countershot. In doing this he is not breaking the narrative illusion, as Dovzhenko's acknowledgments of the viewer do; for the narrative illusion is never allowed to congeal in the first place. When that actor directs attention to something other than himself, the camera sweeps away from his as if obeying his commands, as in the wry proclamation, "You see . . . an eclipse," followed by a skyward pan from his extended arm, truncated, just as the sun comes into the frame, by an obvious splice mark introducing the substitution of black leader for the image, while the voice continues, "manufactured . . . but not yet patented . . . for your pleasure."

Cinema as Seeing

BRAKHAGE'S ALMOST total elimination of shot–countershot in his massive oeuvre results from his insistence that films be about the act of seeing with a camera. The real is what he can observe, or create, with his camera and the juxtaposition of shots. The startling ambition of Brakhage's cinema is to find fresh sights and "deal imagistically with —birth, sex, death, and the search for God." Shot–countershot, which always introduces a fictional mediator into the representation of the act of seeing, diverts the filmmaker from the direct encounter with a vision from which he constructs "the world." The few times that shot–countershot occurs in Brakhage's immense work, it is as if within inverted commas.

Thus, Brakhage follows Olson in his revision of the encounter of Moses and Yahweh. Once the actor steps out of his prophetic role, pulling off his false beard and admitting, "I'm an actor . . . this whole film is about us . . . you're my audience, my captive audience," aspects of the tabernacle scene before Mount Sinai begin to come to the fore.

As *Blue Moses* stands before the screen on which his Pirandellean confession is repeated, he bares *his own back parts* to the light of the interior projector, saying, "You . . . see . . . my back . . . But . . . If I could *really* turn myself around . . . there would be nothing but empty black space . . . and that glaring beam of illumination . . ." (as the camera moves in to a closeup of *his own hand* casting a shadow on the white screen).

For Brakhage, *the implicit countershot of every cinematic image would be the image of the filmmaker behind his camera.* Twice during the film, when the actor declares that "there is a filmmaker in back of every word I speak . . . in back of you, too, so to speak . . ." the camera pivots as if to catch a glimpse of the filmmaker. In the crucial scene of the baring of the back, the parody of Yahweh, we see the filmmaker's shadow on the interior screen as he comes in for the closeup of the hand. There is also an image in the film of another hand giving signals which can be taken as the filmmaker's. It is important to realize that any representation of the filmmaker would merely reduce him to the status of a character in the film. The problem is not one of mirroring the filmmaker or recording how he would look from the actor's perspective.

Instead, Brakhage insists that the cinematic image (as a mediation through the limited scope of the technical apparatus—a severe diminution of human eyesight— of the filmmaker's vision and of the object of his gaze) is immanently reflexive. It would follow in his thought that editing strategies such as shot–countershot, which disguise the presence of the camera, are regressive dramatic ploys for "hooking" the hypothetical viewer into the displaced, fictional subjectivity of invented characters—false prophets—and constitute a lapse of the "self-reliance" of the filmmaker as an artificer of images. One of the consequences of this immanence would be that the sublime, for Brakhage, is wholly naturalized and concretely visible, as it was for his major Romantic precursors, Wordsworth and Shelley, Emerson and Whitman. Furthermore, there is no place in Brakhage's theology of art for a divinity that is not immanent in sight. His doctrine of Necessity denies even the validity of a structure that would transcend a film and legislate its organization; that is why he writes of "the search for God" as a function of his cinema, knowing that only the tokens of the *search* can be visible.

Such an emphasis on the redemptive power of sight complicates or even contradicts the argument of this book. Furthermore, Olson's dramatic opening of "Letter 6" in *The Maximus Poems* ("Polis is/ eyes") confirms his place as well in the Emersonian tradition of extolling vision. It is important to keep in mind that within this American mode the modernist writer or filmmaker does not take the power or truth of sight for granted; it must be won again and again at great expense. The optical world that Brakhage creates is that of a second sight, after the exhausted names of things and failed gods have been blanked out.

The Anti-Sublime Landscape

IF WE look at a European work at this point, the Emersonian theology of Brakhage's project may stand out more clearly by contrast. The opening sequence of Jean-Marie Straub and Danielle Huillet's *Moses und Aron* is one of the most rigorous and systematic avoidances of shot–countershot in the history of the cinema. It introduces an extraordinarily ambitious film which, as a whole, strives to remain faithful to Schoenberg's unfinished opera of 1928–31. As such it is the most successful film yet made that adapts a major modernist source text to cinema. The entire text, as written by the composer, occurs on the screen, including the unscored third act. Straub and Huillet make this awkward, self-imposed ordeal all the more difficult for themselves by rigidly adhering to their doctrine of never dubbing sound. All of their films have direct sound; often featuring the stylistic peculiarity of an empty frame at the end of a shot while the filmic space reverberates with offscreen sounds.

The opera's first act, "The Calling of Moses," requires the *Sprechstimme* of the lone singer as Moses against an unseen chorus representing the voice of Yahweh. The film renders this act with a single nine-minute shot. For several long minutes it dwells on the back of Moses' head, with glimpses of his profile, then unexpectedly begins to pan, drifting upward and to the left, slowly revealing the ancient, weedy Roman amphitheater in which the actor stands, praying. Then it climbs to the tree-lined horizon, and after some three minutes of seemingly aimless panning, settles for another three minutes on two mountain peaks under a clouded sky. All this time the dialogue of Moses and the Godly voices continues with even modulation.

In a revealing interview with *Cahiers du Cinéma,* Straub claimed that the "theological" aspect of the opera, not its music, attracted him.[13] He also stresses the identity of the chorus of Israelites with the voice of God, literalizing the Roman adage "vox populi vox dei" with a vengeance. Pressing an improbable interpretation of Schoenberg's text, he and Huillet see the opera as an anti-Zionist polemic in which the Promised Land must remain an unreified utopia for a nomadic tribe. More central to my concerns in this book, however, they acknowledge the opposition of language (Moses) and image (Aron) which permeates the opera and the film. For the filmmakers this culminates in the episode of the Golden Calf, with deliberate allusion to the feast of the young bull in Eisenstein's *The Old and the New*.

The very opening of the film establishes the parameters of the dialectic of language and image, presence and absence, which the opera dramatizes. A careful look at the extended sequence-shot will bring us closer to the "theological" dimension of the film. In the four and a half minutes that we peer down on the back of Moses' head, the space around the shot is obscure. A parched bit of ground occupies the left of the frame, but it constitutes nothing more than a blank backdrop to the rhythmic bowing of the patriarch. Our attention fixes on the soundtrack. There, a chorus of voices announces the task set for the unwilling agent of Yahweh. He, in turn, invokes the Deity in the language of negative theology: "Unique . . . eternal . . . invisible . . ." and he protests that he is too old, too tongue-tied to effect the Divine Will. During this initial exchange the radical denial of visualization—the back of a singer's head seems even less than a blank screen—parallels the invisibility of the God, while the position of the camera denies the fascination with human presence that characterizes the opera stage.

The belated movement of the camera, drifting upward and more and more to the left (seeming at first to follow the line of Moses' gaze but soon leaving that path, unless we are to suppose that the now unseen prophet turns as the camera does) has been keyed to the mention of the "thornbush." Lacking the directorial intrusion of a dramatic fire, we can try to anchor that allusion to the passing weeds and parched shrubbery that the camera sweeps as it locates the scene in an amphitheater of the Roman Empire. Immediately, any hope of an illusion of geographical "authenticity" must be abandoned.

The site has been selected for its blatant anachronism. Both polemical and practical reasons have determined the choice. It is manifestly *other* than the state of Israel. On the other hand, clinging to their theoretically motivated refusal to use dubbed sound, Straub and Huillet set a prodigious discipline for themselves in making an opera film. The orchestra was prerecorded and the film shot in the open air at the amphitheater of Alba Fucense (all but the third act), which retains perfect acoustics. This and the spot's geographical isolation make an opera film possible.

The sight of the marble seats of the theater conflates notions of Imperial domination and cruelty with the archaic scenes of Exodus, but, at the same time, gauges the distance of ourselves as film viewers from both post-Augustan Rome and Israel's Egyptian captivity. This strange anachronism and displacement might also quickly recall a page of Exodus we had seen and heard read just before this shot began: the end of chapter 32, in which Moses commanded the massacre of three thousand Israelites for the apostasy of the Golden Calf, links the fierceness of the Old Testament to the excesses of the Roman emperors.

The passing glimpse of the marble theater seats is notable also for its brevity. Even though the oval shape of the ancient enclosure dictates the elliptical revolution of the camera, the filmmakers disguise that relationship by moving the camera past the visible portion of the theater on a diagonal, simultaneously upward and to the left. Furthermore, the site provides no views of objects in the far distance until the appearance of the mountain peaks, so that the nearness of the horizon prevents the viewer from anticipating the landscape contour that the panning motion will reveal. Looking up, from the pit of the amphitheater we see only the trees and, in an ambiguous distance, the clouds which fringe its horizon. Yet, since most of the time we do not have sight of the theater tiers to anchor our sense of presence in this open concavity, the panning movement is disorienting and dramatic. This heightens our sense of purposiveness in the movement, lending emphasis to the near correspondences between text and image.

Thus, at first the parched trees on the horizon seem to "represent" the thornbush of which the chorus chants. But the unhalting movement of the camera soon discredits that connection, or at least diminishes its importance. Then, as the framing moves above the trees and slowly sweeps around the blue sky, spotted with white cumulus clouds, and almost achieves, for an instant, a pure blue frame, the sky itself can be taken for the source of the Divine voice. But again the movement does not hesitate, the tree tops reappear, and the sky grows thick with rain clouds. After three minutes the panning at last halts on twin mountain peaks under a dark gray sky. The movement has gone on so long that we lose sense of the scope of the arc: it could be a complete circle, for we never saw above Moses' head in the long holding frame which began the sequence; the ominous shift of weather could have occurred during the take, or it could have been that clouds were above Moses from the beginning, with the camera movement suggesting, even constructing, a temporal sequence out of what was a spatial difference. One thing is certain: this image was the goal of the camera movement all along; the two-minute-long hold on it assures us of it. It even stays in frame for several seconds after first the chorus, then even the orchestral music fades away. This mountain under threat of a storm is a diminished version of the theophany on Sinai which begins at Exodus 19:16.

The flirtation with representation in this introductory shot of the landscape which dominates most of *Moses und Aron* sets the critical tone for the whole film. The parched grasses and trees around the amphitheater are *not* "a bush burn[ing] with fire . . . and not consumed"; the patch of blue sky is *not* "as it were a paved work of sapphire stone, and as it were the body of heaven in *his* clearness" (Exodus 24:10); the clouds are far from the cloud of "the glory of the Lord" which covered Sinai for six days (24:15, 16) and which Moses entered on the seventh; and finally, the mountain under a threat of rain is *not* a vision of "thunders and lightnings, and a thick cloud upon the mount" from which "the smoke thereof ascended as the smoke of a furnace" (Exodus 20:16, 18). The landscape apprehended in the tour of the ellipse resists sublimation; it is naturalized, and, concomitantly, the mediations of the camera and the tripod come to the fore, dehumanizing the panning motion. In fact, the gap between the mechanical recording of the horizon and the fiction of an encounter of patriarch and Divinity grows so great over these nine minutes that the viewer loses the ability to position Moses in relation to the mountain. The tour of the ellipse in a single sequence-shot inverts the work conventionally relegated to shot–countershot, radically humanizing the Godhead as it naturalizes the landscape (which is numenal in Exodus). The chain of substitutions not only undermines representation by preferring an oblique allusion to a theatrical evocation (e.g., dry vegetation for the burning bush), but also polemically denies the topolotry of Zionism by making an Italian (and virtually anonymous) peak stand in for the eponomous Sinai. It is precisely here that the concreteness of cinema opens a dimension Schoenberg never had to consider as long as he operated within the generic periphery of opera.

Landscape as the Epiphany of the Present

AN AMERICAN avant-garde film provides us with a useful example of a sequence shot with its meaning differently inflected. Bruce Baillie's one-shot film *All My Life* shares a few formal similarities to the opening of *Moses und Aron*. It is a color film with a musical soundtrack in which the camera scans a scene moving to the left and up into the sky; the images include natural vegetation and human artifacts of ambivalent status. On the other hand, there are no human figures in *All My Life,* and the sound was not recorded at the same time as the image.

It is a summer scene of an old, somewhat broken down, wooden fence, in an ill-manicured yard. As the camera pans along the fence, it encounters first a radiant bush of roses; then passing beyond it, in its consistently horizontal movement, it reveals an even fuller, richer rose bush entering from screen left just as the last glimpse of the first passes from screen right; a third and final bush marks the end of the horizontal panning. Two vertical posts seem to direct the camera movement skyward; it tilts up, passing two diagonal telephone or electric wires, until it frames a pure rectangle of blue which becomes the background for the following title:

All My Life
—Ella Fitzgerald
with Teddy Wilson
and his orchestra

Caspar, Summer 1966

This elegantly timed and ravishingly sensuous little film demonstrates Baillie's unique mastery of the limited spectrum of 16mm color film. The instant the film begins we know we are in the unsatisfying domain of 16mm color and, I believe, we subtly adjust our expectations. The grass in the foreground is oddly reddish as if the chemical tints in the film stock were faulty, and the glimpses of sky at the horizon are a feeble bluish white. It is against this initial transcription of "realistic" color that amateur filmmakers must use that Baillie's roses come to look so wondrously red and the final sky appears so sapphire. Even more miraculous is the strangeness of the panning movement, which always seems to maintain a fixed distance from the old fence, even though it is distinctly a pan, and not a tracking shot. In fact, the linearization of the landscape is so exquisitely controlled, unrolling the fence and its bushes as if a scroll, that I saw the film more than a hundred times and lectured on it dozens of times before someone revealed that the fence is, in fact, not straight at all, but pivots at 90 degree angles at the first bush!

One has only to consider the relationship of experience to filmmaking in order to appreciate the intensity of the cinematic imagination operating here. Obviously, the filmmaker must have first encountered this yard and its bushes as a three-dimensional whole in depth. He not only intuited the extraordinary suitability of the natural colors for his film stock, but recognized how the panning movement of the camera would recast the bidirectional fence as a purely horizontal sequence. His genius consisted in realizing that there must be a single point in which to plant his tripod so that the panning movement would seem to keep the fence equidistant at all its moments, while the first bush could camouflage the pivot.

The relationship of the image to the blues song shows comparable sensitivity and tact. The three bushes reflect the song's triadic structure. The first appearance of the roses corresponds to the entrance of Fitzgerald's voice, while the introductory notes suggest happily the association of the boards of the fence with the piano keyboard. Even the scratchy quality of the record matches the weathered look of the yard; both suggest the momentary sustaining of something that is waning or has passed.

Electric wires provide a fitting resolution to the panning movement. At first they seem intrusions on the pastoral scene. But Baillie capitalizes upon them. A first, thinner wire only becomes visible after we see the second rose bush, a glorious explosion of flowers. However, when the movement begins its vertical ascent a heavier wire appears, repeating and enriching the original just as the second bush extravagantly reduplicated the first. If it were not for the wires we would not be able to read the movement into the sky. A camera panning a field of pure color seems to be a camera at rest. Just as the last section of the heavier wire passes out of the lower right hand corner of the frame, the song ends. In fact, the timing is so accurate, with a touching moment of hesitation just before the final push, that I suspect Baillie was listening to the song as he was moving the camera. Finally, the diagonal movement of the dark wire gives the illusion of being the edge of a curtain, pulling down an even darker sheet of blue sky than the blue below it.

The ecstatic wholeness of this single sequence-shot calls to mind the tensions involved in the famous passage from Emerson's "Self-Reliance" cited in chapter 7. Even as Emerson exhorts us to be like the rose, his text lets us understand the impossibility of this ideal. Being human means being complexly temporal, absolutely expelled from the Eden of vegetative presence. Of course, the rose is a hyperbole of the immunity from history the self-reliant man must develop. Emerson continues:

> This should be plain enough. Yet see what strong intellects dare not yet hear God himself unless he speak the phraseology of I know not what David, Jeremiah, or Paul . . . If we live truly, we shall see truly.[14]

His argument contends with the influence of the past and of other men. Baillie's film, like all of his best work, remains under Brakhage's mighty influence. However, in denying both silence and montage in *All My Life,* he turns away from that influence only to create his most Brakhage-like epiphany of the "present moment." Fitzgerald's song describes a prolonged expectation culminating in erotic satisfaction: "All my life I've been waiting for you, my one and my true." The audio-visual marriage of the extended panning shot with the song has at least two effects: the music becomes environmental, as if a subject were hearing the record, with all its nostalgic evocations, as he scanned the fence and looked up to the sky; and, on another plane, the text of the song finds a new referent in the visual field, where "you" might address the weather, the composite epiphany of roses and sky; this unique apprehension of landscape then offers almost erotic satisfaction, and the slow, more-than-human gliding of the frame takes on the sensuality of an optical caress.

Just as Emerson's rhetoric acknowledges that the ideal of atemporal vision eludes human experience, Baillie's film incorporates a sense of its own temporal limitations. It may be said to translate the Emersonian moment into a schematism from Benjamin. The beauty of the landscape he offers us is that of a waning glory. Even electrical wires which provide the exquisite final touch to the sweep of the image gauge the imposition of a technological society on the scene of contemplation. The rotting fence might suggest to the viewer that this yard has not even survived until the time we are seeing the film, just as the very deterioration of the record of Ella Fitzgerald's voice underlines this pastness, so that there is something desperate in the prolonged quality of the sequence-shot, almost as if the imposition of editing, or of any shot change, would destroy what we are seeing for the last time. The song is made to declare that this moment of vision has been purchased by a lifetime of waiting.

All four interpretations of the Sinai dialogue are allegories of poetic calling. For Blanchot the scene in Exodus marks the temporal paradox of language's compulsion to narrate stories of sublime incomprehensibity, which generates the perpetual pursuit of literature. Olson rejects the sublime authority, which Blanchot makes the source of language, in order to tell his own Emersonian story of turning from religion to poetry. Brakhage follows Olson's antinomianism and even parodies Exodus as a false parable of the power of apotheosis. He repudiates the narrative model that invents a desiring Moses and a hidden Yahweh in favor of a cinema centered on the presence of the filmmaker/cameraman. Finally, Straub and Huillet take Moses and Aaron as figures for the image and sound division of cinema; their "Calling of Moses" entails an acceptance of the specific historical and geographical conditions under which a film can be made, where both image and sound are complex palimpsests in which vestiges of struggles for power are recorded. Finally, Baillie does not allude to the Sinai scene; yet in describing an arc and tilting movement quite similar to Straub's and Huillet's he abstracts the native American sublime, an Emersonian "circle" in which the eye, the horizon, and God are identities.

10

Theology vs. Psychoanalysis: Landow's Wit

IN YET another approach to the Sinai encounter, Blanchot returns to the subject after thirty-five years:

> The water in which Narcissus sees what he shouldn't is not a mirror, capable of producing a distinct and definite image. What he sees is the invisible in the visible—in the picture the undepicted [dans la figure l'infigurable], the unstable unknown of representation without presence, which reflects no model: he sees the nameless one whom only the name he does not have could hold at a distance . . . These are the words of Ovid on Narcissus that should be retained: *He perishes by his eyes* (by seeing himself as a god—which recalls: Whoever sees God dies). It is madness he sees and death.

Implicit in these observations is the identification of autobiography with encountering death. Blanchot would apply this model to all poets, not only autobiographers: "The poet is Narcissus to the extent that Narcissus is an anti-Narcissus: he who, turned away from himself—causing the detour of which he is the effect, dying of not re-cognizing himself—leaves the trace of what has not occurred."[1]

The avant-garde filmmakers of the sixties and seventies who attempted to make diachronic autobiographies focused on both their artistic incarnations as filmmakers and their mortality in images of self-alienation.[2] Jerome Hill, who organized his *Film Portrait* around a meditation before a mirror while shaving, used color negative, still photographs, home movies of his childhood, and his own original films, along with a verbal monologue to articulate his version of "the stable unknown of a representation without presence." Brakhage made the constitutive moment of his *Sincerity* (reel one) the occasion of his looking into the eyes of his grandmother and mother in still photographs and ended his film with a parallel false countershot, intercutting his gaze into the camera in 1973 with a similar clip from the outtakes of his first film, *Interim,* twenty years earlier.

It was Hollis Frampton, however, who identified the still photograph as the emblem of the unrecoverability of the past in his autobiographical (*nostaliga*). That unrecoverability registers on the soundtrack through two displacements: in the first place, through a Steinian ploy, Michael Snow reads Frampton's text to us as if his were the voice of the autobiographer; then more crucially, the narrative description and contextualization of each photograph refers to the one we are about to see, while the one previously described burns up on a hotplate. That is all we see: one photograph after another slowly turning to ash. We hear one more description than the images illustrate. Ironically, the final image receives the most dramatic buildup; it is the frightening picture that made him give up still photography. In the end, he directs us to look at the ambiguous, multiply blown-up image, asking "Do you see what I see?" But instead of the anticipated image we see only his monogram, by which he signs his films. Ultimately, Frampton's question challenges the assumptions of Brakhage's identification of the camera with the eye of the filmmaker, and the film with the trace of his visual experience (a notion that Brakhage himself had often implicitly challenged).

The elaborate punning and playing with the word "see" in George Landow's *Wide Angle Saxon* and the pun on the word "cited" in his subsequent film, *On the Marriage Broker Joke as Cited by Sigmund Freud in his Wit and Its Relation to the Unconscious or Can the Avant-Garde Artist by Wholed?,* are his responses to both Brakhage and Frampton. Earlier, as he was reaching his maturity as a filmmaker, he had proposed a correction to both Deren and Brakhage with *Remedial Reading Comprehension* where he represented himself running, as Deren did herself in *At Land,* but in an image that was merely a flattened, superimposed projection, as in *Blue Moses.* The text printed over it asserts, "This is a film about you . . . not about its maker." In the center of that film there is a parody of direct address montage. The voice-over says, "Suppose your name is Madge and you've just cooked some rice." Landow, a lover of puns, anagrams, and palindromes, may have chosen that name for the joke on the hypothetical viewer who would call himself or herself "I, Madge" or *image*. In any case, the voice-over suggests that the woman, the image, we next see on the screen must be the imaginary Madge, but she looks right into the camera, saying, "This rice is delicious, Madge" as she introduces a bogus advertisement. "Madge," thus, remains an imaginary, unseen image. Landow's film was not only a declaration of his (limited) independence from his avant-garde tradition, but a reaffirmation of the unbridgeable transcendance of the "maker,"and a rejection of the immanence of the artist in the filmic image.

Wit Work and Dream Work

SINCE 1969 when he released *Institutional Quality* and thereby found a place for his astonishing verbal wit in his cinema, Landow has produced a coherent body of aggressively original films and has asserted, through those films, a unique position in opposition to the very genre in which he works. That theoretical position has not always been immediately clear. In fact, each successive Landow film seems to illuminate the ambiguities of the previous work while engendering its own obscurities. If we assume that all of the films from *Institutional Quality* to *On The Marriage Broker Joke* (1980) address a single urgent problem, then that problem would be the relationship of the self to truth. Rather than "solving" the problem or defining its limits, Landow's films have dramatized the elusiveness of that truth, the instability of the self, the inadequacy of cinema to represent either self or truth, and the urgency of the need to do this very thing for which it is ill equipped, and to do nothing else. Landow cultivates the paradox. It is not surprising that his films are enthusiastically received even by those whom he attacks; for he instinctively locates the axis of truth at the point of maximal absurdity in his films.

Many of his most exciting films contain an elaborate network of allusions and quotations. Primary among the references are earlier Landow films. When he mocks and criticizes the dimensions of his own artistic aspiration, the filmmaker cautiously offers us sly hints about his earlier intensions and their pitfalls. The written notes he has occasionally provided for catalogues demonstrate the same reluctant generosity and guarded suspicion. As starting points of the interpretation of his work, they are quite useful.

Here is what he has written for the American Federation of Arts catalogue about *On the Marriage Broker Joke:*

213

John Milton (played by British actor Keith Anderson) recites his famous lines from "Comus," "How charming is divine philosophy . . . ," then is reincarnated as a modern Milquetoast of a poetaster (played by avant-garde filmmaker Morgan Fisher) who recites an ode to the sprocket hole. Thus the two poles of the film which follows, theology and film as static, flat medium with illusory movement and depth, are established. Two pandas, who exist only because of a textual error (the word "pander" was misread) run a shell game for the viewer in an environment with false perspectives. They posit the existence of various films and characters, one of which is interpreted by an academic exegete as containing religious symbolism. Finally, Sigmund Freud's own explanation is given by a sleeper awakened by an alarm clock.

I detect no direct references to any of his earlier films in this work. There is, nevertheless, a moment mocking a tendency that marks all of his films of the past two decades. One of the pandas, while explaining the structure of the film we are watching, admits that he does not know what version of the film is being projected. Landow has obsessively revised his films after their initial release. If, indeed, the two pandas are competing filmmakers, making different avant-garde films about marriage broker jokes, then we have yet to see the second film-within-the-film. Landow has said that this will be a cartoon called *Noneuhemeristic Henotheism*. The religious theories of Euhemerus entailed the assertion that gods are vestiges of human imagination. The only cartoons Landow has made in his public oeuvre appear in *The Film That Rises to the Surface of Clarified Butter*. They approximate the semblance of Tibetan deities.

The urge to revise a film which has already had a public life is coupled with the nearly compulsive announcement of series which seldom materialize. The most obvious examples would be the two films called *What's Wrong with This Picture?* and the two versions of *Institutional Quality*. *Thank You, Jesus, For the Eternal Present* was to be a series and the second part was released. But then *No Sir, Orison* was supposed to be the first of a number of films ending with that palindrome; *Wide Angle Saxon* was to have been the first of several works ending with the declaration, "Oh, it was a dream!"; but the subsequent parts never were made. There was even a series to be called *Baroque Slippages* of which the one part-in-progress may be lost. The need to revise and the fantasies of a series are indications of the underlying continuity of the films since *Institutional Quality*. The negative side of that continuity is the filmmaker's sense of the inadequacy of each individual work. Continuity and inadequacy are paired attributes of the artistic imagination as Landow's cinema has attempted to define it. In the remainder of this chapter I hope to tie together the scattered insights into that version of the artistic imagination. But a preliminary step must be an analysis of Landow's "theology."

This brings us to the very heart of *On the Marriage Broker Joke*. The film turns upon an opposition of Freudian analysis and Christian hermeneutics. Landow is fully aware that at the present moment in the history of the theory of interpretation the former mode has as much orthodox acceptance as the latter has the appearance of an antiquated absurdity. The character within the film who attempts a synthesis is the comical academic poet who reveals that the pandas we have been watching originated with the misunderstanding of the word "pander" from a marriage broker joke. Without committing himself—thus preserving his academic objectivity—he points out that one school of thought holds the marriage broker to be God, the suitor, or bridegroom Christ, and the prospective bride fallen mankind. This is as big a howler as the misinterpretation of the man distractedly watching the film on television who tells his wife that it is about "a broken marriage, a suitcase, and bribing a prospector." If humor reveals the structure of this film (one of the pandas defines a "structural film" as one that demonstrates where the points of stress are to be found) then the message of the film is chicly contemporary: the authority of the text does not hold; this, like all films, is a jumbled web of misinterpretations.

There is nothing in the film to disprove such a fashionable interpretation. Still, the theological references are naggingly persistent. In the opening shot we read the preface to Evelyn Underhill's *Mysticism,* just as at the end we read, and hear read to us, an ecstatic passage from the diary of Mrs. Jonathan Edwards. Landow has said that he found this passage in William James' *The Varieties of Religious Experience,* a classical study which Underhill mentions in the very page we see as the film opens. Add to these texts the quotation from Milton that Landow describes in his note. Finally there is a speech by one "Diminutive Dick" to the effect that the truth of Christianity cannot be diminished by the absurdities and atrocities committed in its name. One character who does not make it into the current version of the film, although he is mentioned, is the Swoony Devout. Presumably he would further illuminate and muddy the theological context.

None of the theological issues are presented without irony. We read Underhill as we watch and hear the orgasm of a beautiful woman. Mrs. Edwards competes for our attention with the superimposed image and voice of a woman who reacts to being awakened by her alarm clock with a recitation of Freud's interpretation of marriage broker jokes. The path is opened to the viewer to see the film as a somewhat obscure and certainly oblique affirmation of the psychological or psychoanalytical interpretation of religion.

The name of Diminutive Dick, as well as his hyperactive, nearly hysterical stance, encourages an analysis of his "faith" as the symptom of a sexual problem. Even John Milton quotes himself through a veil of irony in this film. He appears as a stage Puritan, calling to mind the sexual stereotype we are apt to associate with the uniform. The tone with which he incants the lines from Comus:

> How charming is divine Philosophy!
> Not harsh, and crabbed as dull fools suppose,
> But musical as is Apollo's lute . . . (ll. 476–78)

argues against the message he asserts; in this context it forbodes a "crabbed" and unmusical didacticism.

We cannot assume that Landow quotes these famous lines without sufficient knowledge of their source, the Masque *Comus*. The play was written for and performed by the Egerton family in 1634. The words were not sounded by a puritan gentleman, but by a nine-year-old boy, responding to the eloquence of his older brother, himself all of eleven, who had been extolling the supernatural power of their sister's (fifteen years old) chastity. The comedy grows hilarious when we imagine the older brother theologizing to the younger:

> But when lust
> By unchaste looks, loose gestures, and foul talk,
> But most by lewd and lavish act of sin,
> Lets in defilement to the inward parts,
> The soul grows clotted by contagion,
> Imbodies, and imbrutes, till she quite lose
> The divine property of her first being.[3]

After seven more lines depicting "carnal sensuality" the younger brother gushes forth his admiration of theology. The meticulous Milton chose the word "charming" to indicate the delusive, magical persuasiveness of the elder brother on a subject about which he knew as little as his listener.

Freud tells us, in a passage Landow's awakened woman quotes that "the wit work follows the dream work."[4] If we accept even this much of Freud's doctrine, we must conclude that rejection of the film as nothing but a joke (or rather, an "in" joke as Landow's detractors have called his films) is as superficial as the ironical conclusion of *Wide Angle Saxon:* "Oh, it was a dream!"

On the Marriage Broker Joke comments on the humor of *Wide Angle Saxon* when Freud speaks through the woman awakened from her dream: "We shall not err if we assume that all stories with logical facades really mean what they assert even if those assertions are deliberately or falsely motivated." This is the truth about *Wide Angle Saxon:* when it is most ridiculous, when it gets its biggest laughs, is when it is most in earnest. Two such points immediately stand out. Early in the film the dead-pan narrator tells us that the fat (wide angle) white Anglo-Saxon Everyman "hero" experienced a religious conversion while watching a boring "avant-garde film at the Walker Art Center." The detail of location detonates the laugh; for, in its insistence on a particular, it reminds the viewer of how far he is from having a similar experience as he watches this film in whatever place he sees it. It is a rare occasion when that place is not much like the Walker Art Center of Minneapolis. Perhaps an even surer laugh attends the earnest speech of the Christian rock musician when he naively assures us of the way in which Christ fulfilled the Old Testament's prophecies of the Messiah. Had Judas betrayed him for gold or for thirty-one pieces of silver "he would have been a phony." We laugh, I think, because this hyperbolically sincere musician unintentionally offers us the very word we have been grasping for to describe him, to label his argument, to ridicule the whole theological dimension of the film: *phony.*

Typological Interpretation

IN *WIDE Angle Saxon* this singer is the exemplar of typology, the figural mode of interpretation of which I found traces in the works of Bresson and Blanchot. It reads all of the events of the Old Testament as prefigurations of the *New.* In fact, it sees the entire history of the Hebrews as a form of writing, in historical time with real people, by God Himself. That history points toward the one authentic pivot of time, the Christ event. From it all meaning flows, according to typological interpretation. Thus, it is as radical and as elaborate as the hermeneutics of Freud which operate in the multiple "condensations" and "displacements" of repetitive imagery throughout the film, even though the name of Freud is not invoked.

When we look at *Wide Angle Saxon* and *On the Marriage Broker Joke* as part of a "series"—as two versions of "Oh, it was a dream!"—it becomes clear that the tension between theology and dream or wit analysis operates in both of them. Furthermore, the later film throws light on the hidden sexual thematics of the earlier. An important step in the preparation for the "hero's" conversion was the accidental meeting with an attractive young woman across the threshold of a store. The title which is superimposed over their passing tells us that he retained her image in his memory. This retention is crucial to Landow's Augustinian theory of imagination which I shall discuss later. At this point I wish to call attention to the fact that the woman never noticed the unattractive man. We see their passing twice: the same shot recurs, first conventionally; then, in solarized negative. The filmmaker pointedly avoids shot–countershot here where we should expect it. The only reverse angle in the whole film follows the screening which effects the hero's conversion. After we see *Regrettable Redding Condescension,* he shows us the wide angle Saxon clapping in the audience. Landow invented a pun in the superimposed title to describe the young woman's nescience: she does "nazi" him. In this film to "not see" is called a sin. In its most sinister form this blindness was the refusal of the Nazi movement to see the historical mission of the Jewish people. This deliberate refusal to see took the form of a genocidal removal of the Jews from the visible landscape.

A singer, presumably associated with the proponent of typology, croons, "How can I express the anguish of my soul when sin obscures my vision of You, my only Lord?" This is the point at which a hitherto unheard female voice orders the film rolled backward to the key word, "sin." The forward/backward movement of the filmstrip reflects the typological vision of time which moves either toward or away from the central point of the incarnation of Jesus. Landow makes us realize, at this point, that the normal progression of any film is a mere convention. It is, perhaps, even a trap to blind us to an authentic insight which is obscured by the linear movement of cinematic succession. Yet the filmmaker, in his capacity as an editor, is continually running his work-in-progress back and forth until it assumes the form that satisfies him.

The two palindromes printed on the screen at widely separated intervals reinforce the circularity of reading. Vera Dika has wittily observed that the central letter of each palindrome forms a word. From "A man, a plan, a canal: Panama!" only the "c" is not cancelled out. Likewise, from the name of the language "Malayalam" which the cook who parodies the theories of filmmaker, Peter Kubelka, speaks, we get a central "y." The hidden palindrome of the film, its secret motto, would then become yc/cy.[5] The question "Why see?" can be answered in this context only by a leap of faith, not by a logical argument or a biblical "proof." It demands assent, in response to the rhetorical "See why?"

Why See?

THE FILM which converted the wide angle Saxon, or rather the film during which he was converted through the condensations and displacements of his own memory, was *Regrettable Redding Condescension,* by the hypothetical Al Rucurts, whose name is a near-palindrome of "structural." This is one of Landow's several bitter jokes about my own article "Structural Film" which emphasized the formal similarities of his films of the 1960s to those of Hollis Frampton and others. *Regrettable Redding Condescension* is a close parody of Frampton's (*nostalgia*) which Landow attacks as a work of specious self-inflation, a piece of *fiat* art in which the filmmaker asserts his creativity by obscuring things in a repeated gesture which stands for a signature. Both (*nostalgia*) and the parody end with the unanswerable question, "Do you see what I see?"

Landow hilariously, and unfairly, mocks Frampton by suggesting that he subscribes to a severely self-limited form of the claim Stan Brakhage has often made—again with more openness than Landow's satire would admit—that cinema should attempt to reproduce as fully as it can the artist's vision. In *Wide Angle Saxon* seeing becomes a mode of interpreting the world which leads to salvation.

Both Frampton and Landow owe debts to the word play of Marcel Duchamp. Frampton, in fact, preceded Landow in claiming the palindrome as a filmic model. His abstract film *Palindrome* opens with the elegant late Latin example: *In girum imus nocte et consumimur igni.* A literal translation would be, "into the gyre we go at night and we are consumed by fire." It could be an allegory of death or a description of nightmares. If we translate *girum* as "spiral," keeping Duchamp's *Anémic cinéma* in mind, the palindrome becomes a description of erotic love.

The early Church recognized the magical quality of palindromes. Around the baptismal fount of Hagia Sophia in Constantinople one could read, clockwise and counterclockwise: [NIΨONANOMHMAMH-MONANOΨIN] "Wash your sins not only your face."

The explicit themes of *On the Marriage Broker Joke* suggest that a deeper, and certainly more contemporary, dilemma haunts the spiritual longings of *Wide Angle Saxon* than the one which the film makes much of. There the "hero" is moved by a passage in the Gospel of Matthew to sell his possessions and give the money to the poor. In a parody of

Kenneth Anger's film *Kustom Kar Kommandoes* we saw the wide angle Saxon lovingly polishing the grille of his Cadillac. The issue of Anger's fragment is not material possessions but sexuality. The young man who fetishistically caresses his hot rod with a giant powder puff is the "Dream Lover" of the song we hear on the sound track. Sex, not the idolatry of possessions, is the obstacle to salvation in Landow's theological scheme.

This opposition dominates the allusions of *On the Marriage Broker Joke as Cited by Sigmund Freud in his Wit and Its Relation to the Unconscious or Can the Avant-Garde Artist be Wholed?* Is there, then, a triple pun in the final two words of the grotesquely long title? Can the avant-garde filmmaker unite and make a holistic vision of sexual ecstasy and the mystical insight *Wide Angle Saxon* describes? Despite the superimpositions of Underhill's text over the face of the woman in sexual spasms and the fusion of Freud and Mrs. Edwards, which insures an erotic reading of the "constant flowing and reflowing of Christ's excellent love" in her journal passage, the answer seems to be "No." Yet the very formulation of the tension, the highlighting of the stress points, clarifies not only *Wide Angle Saxon* but even the earlier *Thank You, Jesus, for the Eternal Present,* in which the barely clad body of a woman, calling attention to an unseen car at a trade fair, conflicted with the Pentecostal prayers recited on the sound track.

Filmic superimposition does not constitute moral resolution or mystical union. What then is the status of cinema? This is a continual question in Landow's work. After the quotation from Milton, the filmmaker Morgan Fisher recits a Landow poem, a rhyming ode on the nativity of cinema and the naming of the sprocket hole. So the pun is quadrupled. The avant-garde artist can be sprocket-holed, for sure.

Visual and Verbal Illusions

IN THE "Conclusions" to James' lectures on *The Varieties of Religious Experience,* Landow would have read the following metaphor:

> Individuality is founded in feeling; and the recesses of feeling, the darker, blinder strata of character, are the only places in the world in which we catch real fact in the making, and directly perceive how events happen, how work is actually done. Compared with this world of living individualized feelings, the world of generalized objects which the intellect contemplates is without solidity or life. As in stereoscopic or kinetoscopic pictures seen outside the instrument, the third dimension, the movement, the vital element,

are not there. We get a beautiful picture of an express train supposed to be moving, but where in the picture, as I have heard a
friend say, is the energy or the fifty miles an hour?[6]

It would seem that by 1902 James was familiar with the first film of
the Lumière Brothers. The distinction between the filmstrip "seen outside the instrument" and the illusion of movement has been illustrated
many times in Landow's films. Here he repeats the sprocket-hole poem
examining the strip on which it is recorded. In doing this, not only does
he repeat gestures from his earlier films, but he parodies the works of
filmmakers Fisher and Paul Sharits, the latter known in part for his use
of filmstrip imagery, who makes an appearance in this masque as the
very fey Liveraccio.

Turning back to Landow's notes on the film, we find the fundamental opposition is not eros and salvation but theology and cinematic
illusionism. Freud and Milton are the avatars of meaning and interpretation while Fisher and Sharits are reduced to being skeptical artificers
of the medium. Of course, Landow finds his actors wherever he can,
and it would be wrong to overemphasize the emblematic presence of
the other filmmakers. The satiric energy which he focused on Frampton, Anger, and Kubelka in *Wide Angle Saxon* has no place in the later
film.

The dynamics of the cinematic imagination which Landow explored
in both versions of *Institutional Quality* and in *Remedial Reading Comprehension* are amplified in *On the Marriage Broker Joke*. Again, the filmmaker insists that the genealogy of new films can be traced to the condensations and displacements of earlier works. In *Wide Angle Saxon,* he
made a rhythmic structure by repeating outtakes of a newscaster before
the Panama Canal. This victim of what Freud called "the psychopa-
thology of everyday life" cannot tell the camera the names of the Pan-
amanian boss and figurehead without a memory lapse or a verbal error.
Yet from his recurring mistakes reecho the terms "nominal" and "real"
which recall a once vital debate in medieval philosophy of language (and
theology) which is central to the theme of the film.[7] In *On the Marriage
Broker Joke* the trichotomy of the suitor, the marriage broker, and the
prospective bride engenders a chain of misinterpretations and confusions
which give a rhythm to that film.

As in *Remedial Reading Comprehension,* an advertisement occupies the
center. Advertising is always a pernicious factor in a Landow film. Here
we see, in an extremely long static take, a Japanese advertising expert
arguing with unseen associates about how to package and promote
"Marriage Broker Brand Plums." The debate centers around the effects

upon consumer psychology of distinctions between large and small. It concludes with a bewildering concatenation of sizes in which the possibility of discrimination is obfuscated. This episode is remarkably like Polonius' speech to Hamlet's actors both in its folly and its very denial of the moral genre in which it occurs. After Hamlet's sarcastic comment on actors, Polonius babbles:

> HAMLET: Then came each actor on his ass, —
> POLONIUS: The best actors in the world, either for tragedy, comedy, history, pastoral, pastoral-comical, historical-pastoral, tragical-historical, tragical-comical-historical-pastoral, scene individable, or poem unlimited: Seneca cannot be too heavy, nor Plautus too light. For the law of writ, and the liberty, these are the only men. (act 2, scene 2)

Freud's marriage broker ("Schadchen") jokes all involve Jews. Landow has made them Japanese. His humor is quite subtle here. Where we expect to hear the conventional confusion of liquid sounds ("l" and "r") in the words "marriage broker" and in the excruciating Asian tongue twister "Marriage Broker Brand Plums," his Japanese actors pronounce English flawlessly. As the phrases are repeated ad nauseum their suave linguistic success becomes an increasingly funny running joke.

In 1972 Landow published a note on *Remedial Reading Comprehension* in which he drew significant conclusions from the falsity of the advertisement he inserted in that film, which affirms the superiority of pre-cooked rice over the whole grain despite the visual evidence on behalf of the latter. He wrote:

> Compare the two grains of rice—whole grain (brown) and processed (white). The white rice grain has lost its "essence" (the germ) just as the silhouette has lost its three dimensionality. One thing this suggests is the process of removing substance, which is done to food, art, environment, religion, etc. An art that becomes personal removes some of the substance to get a "purer" product.

One aspect of the removal of substance is the leveling of differences. Just as the different containers for Marriage Broker Brand Plums confuse real distinctions, the Japanese of the film have been thoroughly assimilated. They speak correct English and behave according to the pattern of Jewish jokes.

The behavior of language has always been a major aspect of Landow's cinema. One of his early 8mm works was entitled *Faulty Pronoun*

Reference, Comparison and Punctuation of the Restrictive or Non-Restrictive Element. In the subtitle of *New Improved Institutional Quality* we encounter the description of the conditions for an anaptyptic vowel: *In the Environment of Liquids and Nasals a Parasitic Vowel Sometimes Develops.* The connotation of the linguistic terms "liquids," "nasals," and "parasitic" suggests that the "environment" is the human body and the phenomenon is a form of virus. The linguistic description, and indeed the medical overtone, are analogies for the cinematic imagination in this film which mocks the notion of creative parthenogenesis. Landow suggests that films are not simply the imaginative assertions of their makers. Rather, like language and disease, they develop under their own predetermined conditions. The whole film is a repetition from a shifted perspective of the earlier *Institutional Quality.* Experienced viewers of Landow's films should know to be on guard when they read the advertising jargon "new improved . . ." At the end of that film, in the filmmaker's words, another Everyman wanders:

> through the images of the filmmaker's mind . . . in a trancelike state, and is carried along by some unseen force. This is an allusion to the "trance film" and the "triumph of the imagination" described in P. Adams Sitney's *Visionary Film.* At the end of the film the test taker is back at his desk, still following directions. His "escape" was only temporary, and thus not a true escape at all.

The images of the "filmmaker's mind" are comic incarnations of a static blinking woman from *Film in Which There Appear Edge Lettering, Dirt Particles, Sprocket Holes, etc.* and a man running, bearing the words, "This is a film about you," from *Remedial Reading Comprehension.*

The slogan "This is a film about you" is itself a paradox; for it first appeared superimposed over images of the filmmaker. It invites the viewer into the film. Yet, from *Wide Angle Saxon* we know that the affective response to avant-garde cinema is not predictable. Even the worst of films, films which condescendingly assert nothing but "I," can occasion a revelation of what in Christian theology is called the Great Condescension, the emptying out of God for the salvation of Man through the incarnation of Himself as Christ. Here Landow's theology comes into contact with his sense of the function of cinema. *Wide Angle Saxon* jeers at the reductiveness of all propaganda films essentially because they fail to understand the complexity of conversion. It recognizes that a Landow film has no more authority than any other in effecting its goal upon an individual viewer "at the Walker Art Center" on a given night. One of the things wrong with one of the films called *What's Wrong with*

This Picture? has nothing to do with the numerous "errors" of printing and solarization we see on the screen; it is wrong because it attempts to teach moral behavior. In Landow's terms didactic preaching is comedy.

You = Viewer

THE SUBTITLE of *New Improved Institutional Quality* is itself a test. The liquids "l" and "r" and the nasals of "m" and "n" create problems of pronunciation when they come into contact with one another. The crucial example must surely be the word "film." Often it is mispronounced "filum." So it turns out, in a devious way, this too is a "filum" about "u," a parasitic vowel which smuggles itself into the pure abstraction of spoken language.

In Landow's films, "you" means the viewer. The conventions of cinematic identification indicate that the viewer not be reminded of his condition. Landow insists on naming the viewer, just as he refuses the editing strategies that would engage the viewer with the fiction of the film. Shot–countershot is the most decisive of these strategies. I have noted how he avoids it in the crucial passing of the woman and the future convert in *Wide Angle Saxon*. In *On the Marriage Broker Joke* there are several offscreen voices addressing the characters we do see, but they never appear in the expected countershots. Even when he shows a young Japanese suitor surprising his prospective bride as she dances with the marriage broker, he quickly intercuts very short bursts of frames of the suitor and the dancers so that the montage is simultaneous, creating a virtual superimposition, rather than giving us a shot–countershot encounter. This is reserved for the moment when the poet's academic interpretation of the allegory suddenly cuts away to a family living room where the film seems to be playing on the television.

In both *Wide Angle Saxon* and *On the Marriage Broker Joke* shot–countershot marks a viewer's relationship to the image, rather than an exchange of glances between fictional characters, or the scopic relationship of one character to the things of the world. According to the evidence of these films, viewing is interpretation. At one extreme it may be either the parapraxis of a father reading a newspaper while half-attending to television, or the strained analysis of a professor; at the other, it is the "miraculous" conversion of an Everyman who follows a chain of associations triggered by a banal film.

In these films by George Landow the model of modernism I drew from Sidney Peterson's *Mr. Frenhofer and the Minotaur* crosses the one I drew from Mallarmé's "Sonnet allégorique de lui-même." When Landow has the Malayalam speaker say that the process of making one film is like cooking, he is not only having a joke on Kubelka's theoretical lectures; he is also acknowledging the synthetic dynamics of the combination of foreign elements in the work. Similarly, the film-imagining pandas in another film are trapped in an illusionary room that indirectly makes reference to the landscape of Henri Rousseau's *Dream,* which inspired the backdrop for another scene in the film. The obsessive references to *Comus,* "nominalism and realism," the Psalms, Rousseau, as well as the barrage of allusions to contemporary filmmakers are his cinematic versions of the "ptyx" of Mallarmé.

Insofar as Mallarmé's self-imposed discipline of rhyming in -ix helped him to generate the extraordinary liminal vision of the sonnet, we can see what was to become Peterson's use of form as the driving force for an aesthetic discovery, unanticipated in the intentional origin of the work, already in place in Mallarmé's poetics. However, in *Mr. Frenhofer and the Minotaur* the interaction of divergent elements is more clearly manifested.

Perhaps it is true that these two models continually cross over each other. Although *Au moment voulu* clearly follows through on Blanchot's early, and explicit, aspiration to write Mallarméan novels, with the phrase "nescio vos" being the ptyxlike moment that opens up the idea of the *récit* as an allegory of the parable form, it is just as true that its play of opening and closing doors, both confirming and reversing the parable of the foolish virgins, has Petersonian dimensions: they inscribe the reader in a labyrinth in which a castrating Judith lurks despite the uncertainty about who bears her name.

Olson's passing two classical statues in a castle in Gloucester, Massachusetts, ultimately brings him in "The Distances" to a vortex of allusions and conflicting iconographies—Melvillean and Alexandrian—as disorienting as his explicitly oneiric poem "The Librarian"; while Bergman's *Persona* embeds a psychological agon between two women in such a network of personal, and classical, allusions that the film becomes a Petersonian instrument for the filmmaker's discovery of tensions at the source of his impulse to make films.

The fragmented quotations, nagging allusions, and self-allegorizing forms that play such a large role in modernist literature and cinema repeatedly call into question the clarity and authority of sight. Yet their strength derives in part at least from the intensity with which they posit an Edenic moment of sight's authority, clarity, and finality.

225

Notes

Introduction

1. See James Bradbury and James McFarlane, eds., *Modernism: 1890–1930;* Eugene Lunn, *Marxism and Modernism;* Monique Chefdor, Ricardo Quinones, and Albert Wachtel, eds., *Modernism: Challenges and Perspectives;* and especially Gabriel Josipovici, "Modernism and Romanticism," in *The World and the Book.*

2. Noulet made two fine observations about the final tercet. "Le septuor," she pointed out, "is a musical term substituting for an astronomical one, 'le septemtrion.' " To this she added the insight that the seven stars, together with their reflection in the mirror, constitute fourteen points of light corresponding to the rhymes of a sonnet. Emilie Noulet, *Vingt poèmes de Stéphane Mallarmé*, p. 191.

3. Stéphane Mallarmé, *Correspondance 1862–1871*, pp. 278–79.

4. See Ellen Burt, "Mallarmé's 'Sonnet in yx' "; Emilie Noulet, *Vingt poèmes de Stéphane Mallarmé*; Michael Riffaterre, *The Semiotics of Poetry*; Frederick R. Karl, *Modern and Modernism*; and Octavio Paz, "Stéphane Mallarmé: Sonnet in 'ix.' " Paz gives the most attention to the historical condition of the sonnet form.

5. Mallarmé, *Correspondance*, p. 274.

6. Describing the Phoenix Ovid wrote: "unguibus et puro nidum sibi construit ore . . ." [with her talons and wide bill constructs her nest], *Metamorphoses* XV. 391 ff. "Unguibus" and "puro" correspond to "purs ongles" (1887 version), even more directly to "ongles au pur" (1868). The "lacrimis" of l. 393 might have influenced the change from "l'eau" to "pleurs" in the rewriting.

L. 403, "cum dedit huic aetas vires, onerique ferendo est" [when age gives her strength, and the burden can be borne], gives us the word and enclitic "onerique" which can be perversely misread as "onirique," a source for the "rêve" of the sonnet; and the winds (auras) of l. 406, "perque leves auras Hyperionis urbe potitus" [and through light breezes having reached Hyperion's city] might have rendered the false association of "aurum"—gold—as the dying "or" of the first tercet. In this case Mallarmé's sonnet is reborn from the dying and now confused echoes of Ovid's incantation, like the Phoenix which is their common emblem.

7. Sidney Peterson, *The Dark of the Screen*, p. 32. Ellipsis mine.

8. Honoré de Balzac, *Le chef-d'oeuvre inconnu*, pp. 414–15.

9. P. Adams Sitney, *Visionary Film*, p. 73.

10. Peterson, *The Dark of the Screen*, p. 104.

11. Picasso's "Minotauromachie" had been the focus of psychoanalytically informed essays which Peterson might have seen: Robert Melville's "Picasso in the Light of Chirico" in 1942 and Dr. Daniel E. Schneider's "The Painting of Pablo Picasso: A Psychoanalytic Study," in 1948.

12. The phrase is Peterson's, from a telephone interview, January 24, 1989.

13. Blanchot, *The Gaze of Orpheus*, p. 20.

1. The Instant of Love: Image and Title in Surrealist Cinema

1. Jean-Pierre Oudart, "La suture," and "Cinema and Suture"; Daniel Dayan, "The Tudor Code of Classical Cinema"; William Rothman, "Against the System of the Suture"; Stephen Heath, *Questions of Cinema*; Barry Salt, *Film Style and Technique*; David Bordwell, *Narration in the Fiction Film*; and Noël Carroll, *Mystifying Movies*.

2. Alfred Hitchcock, "Film Production," *Enclyclopaedia Britannica*, Chicago, 1968, 15:908.

3. V. I. Pudovkin, *Film Technique*, p. 168.

4. Hitchcock, p. 908.

5. Jean Epstein, "Pour une avant-garde nouvelle," in *Ecrits*, 1:148.

6. Robert Desnos. "Musique et sous-titres," in *Cinéma*, p. 98.

7. Robert Desnos, *Corps et biens*, pp. 33, 46.

8. Because the titles are puns they pose obvious translation problems. One literal rendering might be:

Baths of fat tea for beauty marks without too much Bengay.

The infant who feeds at the breast is an inhaler of hot flesh who does not like hothouse cauliflowers.

If I give you a penny, will you give me a pair of scissors?

One needs domestic mosquitoes (demi-stock) for the nitrogen cure on the Riviera.

Incest or family passion, with too much stroking.

Let's avoid the welts of Esquimos who have exquisite words.

Have you already put the marrow of the sword in the oven of your beloved?

Among our articles of lazy hardware, we recommend the faucet which doesn't stop dripping when no one hears it.

The candidate inhabits Javel and I had the spiral costume.

For a more elaborate, annotated translation, see Katrina Martin, "Marcel Duchamp's *Anémic cinéma*" pp. 53–60.

9. Mary Ann Caws, *The Surrealist Voice of Robert Desnos*.

10. "Robert Desnos's and Man Ray's Scenario for *L'Etoile de mer*," in Rudolf E. Kuenzli, ed. *Dada and Surrealist Film*, pp. 207–19. As Inez Hedges notes in her commentary on the manuscript, it represents a stage of collaboration Man Ray does not acknowledge in his autobiography, *Self Portrait*, pp. 276ff.

11. Inez Hedges, "Constellated Visions," pp. 103–4.

12. André Breton, *Nadja*, p. 152.

13. *Ibid.*, p. 18.

14. One collection of Desnos' poetry from this period is entitled *A la mystèrieuse*, another, *Les ténèbres*.

15. Robert Desnos, "Cinéma d'avant-garde," in *Cinéma*, p. 189.

16. *Les Cahiers du Mois* (Paris, 1925), no. 16/17, p. 85.

17. Jean Epstein, "Le Regard du verre," *Les Cahiers du Mois*, no. 16/17, p. 11.

18. Lionel Landry, "La Formation de la Sensibilité: Le rôle du 'sujet,' " pp. 36, 37.

2. Revolutionary Time: Image and Title in Soviet Cinema

1. Lev Kuleshov, *Kuleshov on Film*, p. 52.

2. Dziga Vertov, *Kino-Eye*, pp. 16–17.

3. Kuleshov, p. 53.

4. Sergei Eisenstein, *Film Form*, p. 11.

5. See Annette Michelson, "From Magician to Epistemologist," in Sitney, *The Essential Cinema*, pp. 95–111.

6. Boris Eikhenbaum, "Problems of Film Stylistics," pp. 14–15.

7. Vertov, p. 8.

8. Sergei Eisenstein, "On the Question of a Materialist Approach to Form," p. 19.

9. Jay Leyda, *Kino*, pp. 243–44.

10. Alexander Dovzhenko, *The Poet as Film-Maker*, p. 13.

11. Jean and Luda Schnitzer, *Alexandre Dovjenko*, p. 184.

12. Quoted in Vladimir Markov, *The Long Poems of V. Khlebnikov*, p. 58.

13. See Jurij Streidter, "The 'New Myth' of Revolution: A Study of May-akovsky's Early Poetry," for a discussion of the priority of Christian mythology in Soviet revolutionary literature.

14. Dovzhenko, p. 14.

15. Karl Marx, "*The Class Struggles in France*," p. 221.

16. See P. Adams Sitney, "Dovzhenko's Intellectual Montage," in *The Essential Cinema*, pp. 88–94.

17. Sergei Eisenstein, *Film Essays and a Lecture*, pp. 42–43.

18. Richard Stites, *Revolutionary Dreams*.

3. Moments of Revelation: Dreyer's Anachronistic Modernity

1. Carl Theodore Dreyer, *Dreyer in Double Reflection*, pp. 177, 167.

2. *Ibid.*, pp. 53–54.

3. Carl Theodore Dreyer, *Four Screen Plays*, p. 20, n. 2.

4. Carl Dreyer, *Jesus*, p. 252.

5. Dreyer, *Dreyer in Double Reflection*, p. 52.

6. *Ibid.*, p. 184.

7. *Ibid.*, p. 179.

8. *Ibid.*, p. 185.

9. David Bordwell's *The Films of Carl-Theodore Dreyer*, formalist in the extreme, does treat *Ordet* in great detail, also without acknowledgment of the film's theological import. His is, in fact, a massive effort to rescue Dreyer's oeuvre from its thematics and to locate the master as a modernist, in terms very different from those I have been elaborating. See also Philippe Parrain, *Dreyer: cadres et mouvements*; Mark Nash, *Dreyer*; Noel Burch and Jorge Dana, "Propositions."

10. Dreyer, *Four Screenplays*, p. 117.

11. "The sense of constriction about these characters—the sense that they are limited or condemned to the same views of themselves that we are given —produces a sense that it is they who are selecting these views, as if their spiritual energies are exhausted in the effort to find some perfect or complete view of themselves to offer and to retain." Stanley Cavell, *The World Viewed*, p. 206.

4. Cinematography vs. the Cinema: Bresson's Figures

1. Robert Bresson, *Notes on Cinematography*, p. 18. Hereafter cited as *Notes*; translation modified to follow Bresson's punctuation.

2. See n. 1, chapter 1.

3. Bresson, *Notes*, pp. 63, translation modified; p. 59.

4. P. Adams Sitney, "The Rhetoric of Robert Bresson," in *The Essential Cinema*, pp. 186–89.

5. I use the word, keeping in mind Bresson's dictum: "No psychology (of

the kind which discovers only what it can explain)." This is rather a case of what he indentified as "Expression through compression. To put into an image what a writer would spin out over ten pages." *Notes*, p. 47. In my reconsideration of this film I am guided by a reading of René Girard's *Deceit, Desire, and the Novel*.

6. Georges Bernanos, *Mouchette*, pp. 115, 123.

7. *Ibid.*, pp. 118–119, ellipsis and emphasis mine.

8. Bresson, *Notes*, p. 6, translation modified, my ellipsis.

9. *Notes*, p. 37, translation modified.

10. *Mouchette*, pp. 121–22.

11. George Lukács, *The Theory of the Novel*, pp. 74–75; ellipsis mine. I have corrected the apparent typographical error "understand" to "understands" to make the passage legible.

12. See David Bordwell, *Narration in the Fiction Film*. Bordwell argues perceptively that Bresson's inflection of "shot/reverse shot" is "well suited for the neutral transmission of story information" (p. 293). As often, so it would seem, he and I are interested in the same cinematic phenomena, but we are never more in disagreement than when he writes: "*Pickpocket's* stubborn resistance to interpretation, its preference for order over meaning, reappears in the final four segments" (p. 306). In general, his description of what he calls "Parametric Narration" corresponds to several of the issues in this book, although he takes a very different approach. Note, in this regard, his discussion of "The Problem of Modernism," p. 310.

13. Blanchot, *The Gaze of Orpheus*, pp. 71–72.

14. Fyodor Dostoevsky, *Crime and Punishment*, p. 465. Hereafter page references given parenthetically in text.

15. Bresson, *Notes*, p. 13.

5. The Récit and the Figure: Blanchot's *Au moment voulu*

1. Noel Burch, *The Theory of Film Practice*, pp. 150–51.

2. Maurice Blanchot, *The Space of Literature*, pp. 254, 257.

3. Maurice Blanchot, *The Gaze of Orpheus*, p. 42.

4. Blanchot, *The Space of Literature*, p. 260.

5. Blanchot, *Au moment voulu*, p. 7. I have provided literal translations of the passages from the tale for the purposes of this chapter. Readers of English should consult Lydia Davis' elegant translation for a literary version.

6. *Ibid.*, pp. 165–66.

7. Geoffrey Hartman, "Introduction," to Blanchot's *Death Sentence*, p. 380.

8. Blanchot, *Au moment voulu*, pp. 139–47. There is a hardly veiled invitation by the author to read the narrator as a version of Zarathustra. Compare the relationship of *Le Dernier Homme* to the fifth section of Zarathustra's "Vorrede." Ultimately the Zarathustrian hints in *Au moment voulu* are foils for a meditation on death and time that takes us far from *Also sprach Zarathustra*.

9. Maurice Blanchot, *The Siren's Song: Selected Essays*, p. 68.

10. *The Siren's Song*, p. 73.

11. Occurring twenty-five times in the text, the word "figure" tends to repeat itself in clusters; the narrator uses it four times in the first two paragraphs, five times in the last three. The initial use is within a cliché, "Mon Dieu! encore une figure de connaissance!" (My God! a familiar face!). Even in the first inscriptions of "figure" there is a hint of paradox and an ambiguity of reference between person and face. By the end of the *récit* the depletion of reference is complete: we read the phrase "pas de nom et pas de figure" twice (*Au moment voulu*, p. 161). These are the very words he used to describe the narrating "I" and the "It of sovereign Death" in his review of *L'Age d'homme*; in *La Part du feu*, p. 248. Near the end he poses the verbless question, "une figure?" twice, when asking himself what he meant to the glimmer ["lueur"] which leaves him free in his solitude.

12. Blanchot, *Au moment voulu*, p. 165.

13. Blanchot, *The Space of Literature*, pp. 79–80.

14. The Gallimard edition of *Au moment voulu* has 166 pp., with the text beginning on p. 7; *When the Time Comes* has 74 pages.

15. Blanchot, *Au moment voulu*, pp. 39 ff.

16. *Ibid.*, pp. 71, 79, 84, 86, two on 137.

17. As a whole Heine's poem "Ich grolle nicht" comes closer to the world of his friend and translator Gérard de Nerval and his *Aurélia* than to Hölderlin's. Nerval is a crucial figure for Blanchot. I believe the description of his guide in *Aurélia* ("mais celui qui m'accompagnait lui fit signe d'éloigner," Gérard de Nerval, *Oeuvres complètes*, 1:370) is the source of the odd title of the *récit, Celui qui ne m'accompagnait pas.*

18. Ovid uses a very similar image to describe the affectionate relationship of the terrible Scylla for the sea-nymph, Galatea. In *Metamorphoses* (XIII.736–38) Scylla, once a beautiful girl, loves to tell the nymphs, as she combs Galatea's hair, of how she rejected her suitors.

19. Friedrich Hölderlin, *Werke und Briefe*, 1:136, and *Poems and Fragments*, p. 375. Blanchot was familiar with the poem and with Heidegger's extensive commentary on it. See "La parole 'sacrée' de Hölderlin," which first appeared in *Critique* (1946), no. 7.

20. Blanchot, *La Part du feu*, pp. 120, 132.

21. Hölderlin, *Werke*, 1:136–37, *Poems and Fragments* pp. 375, 377. See also Martin Heidegger, *Erläuterungen zu Hölderlins Dichtung*, pp. 71–74, for his commentary on the "Stral des Vaters."

22. Frank Kermode, *The Genesis of Secrecy*, pp. 23, 27; ellipsis mine.

28. Friedrich Nietzsche, *Thus Spake Zarathustra*, "Voluntary Death," in *The Philosophy of Nietzsche*, pp. 76–77.

24. Blanchot, *The Writing of the Disaster*, p. 142.

25. See "Le Chant des Sirènes": Blanchot mistakenly calls Plato's fable [récit] in the *Gorgias* a story of the last Judgment. *The Gaze of Orpheus*, pp. 108–109.

26. Blanchot, *La Part du feu*, p. 248.

27. *Fear and Trembling* contains numerous linguistic turns which the reader

of *Au moment voulu* would be tempted to read as sources for the language of the *récit*: an expression of being "unspeakably happy" when we would expect anguish; the emphasis on the "infinite movement" of resignation as the first stage of faith; the responsibility of silence in order to dwell within a paradox; and even the repeated emphasis on problems of the appropriate moment "so that if ever the moment were to come, the moment which does not concern them finitely . . . if ever the moment were to come . . . they would be capable of beginning precisely at the point where they would have begun if originally they had been united." Søren Kierkegaard, *Fear and Trembling and Sickness Unto Death*, p. 56.

28. Blanchot, *The Siren's Song*, p. 124. The difference between Kafka and Kierkegaard, Blanchot suggests, reading the parable biographically, is that the Danish philosopher can give up Regine and gain access to the religious life thereby, while Kafka gives up the Promised Land when he breaks with Felice.

29. Blanchot, *The Siren's Song*, pp. 71–72.

30. Walter Benjamin, *Illuminations* pp. 93, 100; Harry Zohn's translation, slightly modified by me to reflect Klossowski's version in the French. Blanchot gives no concrete evidence of having read Benjamin in German. However the isolated lines "Ach, du warst in abgelebten Zeiten/ meine Schwester oder meine Frau" from Goethe's poem "Warum gabst du uns die tiefen Blicke" (An Charlotte von Stein, Weimar 14, April 1776) turn up in a remarkably similar context in both "Le Chant des Sirènes" and Benjamin's "Über einige Motive bein Baudelaire (*Zeitschriften Sozialforschung*, 1939, 8:1–2) where he wrote of them: "What prevents our delight in the beautiful from ever being satisfied in the image of the past . . . Insofar as art aims at the beautiful and, on however modest a scale, 'reproduces' it, it conjures it up (as Faust does Helen) out of the womb of time. This no longer happens in the case of technical reproduction. (The beautiful has no place in it.)" *Illuminations*, p. 187. Blanchot could also have seen "Der Erzähler" in *Orient* as early as 1939, or he might have had access to Pierre Klossowski's translation. Blanchot's isolated reference to the transforming power of technology, in "Le Chant des Sirènes," indicates that he accepted Benjamin's view on that issue.

6. Saying "Nothing": *Persona* as an Allegory of Psychoanalysis

1. I am deeply indebted to Dr. Leon Balter for his advice and encouragement in writing this chapter. Charles Edward Robins, whose knowledge of Bergman's work far exceeds mine, has also been generous in answering my questions.

2. Perhaps the first writer to point toward the allegory of psychoanalysis in *Persona* was the psychoanalyst Otto Kernberg, who, in his book *Borderline Conditions and Pathological Narcissism* (p. 246) noted that *Persona* "reproduces in essence the transference–countertransference situations that develop in the treatment of severely narcissistic patients." Richard Drake first brought this to my attention. Nick Browne may have been the first to note this in his essay "*Persona*

de Bergman: Dispositif/Inconscient/Spectateur," pp. 198–207. Several points in Browne's study coincide with my reading of the film. His emphasis, however, is on the film's relationship to the spectator.

3. Vilgot Sjöman, *L 136: Diary with Ingmar Bergman*, p. 190.

4. Stig Björkman, Torsten Manns, and Jonas Sima, *Bergman on Bergman: Interviews with Ingmar Bergman*, pp. 198–199.

5. Henry Edelheit, "Crucifixion Fantasies and Their Relation to the Primal Scene," p. 194.

6. Edelheit, "Crucifixion Fantasies," pp. 198–199.

7. Henry Edelheit, "Mythopoeiesis and the Primal Scene."

8. Dr. Balter has shared his work on the "play within a play" as a sign of reality testing with me. See Jacob Arlow's "The Revenge Motive in the Primal Scene" which contains an extended and masterful interpretation of Antonioni's *Blow Up*. In Arlow's "Fantasy, Memory, and Reality Testing," we find the background for Balter's observation on the play within a play. In this context, Bertram Lewin's "The Nature of Reality, the Meaning of Nothing, with an addendum on Concentration," provides an interesting hint for interpreting Elisabet Vogler's one word speech, "Nothing," as a declaration of castration anxiety.

9. See Otto Fenichel, "On the Psychology of Boredom," pp. 295–96: "Sounds like, say, a dripping tap or snoring put the child into a state of excitation or of anxiety and give it 'unpleasure from interruption.' When we discover excitations or fears of this kind we rightly think at once of experiences in the nature of a primal scene. But in making this interpretation we must not forget that excitement, anxiety, and restlessness can also correspond to those situations in which the child, having on one occasion experienced a primal scene, expects its repetition in vain."

10. See P. Adams Sitney, "Autobiography in the Avant-Garde Film," Sitney, ed. *The Avant-Garde Film*, pp.199–246.

7. The Sentiment of Doing Nothing: Stein's Autobiographies

1. Charles Feidelson Jr., *Symbolism and American Literature*, p. 43; Roy Harvey Pearce, *The Continuity of American Poetry*, p. 5; Carolyn Porter, *Seeing and Being: The Plight of the Particular Observer in Emerson, James, Adams, and Faulkner*, pp. 21–22.

2. Gertrude Stein, "Transatlantic Interview 1946," in *A Primer for the Gradual Understanding of Gertrude Stein*, pp. 31, and 26–27.

3. *Ibid.*, p. 18.

4. Ralph Waldo Emerson, *Selected Essays*, p. 153.

5. Emerson, "Self-Reliance," in *Selected Essays*, p. 157.

6. Gertrude Stein, *Writings and Lectures: 1909–1945*, p. 22. Page references hereafter given parenthetically in text.

7. Gertrude Stein, *The Autobiography of Alice B. Toklas*, p. 146.

8. Stéphane Mallarmé, *Oeuvres complètes*, p. 368.
9. Stein, *Writings and Lectures, 1909–1945*, pp. 213–14.
10. Stein, *Lectures in America*, p. 63.
11. Stein, *Everybody's Autobiography*, p. 303.
12. Emerson, *Selected Essays*, pp. 310–11.
13. Charles Chaplin, *My Autobiography*, pp. 306–7.
14. Stein, *A Primer*, pp. 29, 15.
15. Gertrude Stein, *Narration*, p. 57.

8. Out Via Nothing: Olson's Genealogy of the Proper Poem

1. Alfred North Whitehead, *Process and Reality: An Essay in Cosmology*. Olson used the 1929 Cambridge University Press edition, perhaps among others. Its pagination differs from the 1960 edition I have cited even when referring to Olson's annotations. The 1960 edition, by an extraordinary coincidence, prints the passage to which I most frequently refer as a "corrigenda" on p. 544 because it was deleted accidentally from p. 459.
2. Whitehead, *Process and Reality*, p. 44.
3. Olson, *The Human Universe*, p. 97.
4. *Ibid.*
5. Charles Olson, *Additional Prose*, p. 40.
6. Olson, *The Human Universe*, p. 98.
7. Olson, *Additional Prose*, p. 39; ellipsis mine.
8. In a telephone interview, March 1980, George Butterick informed me that Olson had never been legally married.
9. William Carlos Williams, *Collected Earlier Poems*, "The Yachts," p. 107; "Perpetuum Mobile: The City," p. 387.
10. Henry Edelheit, "Mythopoeisis and the Primal Scene," p. 231. I am deeply indebted to Dr. Leon Balter, a member of the psychoanalytic faculty of Albert Einstein Hospital, who discussed "The Librarian" with me and suggested the articles by Edelheit and Arlow in this and chapter 6.
11. Sigmund Freud, *Moses and Monotheism*, pp. 98–101.
12. Charles Olson, "Letter to Vincent Ferrini," *Origin* (Spring 1951), no. 1, p. 42; Geroge Butterick, *Guide*, p. 127.
13. Charles Olson, *Mythologos*, 1:169, 172–73.
14. Jacob A. Arlow, "The Only Child," p. 533.
15. *Ibid.* p. 518.
16. Harold Bloom, *Poetry and Repression*.
17. Walt Whitman, *Leaves of Grass: First (1855) Edition*, pp. 105–16. Olson wrote an academic paper, "Whitman and the Orient," in 1933. He appears to have had a knowledge of Whitman's texts which extended beyond the slightly annotated copy of the poet's final assemblage of *Leaves of Grass* which is part of his library in the Special Collections of the Library of the University of Connecticut.

18. Charles Olson, *In Adullam's Lair*, p. 6. The title and the allusion to 1 Samuel 22:1, in this initial chapter of the book which later became *Call Me Ishmael*, are further instances of the claustral fantasies which dominate "The Librarian."

19. Charles Olson, *Call Me Ishamel*, p. 82. See Sherman Paul, *Olson's Push: Origin, Black Mountain, and Recent American Poetry*, p. 259, n. 3. In this note, Paul usefully cites the passage I have quoted from *Call Me Ishmael*. I quote his note which predicts my reading of "The Distances": "he identifies with Melville's agony of paternity in a passage (82–85) which provides the best gloss of 'The Distances,' one of the great poems on this theme. Here the homoeroticism in respect to fathers calls up the treatment of Hawthorne and Melville in *Call Me Ishmael . . .*"

20. Butterick, *Guide*, p. 249. I am deeply indebted to Robert Kelly for an interview, Sept. 20, 1979, in which he gave me the details of Olson's acquaintance with Hammond and Martin, insofar as he knew of it. The statues are a nineteenth century copy of a Roman bust of Augustus (Hammond Museum 396) and a Greek head (H. M. 399).

21. Paul Christensen, *Charles Olson: Call Him Ishmael*, p. 115.

22. The first and fourth lines of Olson's poem are actually variations on the twelfth stanza of "Crossing Brooklyn Ferry": Whatever it is, it avails not— distance avails not, and/ place avails not." "Crossing Brooklyn Ferry" seems to have been a particularly important poem for Olson. Boer vividly describes him reading it aloud to a seminar at SUNY/Buffalo. Boer, *Olson in Connecticut*, pp. 61–62. Curiously, echoes of its repetitious "avails not" recur in the poem which first attracted Olson to Robert Duncan's verse, "The Years as Catches." In an interview from 1966 Olson associates "Crossing Brooklyn Ferry" with Melville. Olson, *Mythologos*, 1:49.

23. Herman Melville, *Moby Dick*, p. 174.

24. See Olson, *Mythologos*, 1:133 for further remarks on the opposition of love to power.

25. *Anthologie Grecque: Anthologie Palatine*, 7:123. The epigram is no. 307 in bk. 9. See *Olson* (Spring 1978), no. 9, p. 29, for "from the Greek PALATINE ANTHOLOGY."

26. Suetonius, *De Vita Caesarum Libri*, p. 85; *Divus Augustus*, Cap. 68: ". . . he won adoption by his uncle through perversion."

27. See "After the Pleasure Party," in Herman Melville, *Selected Poems of Herman Melville*, pp. 132–36.

28. *Bucolici Graeci*, p. 44. See Olson, *The Human Universe*, pp. 145–48, for a discussion of Theocritus.

29. I understand the phrase "The girl who makes you weep," to be a reference to the mournful Polyphemus of Theocritus' "Idyll XI." For another aspect of Polyphemus, see *Olson*, no. 10, p. 70.

30. The phrase "the poet slept within the statue" from Robert Duncan's "The Venice Poem" (*The First Decade*, p. 98) may be a source for the conclusion of "The Distances."

9. Whoever Sees God Dies: Cinematic Epiphanies

1. Maurice Blanchot, *The Gaze of Orpheus*, pp. 45–46. See my "Afterword" for an analysis of this essay.
2. Charles Olson, "The Chiasma," p. 64.
3. *Ibid.*, pp. 64, 65.
4. Clement Greenberg, *Art and Culture*, p. 157.
5. Charles Olson, *Additional Prose*, p. 21.
6. Herman Melville, *Moby Dick*, p. 356.
7. Olson, "The Chiasma," p. 65.
8. William Carlos Williams, *The Collected Earlier Poems*, p. 148.
9. Victor Bérard, *Did Homer Live?* p. 203.
10. Stan Brakhage, *Metaphors on Vision*, reprinted in Sitney, ed., *The Avant-Garde Film: A Reader of Theory and Criticism*, p. 120.
11. Ralph Waldo Emerson, "The American Scholar," in *Selected Essays*, p. 97.
12. Maya Deren, "Cinematography: The Creative Use of Reality," p. 68.
13. Jacques Bontemps, Pascal Bonitzer, Serge Daney, "Conversation avec J.-M. Straub et Danielle Huillet," p. 6.
14. Emerson, "Self-Reliance," *Selected Essays*, p. 189.

10. Theology vs. Psychoanalysis: Landow's Wit

1. Maurice Blanchot, *The Writing of the Disaster*, pp. 134–35.
2. See P. Adams Sitney, "Autobiography in Avant-Garde Film," in Sitney, ed., *The Avant-Garde Film*, pp. 199–246.
3. John Milton, *The Complete Poems of John Milton*, "A Mask," p. 137, pp. 463–69.
4. Sigmund Freud, *The Basic Writings of Sigmund Freud*, p. 701.
5. See Vera Dika, *Wide Angle Saxon*: An Examination of the Film Viewer as Reader."
6. William James, *The Varieties of Religious Experience*, pp. 501–2.
7. The eleventh-century debate between Realists and Nominalists concerned the status of universals, e.g., The Good, Justice. The Realists maintained they were existing entities while the Nominalists considered them empty signs. Landow's affinity for oddly displaced names and images, coupled with the theological gestures of his recent films, makes this archaic quarrel relevant to his work. Nevertheless, his closest ties seem to be to St. Augustine, an even earlier philosopher and theologian. I doubt that Landow has studied his treatise *De Musica*. Still, one finds a theory of memory and imagination articulated in ch. 12, par. 35 ff., which is curiously close to the operations of *Wide Angle Saxon*, *New Improved Institutional Quality*, and *On the Marriage Broker Joke*. Similar connections could be made to the theory of language in *De Magistro* and the function of memory in book 11, ch. 28, of *The Confessions*.

Bibliography

Amengual, Barthelemy. *Que viva Eisenstein,* Lausanne. Age d'homme, 1980.

Anthologie Grecque: Anthologie Palatine. 8 Vols. Pierre Waltz, ed.; Guy Soury, trans. Paris: L'Association Guillaume Budé, Societé d'edition "Les belles lettres," 1957.

Arlow, Jacob. "The Only Child." *Psychoanalytic Quarterly,* (1972), 41:507–536.

Arlow, Jacob. "Fantasy, Memory, and Reality Testing." *Psychoanalytic Quarterly* (1969), 38:28–51.

Arlow, Jacob. "The Revenge Motive in the Primal Scene." *Journal of American Psychoanalytical Association* (1980), 28(3):519–541.

Arthur, Paul. "The Calisthenics of Vision: Open Instructions on the Films of George Landow." *Artforum,* (September 1971), 10(1):74–79.

Ashton, Dore. *A Fable of Modern Art.* New York: Thames and Hudson, 1980.

Balzac, Honoré de. "Le chef-d'oeuvre inconnu." In *La Comédie Humaine IX, études philosophiques 1.* Marcel Bouteron, ed., Bibliothèque de la Pléiade. Paris: Gallimard, 1950. pp. 389–414.

Benjamin, Walter. *Illuminations.* Hannah Arendt, ed., intro.; Harry Zohn, trans. New York: Schocken, 1968.

Bérard, Victor. *Did Homer Live?* Brian Rhys, trans. London: J. M. Dent, 1931.

Bernanos, Georges. *Mouchette.* J. C. Whithouse, trans. New York: Holt, Rinehart, and Winston, 1966.

Bjökman, Stig, Torsten Manns, and Jonas Sima. *Bergman on Bergman: Interviews with Ingmar Bergman.* Paul Britten Austin, trans. New York: Simon and Schuster, 1973.

239

Blackwell, Marilyn Johns. *Persona: The Transcendent Image*. Urbana: Univ. of Illinois Press, 1986.

Blanchot, Maurice. *Au moment voulu*. Paris: Gallimard, 1951.

Blanchot, Maurice. *L'Ecriture du désastre*. Paris: Gallimard, 1980.

Blanchot, Maurice. *La Part du feu*. Paris:Gallimard, 1948.

Blanchot, Maurice. *The Gaze of Orpheus*. P. Adams Sitney, ed. and afterword, Lydia Davis, trans., Geoffrey Hartman, preface. Barrytown: Station Hill, 1981.

Blanchot, Maurice. *The Siren's Song: Selected Essays*. Gabriel Josipovici, intro. and ed.; Sacha Rabinovitch, trans. Bloomington: Indiana Univ. Press, 1982.

Blanchot, Maurice. *The Space of Literature*. Ann Smock, trans. and intro. Lincoln: Univ. of Nebraska Press, 1982.

Blanchot, Maurice. *The Writing of the Disaster*. Ann Smock, trans. Lincoln: Univ. of Nebraska Press, 1986.

Blanchot, Maurice. *When the Time Comes*. Lydia Davis, trans. Barrytown: Station Hill, 1985.

Bloom, Harold. *Agon: Towards a Theory of Revisionism*. New York: Oxford Univ. Press, 1982.

Bloom, Harold. *Poetry and Repression: Revisionism from Blake to Stevens*. New Haven: Yale Univ. Press, 1976.

Bloom, Harold, ed. *Gertrude Stein*. Modern Critical Views. New York: Chelsea House, 1986.

Boer, Charles. *Olson in Connecticut*. Iowa City: Windhover, 1974.

Bontemps, Jacques, Pascal Bonitzer, Serge Daney. "Conversation avec J.-M. Straub et Danielle Huillet." *Cahiers du Cinéma* (Juillet-Août 1975), 258–59: 5–26.

Bordwell, David. *Narration in the Fiction Film*. Madison: Univ. of Wisconsin Press, 1985.

Bordwell, David. *The Films of Carl-Theodore Dreyer*. Berkeley: Univ. of California Press, 1981.

Bové, Paul A. *Destructive Poetics: Heidegger and Modern American Poetry*. New York: Columbia Univ. Press, 1980.

Bradbury, Malcolm and James McFarlane, eds. *Modernism: 1890–1930*. Middlesex: Penguin, 1974.

Brakhage, Stan. *Metaphors on Vision*. P. Adams Sitney, ed. *Film Culture* 30. New York, 1963. Pages unnumbered.

Bresson, Robert. *Notes on Cinematography*. Jonathan Griffith, trans. New York: Urizen, 1977.

Breton, André. *Nadja*. Richard Howard, trans. New York: Grove, 1960.

Bridgman, Richard. *Gertrude Stein in Pieces*. New York: Oxford Univ. Press, 1971.

Browne, Nick. "*Persona* de Bergman: dispositif/ inconscient/ spectateur." In *Cinémas de la modernité: films théories*. Dominique Chateau et al, eds., pp. 199–207. Paris: Colloque de Cerisy.

Bucolici Graeci. A. S. F. Gow, ed. Scriptorum Classicorum Bibliotheca Oxoniensis. Oxford: Oxford Univ. Press, 1952.

Burch, Noel. *The Theory of Film Practice*. Helen R. Lane, trans. New York: Praeger, 1973.

Burch, Noel and Jorge Dana. "Propositions." *Afterimage* (Spring 1975), no. 5, pp. 57–64.

Burt, Ellen. "Mallarmé's 'Sonnet in yx': The Ambiguities of Speculation." *Yale French Studies* (1977), no. 54, pp. 55–82.

Butterick, George. *A Guide to the Maximus Poems of Charles Olson*. Berkeley: Univ. of California Press, 1978.

Byrd, Don. *Charles Olson's Maximus*. Urbana: Univ. of Illinois Press, 1980.

Carney, Raymond. *Speaking the Language of Desire: The Films of Carl Dreyer*. Cambridge: Cambridge Univ. Press, 1989.

Carroll, Noël. *Mystifying Movies: Fads and Fallacies in Contemporary Film Theory*. New York: Columbia Univ. Press, 1988.

Carroll, Noël. "For God and Country." *Artforum* (January 1973), 11(5):56–60.

Cavell, Stanley. *The World Viewed: Reflections on the Ontology of Film*. Enlarged Edition, Cambridge: Harvard Univ. Press, 1981.

Caws, Mary Ann. *The Surrealist Voice of Robert Desnos*. Amherst: Univ. of Massachusetts Press, 1977.

Chaplin, Charles. *My Autobiography*. New York: Simon and Schuster, 1964.

Chateau, Dominique, André Gardies, Françoise Jost, eds. *Cinémas de la modernité: films théories*. Paris: Colloque de Cerisy, 1981.

Chefdor, Monique, Ricardo Quinones, and Albert Wachtel, eds. *Modernism: Challenges and Perspectives*. Urbana: Univ. of Illinois Press, 1986.

Christensen, Paul. *Charles Olson: Call Him Ishmael*. Austin: Univ. of Texas Press, 1979.

Cohen, Phoebe. "*Scenes from Under Childhood.*" *Artforum* (January 1973), 11(5): 51–55.

Colin, Françoise. *Maurice Blanchot et le question de l'écriture*. Paris: Gallimard, 1971.

Crofts, Stephen and Olivia Rose. "An Essay towards *A Man With a Movie Camera*." *Screen* (Spring 1977), 18(1):9–58.

Dayan Daniel. "The Tudor Code of Classical Cinema." *Film Quarterly* (Fall 1974), 10(10):22–31.

Deren, Maya. "Cinematography: The Creative Use of Reality." In *The Avant Garde Film*, pp. 60–73. P. Adams Sitney, ed.

Derrida, Jacques. *Parages*. Paris: Galilée, 1986.

Desnos, Robert. *Cinéma*. André Tchernia, ed. Paris: Gallimard, 1966.

Desnos, Robert. *Corps et biens*. Collection Poésie. Paris: Gallimard, 1966.

Dika, Vera. "*Wide Angle Saxon:* An Examination of the Film Viewer as Reader," *Film Reader* (February 1978), 3:222–38.

Dostoevsky, Fyodor. *Crime and Punishment*. Constance Garnett, trans. New York: Random House, 1958.

Dovzhenko, Alexander. *The Poet as Film-Maker: Selected Writings*. Marco Carynnyk, ed. and trans. Cambridge: M. I. T. Press, 1973.

Dreyer, Carl Theodore. *Dreyer in Double Reflection*. Donald Skoller, ed., trans. unspecified. New York: Dutton, 1973.

Dreyer, Carl Theodore. *Four Screen Plays*. Ole Storm, intro. Oliver Stallybrass, trans. London: Thames and Hudson, 1964.

Dreyer, Carl Theodore. *Jesus*. New York: Dial, 1972.

Duncan, Robert. *The First Decade*. London: Fulcrum, 1968.

Edelheit, Henry, "Crucifixion Fantasies and Their Relation to the Primal Scene," *International Journal of Psycho-analysis* (1974), 55(2):193–199.

Edelheit, Henry. "Mythopoiesis and the Primal Scene." *Psychoanalytic Study of Society* (1972), 5:212–233.

Eikenbaum, Boris. "Problems of Film Stylistics." Thomas Aman, trans. *Screen* (Autumn 1974), 15(3):7–34.

Eisenstein, Sergei. *Film Essays and a Lecture*. Jay Leyda, ed. and trans. Princeton: Princeton Univ. Press, 1981.

Eisenstein, Sergei. *Film Form*. Jay Leyda, ed. and trans. New York: Harcourt Brace, 1949.

Eisenstein, Sergei. "On the Question of a Materialist Approach to Form." In *The Avant-Garde Film,* pp. 15–21. Roberta Reader, trans. Sitney, ed.

Emerson, Ralph Waldo. *Selected Essays*. Lazar Ziff, ed. New York: Penguin, 1982.

Epstein, Jean. *Ecrits sur le cinéma 1921–1954*. vol. 1. Paris: Seghers, 1974.

Estève, Michel, ed. *Etudes Bernanosiennes* no. 9 (*Nouvelle histoire de Mouchette: de Bernanos à Bresson*). *La Révue des lettres modernes* (1968), nos. 175–179.

Feidelson, Charles, Jr. *Symbolism and American Literature*. Chicago: Univ. of Chicago Press, 1953.

Feldman, Seth. *The Evolution of Style in the Early Films of Dziga Vertov*. New York: Arno Press, 1977.

Fenichel, Otto. "On the Psychology of Boredom." In *The Collected Papers of Otto Fenichel: First Series*. New York: Norton, 1953.

Fischer, Lucy. "*Enthusiasm:* From Kino-Eye to Radio-Eye." *Film Quarterly* (Winter 1977–78), 21(2):25–36.

Foster, Hal, ed. *Vision and Visuality*. Discussions in Contemporary Culture 2, Dia Art Foundation. Seattle: Bay Press, 1988.

Freud, Sigmund. *Moses and Monotheism*. Katherine Jones, trans. New York: Vintage, 1957.

Freud, Sigmund. *The Basic Writings of Sigmund Freud*. Dr. A. A. Brill, ed. and trans. New York: Random House, 1938.

Gado, Frank. *The Passion of Ingmar Bergman*. Durham: Duke Univ. Press, 1981.

Gauthier, Guy. "Le cinéma selon Desnos." *Europe* (May–June 1978), (Desnos Issue), nos. 517–18, pp. 129–135.

Girard, René. *Deceit, Desire, and the Novel*. Yvonne Freccero, trans. Baltimore: Johns Hopkins Univ. Press, 1965.

Greenberg, Clement. *Art and Culture*. Boston: Beacon, 1965.

Hallberg, Robert Von. *Charles Olson: The Scholar's Art*. Chicago: Univ. of Chicago Press, 1978.

Hanlon, Lindley. *Fragments: Bresson's Film Style*. Rutherford, N. J.: Fairleigh Dickinson Univ. and Associated University Presses, 1986.

Hartman, Geoffrey. "Introduction." To Maurice Blanchot, *Death Sentence,* Lydia Davis, trans. *Georgia Review* (Summer 1979), 30(2):379–381.

Heath, Stephen. *Questions of Cinema.* Bloomington: Indiana Univ. Press, 1981.

Hedges, Inez. "Constellated Visions: Robert Desnos's and Man Ray's *Etoile de mer.*" Rudolf Kuenzli, ed. *Dada and Surrealist Film.* pp. 99–109.

Heidegger, Martin. *Erläuterungen zu Hölderlins Dichtung.* Frankfurt: Klostermann, 1963.

Hölderlin, Friedrich. *Poems and Fragments.* Michael Hamburger, trans. Cambridge: Cambridge Univ. Press, 1966.

Hölderlin, Friedrich. *Werke und Briefe.* Friedrich Beissner and Jochen Schmidt, eds. 3 vols. Frankfurt: Insel, 1969.

James, William. *The Varieties of Religious Experience.* New York: New American Library, 1963.

Josipovici, Gabriel. *The World and the Book.* London: Macmillan, 1971.

Karl, Frederick R. *Modern and Modernism: The Sovereignty of the Artist 1885–1925.* New York: Atheneum, 1985.

Kawin, Bruce. *Mindscreen: Bergman, Godard, and the First-Person Film.* Princeton: Princeton Univ. Press, 1978.

Kawin, Bruce. "Time and Stasis in *La Jetée.*" *Film Quarterly* (Fall 1982), 36(1): 15–20.

Keller, Marjorie. *The Untutored Eye: Childhood in the Films of Jean Cocteau, Joseph Cornell, and Stan Brakhage.* Rutherford, N. J.: Associated Univ. Presses, 1985.

Kelman Ken. "The Structure of Fate." In *The Essential Cinema,* pp. 208–215. P. Adams Sitney, ed.

Kepley, Vance, Jr. *In the Service of the State: The Cinema of Alexander Dovzhenko.* Madison: Univ. of Wisconsin Press, 1986.

Kepley, Vance, Jr. "The Evolution of Eisenstein's *The Old and the New,*" *Cinema Journal* (Fall 1974), 14(1):34–50.

Kermode, Frank. *The Genesis of Secrecy: On the Interpretation of Narrative.* Cambridge: Harvard Univ. Press, 1979.

Kernberg, Otto. *Borderline Conditions and Pathological Narcissim.* New York: J. Aronson, 1975.

Kierkegaard, Søren. *Fear and Trembling and Sickness unto Death.* Walter Lowrie, trans. New York: Doubleday, 1953.

Kovacs, Steven. *From Enchantment to Rage: The Story of Surrealist Cinema.* Rutherford, N. J.: Associated Univ. Presses, 1980.

Kuenzli, Rudolf E., ed. *Dada and Surrealist Film.* New York: Willis Locker and Owens, 1987.

Kuleshov, Lev. *Kuleshov on Film,* Ronald Levaco, ed., intro., and trans. Berkeley: Univ. of California Press, 1974.

Landry, Lionel. "La Formation de la Sensibilité: le rôle du 'sujet.' " *Les Cahiers du Mois* (1925), No. 16/17.

Lewin, Bertram. "The Nature of Reality, the Meaning of Nothing, with an addendum on Concentration." *Psychoanalytic Quarterly* (1948), 178:524–526.

Leyda, Jay. *Kino: A History of the Russian and Soviet Film.* Princeton: Princeton Univ. Press, 1983.

Londyn, Evelyne, *Maurice Blanchot, romancier*. Paris: Nizet, 1976.

Lukács, Georg. *The Theory of the Novel*. Anna Bostock, trans. Cambridge: M. I. T. Press, 1971.

Lunn, Eugene. *Marxism and Modernism: An Historical Study of Lukács, Brecht, Benjamin and Adorno*. Berkeley: Univ. of California Press, 1982.

Mallarmé, Stéphane. *Corréspondence 1862–1871*. Henri Mondor, ed. Paris: Gallimard, 1959.

Mallarmé, Stéphane. *Oeuvres complètes*. Henri Mondor, ed. Paris: Bibliothèque de la Pléiade, Gallimard, 1945.

Markov, Vladimir. *The Long Poems of V. Khlebnikov*. Univ. of Calfornia Publications in Modern Philology. Vol. 62. Berkeley: Univ. of California Press, 1962.

Martin, Katrina. "Marcel Duchamp's *Anémic cinéma*." *Studio International* (January–February 1975), no. 189, pp. 53–60.

Marx, Karl. "The Class Struggles in France 1848–50." In *On Revolution*, 1:147–242. Saul K. Padover, arr., ed., and trans., Karl Marx Library. New York: McGraw Hill, 1971.

Melville, Herman. *Moby Dick*. Willard Thorp, ed. New York: Oxford Univ. Press, 1947.

Melville, Herman. *Selected Poems of Herman Melville*. Hennig Cohen, ed. Garden City, N. Y.: Anchor, 1974.

Melville, Robert. "Picasso in the Light of Chirico—Mutations of the Bullfight." *View* (February–March 1942), 1 (11):2.

Michelson, Annette. "*Anémic Cinéma:* Reflections on an Emblematic Work." *Artforum* (October 1973), 12(2):64–69.

Michelson, Annette. "Camera Oscura/ Camera Lucida." *Artforum* (January 1973), 11(5):30–37.

Milton, John. *The Complete Poems of John Milton*. John T. Shawcross, ed. Garden City, N. Y.: Doubleday, 1971.

Mykyta, Larysa. "Blanchot's *Au Moment voulu:* Woman as the Eternally Recurring Figure of Writing." *Boundary 2* (Winter 1982), 10(2):77–95.

Nash, Mark. *Dreyer*. London: British Film Institute, 1977.

Nerval, Gérard de. *Oeuvres complètes*. Albert Beguin and Jean Richter, eds. Bibliothèque de la Pléiade. 2 Vols. Paris: Gallimard, 1966.

Neuman, Shirley. *Gertrude Stein: Autobiography and the Problem of Narration*. Victoria, B. C.: Univ. of Victoria Press, 1979.

Nietzsche, Friedrich. *The Philosophy of Nietzsche*. Thomas Common, trans. New York: Random House, 1947.

Noulet, Emilie. *Vingt poèmes de Stéphane Mallarmé*. Geneva: Librairie Droz, 1967.

Odin Roger. "Le film de fiction menacé par la photographie et sauvé par le bande-son (Etude de *La Jetée* de Chris Marker)." In *Cinémas de la modernité: films théories*, pp. 147–171. Dominique Chateau et al., eds., Paris: Colloque de Cerisy, 1981.

Olson, Charles. *Additional Prose: A Bibliography on America, Proprioception, & Other Notes and Essays*. George Butterick, ed. Writing No. 31. Bolinas: Four Seasons, 1974.

Olson, Charles. *Call Me Ishamel.* New York: Grove, 1958.

Olson, Charles. *In Adullam's Lair.* Archetype No. 1. Provincetown: To the Lighthouse, 1975.

Olson, Charles. *Mythologos.* George F. Butterick, ed. 2 vols., Writing No. 22. Bolinas: Four Seasons, 1979.

Olson, Charles. *The Human Universe.* New York: Grove, 1967.

Olson, Charles. "The Chiasma, or Lectures in the New Sciences of Man." George Butterick, ed. *Olson* (Fall 1978), no. 10.

Oudart, Jean-Pierre. "Cinema and Suture." *Screen,* Henry Seggerman, trans. (Winter 1977–78), vol. 18, no. 4.

Oudart, Jean-Pierre. "La suture." *Cahiers du Cinéma* (April 1969), no. 211, pp. 36–39; and (May 1969), no. 212, pp. 50–55.

Parrain, Philippe. *Dreyer: cadres et mouvements. Etudes Cinématographiques,* nos. 53–56. Paris: Lettres Modernes-Minard, 1967.

Paul, Sherman: *Olson's Push: Origin, Black Mountain, and Recent American Poetry.* Baton Rouge: Louisiana State Univ. Press, 1978.

Paz, Octavio. "Stéphane Mallarmé: Sonnet in 'ix,' " Agnes Moncy, trans. *Delos* (1970), no. 4, pp. 16–28.

Pearce, Roy Harvey. *The Continuity of American Poetry.* Princeton: Princeton Univ. Press, 1961.

Peterson, Sidney. *The Dark of the Screen.* New York: Anthology Film Archives, 1980.

Petric, Vladimir. "Dreyer's Concept of Abstraction." *Sight and Sound* (Spring 1975), 44(2):108–112.

Petric, Vladimir, ed. *Films and Dreams: An Approach to Bergman.* New York: Redgrave, 1981.

Porter, Carolyn. *Seeing and Being: The Plight of the Particular Observer in Emerson, James, Adams, and Faulkner.* Middletown, Conn.: Wesleyan Univ. Press, 1981.

Prince, Gerald. "Point of Narration: Blanchot's *Au moment voulu. Substance* (1976), no. 14, pp. 93–98.

Pudovkin, V. I. *Film Technique and Film Acting.* Ivor Montagu, ed. and trans. New York: Grove, 1960.

Ray, Man. *Self Portrait.* Boston: Little, Brown, 1963.

Riffaterre, Michael. *The Semiotics of Poetry.* Bloomington, Indiana Univ. Press, 1967.

Rogers, Joel. "*Moses and Aaron* as an Object of Marxist Reflection." *Jump Cut* (December 1976), nos. 12–13, pp. 61–64.

Rose, Barbara. "The Films of Man Ray and Moholy-Nagy." *Artforum* (September 1971), 10(1):68–73.

Rosenbaum, Jonathan. "Gertrud: Desire for the Image." *Sight and Sound* (Winter 1985–86), 55(1):40–45.

Ross, Andrew. *The Failure of Modernism: Symptoms of American Poetry.* New York: Columbia Univ. Press, 1978.

Rothman, William. "Against the System of the Suture." *Film Quarterly* (Fall 1975), 5(10):45–49.

Salt, Barry. *Film Style and Technique.* London: Starword, 1983.

Schneider, Dr. Daniel E. "The Painting of Pablo Picasso: A Psychoanalytic Study." *College Art Journal* (Winter 1947–48), 7(2):87–95.

Schnitzer, Jean and Luda. "Alexandre Dovjenko." In *Antologie du Cinéma*. Jacques Charrière, ed. vol. 1. Paris: L'Avant-Scène, 1966.

Sitney, P. Adams. *Visionary Film: The American Avant-Garde 1943-1978*. New York: Oxford Univ. Press, 1979.

Sitney, P. Adams, ed. *The Essential Cinema: Essays on the Films in the Collection of Anthology Film Archives*. New York: New York Univ. Press and Anthology Film Archives, 1975.

Sitney, P. Adams, ed. *The Avant-Garde Film: A Reader of Theory and Criticism*. New York: New York Univ. Press and Anthology Film Archives, 1979.

Sjöman, Vilgot. *L 136: Diary with Ingmar Bergman*. Alan Blair, trans. Ann Arbor: Karoma, 1978.

Sontag, Susan. "Bergman's *Persona*." In *Styles of Radical Will*, pp. 123–145. New York: Farrar, Strauss, 1968.

Spanos, William V. *Repetitions: The Postmodern Occassion in Literature and Culture*. Baton Rouge: Louisiana State Univ. Press, 1979.

Stein, Gertrude. *A Primer for the Gradual Understanding of Gertrude Stein*, Robert Bartlett Haas, ed. Los Angeles: Black Sparrow, 1971.

Stein, Gertrude. *Everybody's Autobiography*. New York: Random House, 1937.

Stein, Gertrude. *Lectures in America*. New York: Random House, 1935.

Stein, Gertrude. *Narration*. Chicago: Univ. of Chicago Press, 1935.

Stein, Gertrude. *The Autobiography of Alice B. Toklas*. New York: Random House, 1937.

Stein, Gertrude. *Writings and Lectures: 1909–1945*. New York: Penguin, 1971.

Stites, Richard. *Revolutionary Dreams: Utopian Vision and Experimental Life in the Russian Revolution*. New York: Oxford Univ. Press, 1989.

Streidter, Jurij. "The 'New Myth' of Revolution: A Study of Mayakovsky's Early Poetry." In *New Perspectives in German Literary Criticism*, pp. 357–385. Richard E. Amacher and Victor Lange, eds., David Henry Wilson, trans. Princeton: Princeton Univ. Press, 1979.

Suetonius. *De Vita Caesarum Libri*. M. Ihm, ed. 2 vols. Bibliotheca Teubneriana. Leipzig: Teubner, 1908.

Sutherland, Donald. *Gertrude Stein: A Biography of her Work*. New Haven: Yale Univ. Press, 1951.

Vertov, Dziga. *Kino-Eye: The Writings of Dziga Vertov*. Annette Michelson, ed.; Kevin O'Brien, trans.; Berkeley: Univ. of California Press, 1984.

Walsh, Martin. "Straub and Huillet's Schoenberg." *Jump Cut* (December 1976), nos. 12–13, pp. 57–61.

Whitehead, Alfred North. *Process and Reality: An Essay in Cosmology*. New York: Macmillan, 1960.

Whitman, Walt. *Leaves of Grass: First (1855) Edition*. Malcolm Cowley, ed. New York: Viking, 1968.

Williams, William Carlos. *Collected Earlier Poems*. New York: New Directions, 1951.

Index

247

INDEX

apotheosis 1. elevation to status of god
2 transfiguration to ideal

catachresis 1. misuse or strained
use of words
2. ~~word is of an employed~~
employment of a word
under a false form
derived from false etymolgy
(e.g. causeway, crawfish,
crayfish)